RAND McNALLY

W9-BQW-893

Atlas
of WORLD GEOGRAPHY

Managing Editor
Brett R. Gover

Design
Rand McNally Art & Design

Cartographic Direction
Howard Veregin

Cartography
Robert K. Argersinger
Gregory P. Babiak
Barbara Benstead-Strassheim
Marzee L. Eckhoff
Nina Lusterman
Robert L. Merrill
David R. Simmons
Thomas F. Vitacco

Research
Susan Hudson
Felix Lopez
Raymond Tobiaski

Photograph Credits:

Front cover images provided by © 1997 PhotoDisc, Inc.

H. Armstrong Roberts: © R. Kord, 7, 31 (b); © Zefa, 100; © M. Schneiders, 108; © Smith/Zefa, 150 (b)

© Randall Hyman: 101

© PhotoDisc, Inc.: 135

Odyssey Chicago: © R. Frerck, 152

Tony Stone Images: © K. Wood, 29 (t); © Mark Segal, 68; © David Frazier, 69; © Jacques Jangoux, 98 (t); © John Warden, 98 (b); © Owen Franken, 110; © John Lamb, 122 (t); © Yann Layma, 134; © Paul Chelsey, 153

Information Credits:

Volcano data, pages 29, 32, and 36: Tom Simkin, Smithsonian Institution Global Volcanism Program

Earthquake data, page 37: Paula Dunbar, National Geophysical Data Center, National Oceanic and Atmospheric Administration

Australia information, page 38: Australian Tourist Commission

Much of the information on the destruction of the Amazonian rain forest, page 101, was provided by Fred Engel of the Center for Earth and Planetary Science, National Air and Space Museum, Smithsonian Institution, Washington, D.C.

Atlas of World Geography

Published and printed in the United States of America

ISBN: 0-528-17790-0
10 9 8 7 6 5 4 3 2 1

For information about ordering *Atlas of World Geography*, call 1-800-678-7263 or visit our website:
www.K12online.com

Table of Contents

Using the Atlas

Maps and Atlases

Today, satellite images (Figure 1) and aerial photography show us the face of the Earth in precise detail. It is hard to imagine how difficult it once was to ascertain what our planet looked like—even small parts of it. Yet from earliest history we have evidence of humans trying to depict the world through maps and charts.

Figure 1

Twenty-five hundred years ago, on a tiny clay tablet the size of a hand, the Babylonians inscribed the earth as a flat disk (Figure 2) with Babylon at the center. The section of the Cantino map of 1502 (Figure 3) is an example of a portolan chart used by mariners to chart the newly discovered Americas. Handsome and useful maps have been produced by many cultures. The Mexican map (Figure 4) drawn in 1583 marks hills with wavy lines and roads with footprints between parallel lines. The methods and materials used to create these maps were dependent upon the technology available, and their accuracy suffered considerably. The maps in this atlas show the detail and accuracy that cartographers are now able to achieve. They benefit from our ever-increasing technology, including satellite imagery and computer-assisted cartography.

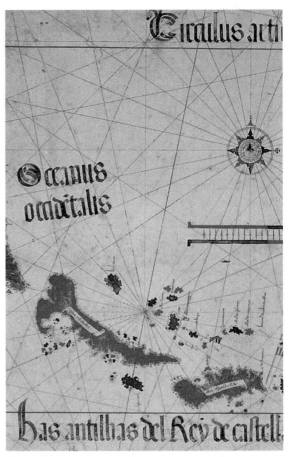

Figure 2

In 1589, Gerardus Mercator used the word "atlas" to describe a collection of maps. Atlases have become a unique and indispensable reference for graphically defining the world and answering the question "Where?" Only on a map can the countries, cities, roads, rivers, and lakes covering a vast area be simultaneously viewed in their relative locations. Routes between places can be traced, trips planned,

Figure 3

Figure 4

boundaries of neighboring states and countries examined, distances between places measured, the meandering of rivers and streams and the sizes of lakes visualized, and remote places imagined.

Getting the Information

An atlas can be used for many purposes, from planning a trip to finding hot spots in the news and supplementing world knowledge. To realize the potential of an atlas, the user must be able to:

1) Find places on the maps
2) Measure distances
3) Determine directions
4) Understand map symbols

Finding Places

One of the most common and important tasks facilitated by an atlas is finding the location of a place in the world. A river's name in a book, a city mentioned in the news, or a potential vacation spot may prompt your need to know where the place is located. The illustrations and text below explain how to find Lagos, Nigeria.

1) Look up the place-name in the index at the back of the atlas. Lagos, Nigeria can be found in the map on page 128, and it can be located on the map by its latitude and longitude, expressed in degrees: 7 North Latitude, 3 East Longitude (Figure 5).

La Fayette, In., U.S. 40N	87W	**90**
Lafayette, La., U.S. 30N	92W	**95**
Laghouat, Alg. 34N	3 E	**128**
Lagos, Nig. 7N	3 E	**128**
La Grande, Or., U.S. 45N	118W	**82**
LaGrange, Ga., U.S. 33N	85W	**92**
Lahore, Pak. 32N	74 E	**143**
Lahti, Fin. 61N	26 E	**116**

Figure 5

2) Turn to the map of Northern Africa on page 128. Note that the latitude appears in the right and left margins of the map, and the longitude in the upper and lower margins.

3) To find Lagos on the map, place your left index finger on the left margin at 7 degrees (between 5 and 10); and your right index finger in the top margin at 3 degrees East (between 0 and 5). Move your left finger across the map and your right finger down the map. Your fingers will meet in the area in which Lagos is located (Figure 6).

Figure 6

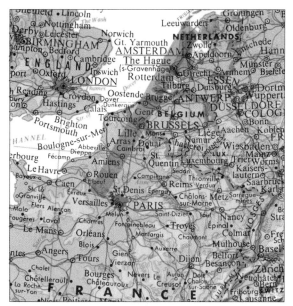

Figure 7

Measuring Distances

In planning trips, determining the distances between two places is essential, and an atlas can help in travel preparation. For instance, to determine the approximate distance between Paris, France and Amsterdam, Netherlands, follow these three steps:

1) Lay a slip of paper on the map on page 117 so that its edge touches the two cities. Adjust the paper so only one corner touches Paris. Mark the paper directly at the spot where Amsterdam is located (Figure 7).

2) Place the paper along the scale of miles beneath the map. Position the corner at 0 and line up the edge of the paper along the scale. The pencil mark on the paper indicates Amsterdam is between 250 and 300 miles from Paris (Figure 8).

3) To find the exact distance, make a second pencil mark at the 250-mile point of the scale. Then slide the paper to the left so that this second mark is lined up with 0 on the scale (Figure 9). The Amsterdam mark now falls at the third 10-mile point on the scale. This means that the Paris and Amsterdam are approximately 250 plus 30—or 280—miles apart.

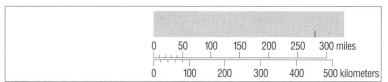

Figure 8

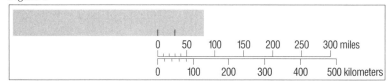

Figure 9

Determining Directions

Most of the maps in the atlas are drawn so that when oriented for normal reading, north is at the top of the map, south is at the bottom, west is at the left, and east is at the right. Most maps have a series of lines drawn across them—the lines of latitude and longitude. Lines of latitude, or parallels of latitude, are drawn east and west. Lines of longitude, or meridians of longitude, are drawn north and south (Figure 10, at bottom of page).

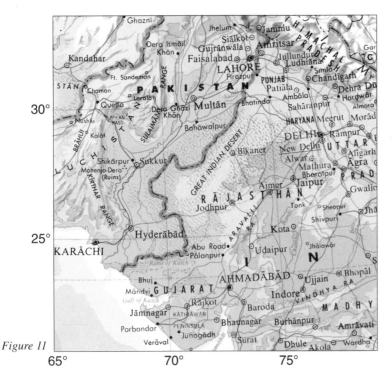

Figure 11

Parallels and meridians appear as either curved or straight lines. For example, in the section of the map of Southwestern Asia (Figure 11), from page 143, the parallels of latitude appear as curved lines. The meridians of longitude are curved vertical lines.

Latitude and longitude lines help locate places on maps. Parallels of latitude are numbered in degrees north and south of the equator. Meridians of longitude are numbered in degrees east and west of a line called the Prime Meridian, running through Greenwich, England, near London. Any place on Earth can be located by the latitude and longitude lines running through it.

To determine directions or locations on the map, you must use the parallels and meridians. For example, suppose you want to know which is farther north, Karachi, Pakistan or Delhi, India. The map in Figure 11 shows that Karachi is south of the 25° parallel of latitude and that Delhi is north of it. Therefore Delhi is farther north than Karachi. By looking at the meridians of longitude, you can determine which city is farther east. Karachi is approximately 2° east of the 65° meridian, and Delhi is about 2° east of the 75° meridian. Delhi is farther east than Karachi.

Understanding Map Symbols

In a very real sense, every map is a symbol representing the world or part of it. It is a reduced representation of the Earth: each of the world's features —cities, rivers, etc.—is represented by a symbol. Map symbols may take the form of points, such as dots or squares (often used for cities, capital cities, or points of interest) or lines (roads, railroads, rivers). Symbols may also occupy an area, showing extent of coverage (terrain, forests, deserts). They seldom look like the feature they represent and therefore must be identified and interpreted. For instance, some of the maps in this atlas define political units by a colored line depicting their boundaries. Neither the colors nor the boundary lines are actually found on the surface of the Earth, but because countries and states are such important political components of the world, strong symbols are used to represent them. The Legend on page 51 of this atlas identifies the symbols used on the maps.

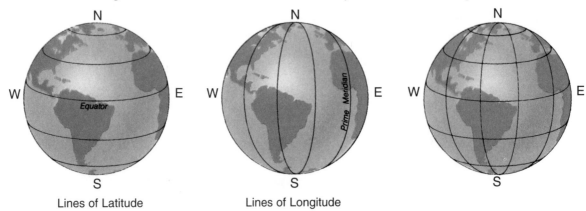

Lines of Latitude   Lines of Longitude

Figure 10

Introduction to Geographic Tables, Charts, and Graphs

Geographic Questions and Answers

This section provides an interesting way to learn key geographic information about your country and the world. Locate places referred to in the questions on Atlas of World Geography maps.

The Universe and Solar System

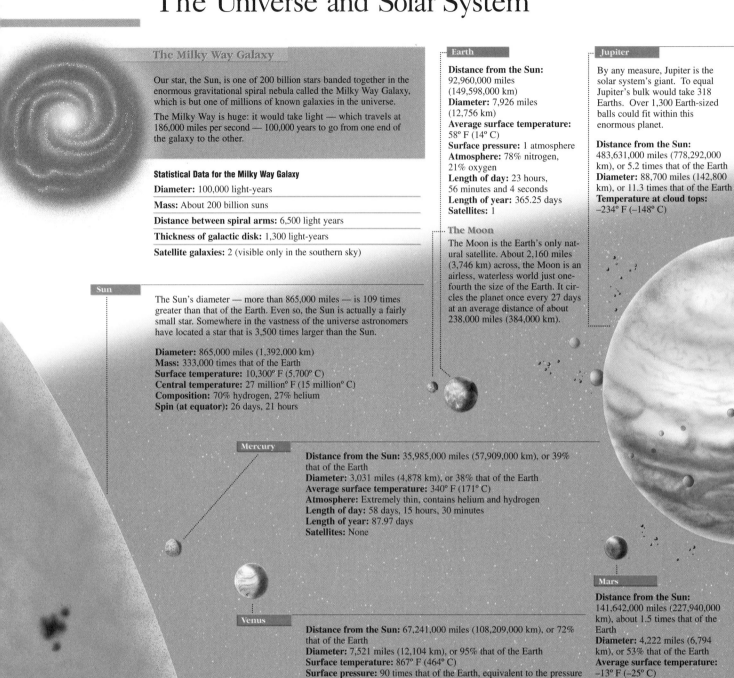

The Milky Way Galaxy

Our star, the Sun, is one of 200 billion stars banded together in the enormous gravitational spiral nebula called the Milky Way Galaxy, which is but one of millions of known galaxies in the universe.

The Milky Way is huge: it would take light — which travels at 186,000 miles per second — 100,000 years to go from one end of the galaxy to the other.

Statistical Data for the Milky Way Galaxy

Diameter: 100,000 light-years

Mass: About 200 billion suns

Distance between spiral arms: 6,500 light years

Thickness of galactic disk: 1,300 light-years

Satellite galaxies: 2 (visible only in the southern sky)

Sun

The Sun's diameter — more than 865,000 miles — is 109 times greater than that of the Earth. Even so, the Sun is actually a fairly small star. Somewhere in the vastness of the universe astronomers have located a star that is 3,500 times larger than the Sun.

Diameter: 865,000 miles (1,392,000 km)
Mass: 333,000 times that of the Earth
Surface temperature: 10,300° F (5,700° C)
Central temperature: 27 million° F (15 million° C)
Composition: 70% hydrogen, 27% helium
Spin (at equator): 26 days, 21 hours

Mercury

Distance from the Sun: 35,985,000 miles (57,909,000 km), or 39% that of the Earth
Diameter: 3,031 miles (4,878 km), or 38% that of the Earth
Average surface temperature: 340° F (171° C)
Atmosphere: Extremely thin, contains helium and hydrogen
Length of day: 58 days, 15 hours, 30 minutes
Length of year: 87.97 days
Satellites: None

Venus

Distance from the Sun: 67,241,000 miles (108,209,000 km), or 72% that of the Earth
Diameter: 7,521 miles (12,104 km), or 95% that of the Earth
Surface temperature: 867° F (464° C)
Surface pressure: 90 times that of the Earth, equivalent to the pressure at a water depth of 3,000 feet (900 meters)
Atmosphere: 96% carbon dioxide
Length of day: 243 days, 14 minutes. The planet spins opposite to the rotation of the Earth.
Length of year: 224.7 days
Satellites: None

Earth

Distance from the Sun: 92,960,000 miles (149,598,000 km)
Diameter: 7,926 miles (12,756 km)
Average surface temperature: 58° F (14° C)
Surface pressure: 1 atmosphere
Atmosphere: 78% nitrogen, 21% oxygen
Length of day: 23 hours, 56 minutes and 4 seconds
Length of year: 365.25 days
Satellites: 1

The Moon

The Moon is the Earth's only natural satellite. About 2,160 miles (3,746 km) across, the Moon is an airless, waterless world just one-fourth the size of the Earth. It circles the planet once every 27 days at an average distance of about 238,000 miles (384,000 km).

Jupiter

By any measure, Jupiter is the solar system's giant. To equal Jupiter's bulk would take 318 Earths. Over 1,300 Earth-sized balls could fit within this enormous planet.

Distance from the Sun: 483,631,000 miles (778,292,000 km), or 5.2 times that of the Earth
Diameter: 88,700 miles (142,800 km), or 11.3 times that of the Earth
Temperature at cloud tops: −234° F (−148° C)

Mars

Distance from the Sun: 141,642,000 miles (227,940,000 km), about 1.5 times that of the Earth
Diameter: 4,222 miles (6,794 km), or 53% that of the Earth
Average surface temperature: −13° F (−25° C)
Surface pressure: 0.7% (1/150 th) that of the Earth
Atmosphere: 95% carbon dioxide, 2.7% nitrogen
Length of day: 24 hours, 37 minutes
Length of year: 1 year, 321.73 days
Satellites: 2

Spatial Relationships of the Sun and the Planets

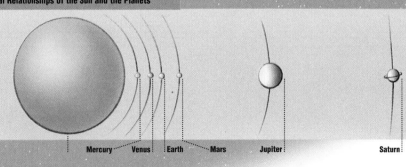

Mercury   Venus   Earth   Mars   Jupiter   Saturn

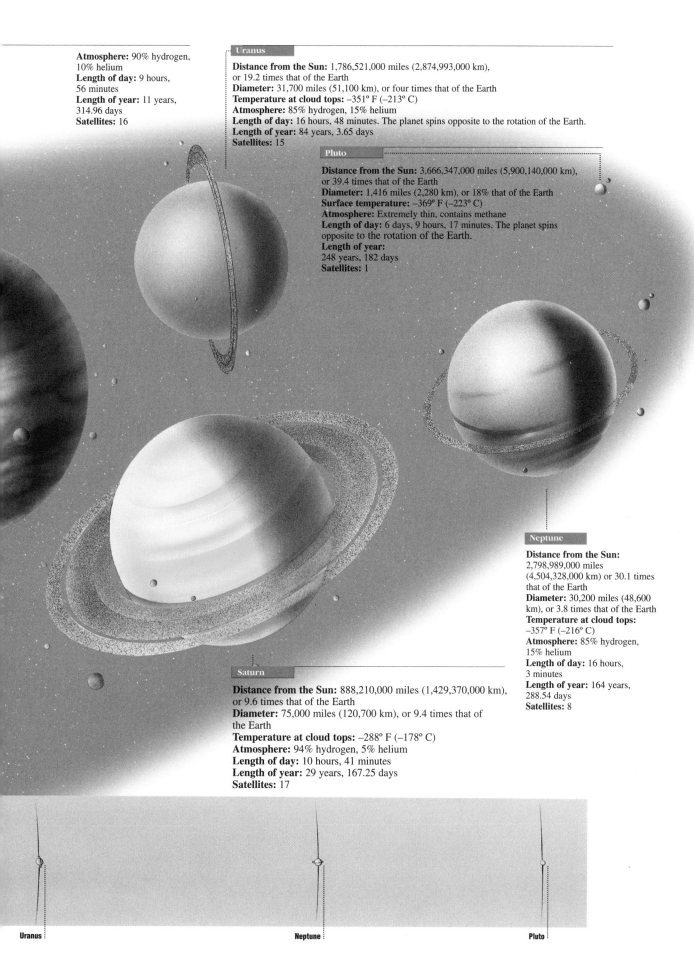

Atmosphere: 90% hydrogen, 10% helium
Length of day: 9 hours, 56 minutes
Length of year: 11 years, 314.96 days
Satellites: 16

Uranus

Distance from the Sun: 1,786,521,000 miles (2,874,993,000 km), or 19.2 times that of the Earth
Diameter: 31,700 miles (51,100 km), or four times that of the Earth
Temperature at cloud tops: –351° F (–213° C)
Atmosphere: 85% hydrogen, 15% helium
Length of day: 16 hours, 48 minutes. The planet spins opposite to the rotation of the Earth.
Length of year: 84 years, 3.65 days
Satellites: 15

Pluto

Distance from the Sun: 3,666,347,000 miles (5,900,140,000 km), or 39.4 times that of the Earth
Diameter: 1,416 miles (2,280 km), or 18% that of the Earth
Surface temperature: –369° F (–223° C)
Atmosphere: Extremely thin, contains methane
Length of day: 6 days, 9 hours, 17 minutes. The planet spins opposite to the rotation of the Earth.
Length of year: 248 years, 182 days
Satellites: 1

Neptune

Distance from the Sun: 2,798,989,000 miles (4,504,328,000 km) or 30.1 times that of the Earth
Diameter: 30,200 miles (48,600 km), or 3.8 times that of the Earth
Temperature at cloud tops: –357° F (–216° C)
Atmosphere: 85% hydrogen, 15% helium
Length of day: 16 hours, 3 minutes
Length of year: 164 years, 288.54 days
Satellites: 8

Saturn

Distance from the Sun: 888,210,000 miles (1,429,370,000 km), or 9.6 times that of the Earth
Diameter: 75,000 miles (120,700 km), or 9.4 times that of the Earth
Temperature at cloud tops: –288° F (–178° C)
Atmosphere: 94% hydrogen, 5% helium
Length of day: 10 hours, 41 minutes
Length of year: 29 years, 167.25 days
Satellites: 17

Uranus

Neptune

Pluto

The Earth

History of the Earth

Estimated age of the Earth:
At least 4.6 billion (4,600,000,000) years.

Formation of the Earth:
It is generally thought that the Earth was formed from a cloud of gas and dust (A) revolving around the early Sun. Gravitational forces pulled the cloud's particles together into an ever denser mass (B), with heavier particles sinking to the center. Heat from radioactive elements caused the materials of the embryonic Earth to melt and gradually settle into core and mantle layers. As the surface cooled, a crust formed. Volcanic activity released vast amounts of steam, carbon dioxide and other gases from the Earth's interior. The steam condensed into water to form the oceans, and the gases, prevented by gravity from escaping, formed the beginnings of the atmosphere (C).

The calm appearance of our planet today (D) belies the intense heat of its interior and the violent tectonic forces which are constantly reshaping its surface.

(A)

(B)

(C)

(D)

Periods in Earth's history

Earth's history is divided into different **eras**, which are subdivided into **periods**.

The most recent periods are themselves subdivided into **epochs**. The main divisions and subdivisions are shown below.

	Began	Ended	
	(million years ago)		
Precambrian Era			
Archean Period	3,800	2,500	Start of life
Proterozoic Period	2,500	590	Life in the seas
Paleozoic Era			
Cambrian Period	590	500	Sea life
Ordovician Period	505	438	First fishes
Silurian Period	438	408	First land plants
Devonian Period	408	360	Amphibians
Carboniferous Period	360	286	First reptiles
Permian Period	286	248	Spread of reptiles
Mesozoic Era			
Triassic Period	248	213	Reptiles and early mammals
Jurassic Period	213	144	Dinosaurs
Cretaceous Period	144	65	Dinosaurs, dying out at the end
Cenozoic Era			
Tertiary Period			
Paleocene	65	55	Large mammals
Eocene	55	38	Primates begin
Oligocene	38	25	Development of primates
Miocene	25	5	Modern-type animals
Pliocene	5	2	*Australopithecus* ape, ancestor to the human race
Quaternary Period			
Pleistocene	2	0.01	Ice ages; true humans
Holocene	0.01	Present	Modern humans

Source: *Atlas of the Universe* by Patrick Moore, Reed International Books Limited, 1994.

Internal Structure of the Earth

In its simplest form, the Earth is composed of a crust, a mantle with an upper and lower layer, and a core, which has an inner region.

Temperatures in the Earth increase with depth, as is observed in a deep mine shaft or borehole, but the prediction of temperatures within the Earth is made difficult by the fact that different rocks conduct heat at different rates: rock salt, for example, has 10 times the heat conductivity of coal. Also, estimates have to take into account the abundance of heat-generating atoms in a rock. Radioactive atoms are concentrated toward the Earth's surface, so the planet has, in effect, a thermal blanket to keep it warm. The temperature at the center of the Earth is believed to be approximately 5,400° F (3,000° C).

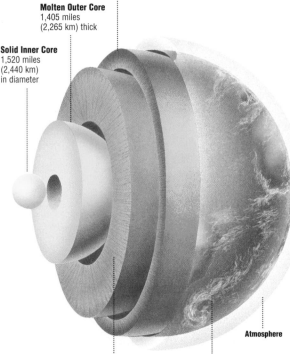

Upper Mantle
415 miles
(667 km) thick

Molten Outer Core
1,405 miles
(2,265 km) thick

Solid Inner Core
1,520 miles
(2,440 km)
in diameter

Atmosphere

Lower Mantle
1,365 miles
(2,200 km) thick

Solid Crust
0–19 miles
(0–33 km) thick

Chemical composition of the Earth:

The chemical composition of the Earth varies from crust to core. The upper crust of continents, called sial, is mainly granite, rich in aluminum and silicon. Oceanic crust, or sima, is largely basalt, made of magnesium and silicon. The mantle is composed of rocks that are rich in magnesium and iron silicates, whereas the core, it is believed, is made of iron and nickel oxides.

- Sial
- Sima
- Upper Mantle
- Lower Mantle
- Outer Core
- Inner Core

A. Silicon
B. Aluminum
C. Iron
D. Calcium
E. Magnesium
F. Nickel
G. Other

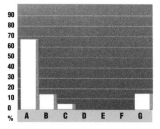
Sial (upper crust of continents)

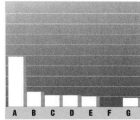
Sima (oceanic crust)

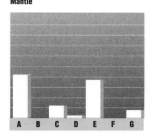
Mantle

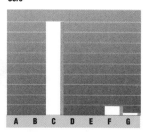
Core

Measurements of the Earth

Equatorial circumference of the Earth: 24,901.45 miles (40,066.43 km)

Polar circumference of the Earth: 24,855.33 miles (39,992.22 km)

Equatorial diameter of the Earth: 7,926.38 miles (12,753.54 km)

Polar diameter of the Earth: 7,899.80 miles (12,710.77 km)

Equatorial radius of the Earth: 3,963.19 miles (6,376.77 km)

Polar radius of the Earth: 3,949.90 miles (6,355.38 km)

Estimated weight of the Earth:
6,600,000,000,000,000,000,000,000 tons, or 6,600 billion billion tons (5,940 billion billion metric tons)

Total surface area of the Earth: 197,000,000 square miles (510,230,000 sq km)

Total land area of the Earth (including inland water and Antarctica): 57,900,000 square miles (150,100,000 sq km)

Total ocean area of the Earth: 139,200,000 square miles (360,528,000 sq km), or 70% of the Earth's surface area

Total area of the Earth's surface covered with water (oceans and all inland water): 147,750,000 square miles (382,672,500 sq km), or 75% of the Earth's surface area

Types of water: 97% of the Earth's water is salt water; 3% is fresh water

Life on Earth

Number of plant species on Earth: About 350,000

Number of animal species on Earth: More than one million

Estimated total human population of the Earth: 6,195,885,000

Movements of the Earth

Mean distance of the Earth from the Sun: About 93 million miles (149.6 million km)

Period in which the Earth makes one complete orbit around the Sun: 365 days, 5 hours, 48 minutes, and 46 seconds

Speed of the Earth as it orbits the Sun: 66,700 miles (107,320 km) per hour

Period in which the Earth makes one complete rotation on its axis: 23 hours, 56 minutes and 4 seconds

Equatorial speed at which the Earth rotates on its axis: More than 1,000 miles (1,600 km) per hour

The Shape of the Earth

Comparing the Earth's equatorial and polar dimensions reveals that our planet is actually not a perfect sphere but rather an oblate spheroid, flattened at the poles and bulging at the equator. This is the result of a combination of gravitational and centrifugal forces.

An even more precise term for the Earth's shape is "geoid" — the actual shape of sea level, which is lumpy, with variations away from spheroid of up to 260 feet (80 m). This lumpiness reflects major variations in density in the Earth's outer layers.

The Seasons
(Northern Hemisphere)

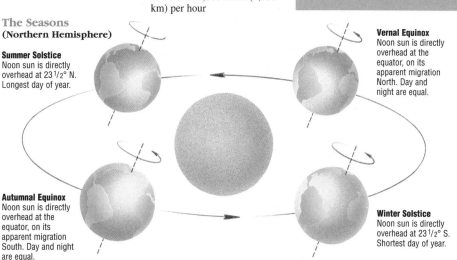

Summer Solstice
Noon sun is directly overhead at 23 1/2° N. Longest day of year.

Vernal Equinox
Noon sun is directly overhead at the equator, on its apparent migration North. Day and night are equal.

Autumnal Equinox
Noon sun is directly overhead at the equator, on its apparent migration South. Day and night are equal.

Winter Solstice
Noon sun is directly overhead at 23 1/2° S. Shortest day of year.

Plate Tectonics

Continental Drift

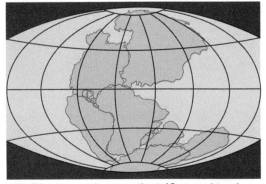

225 million years ago the supercontinent of Pangaea exists and Panthalassa forms the ancestral ocean. Tethys Sea separates Eurasia and Africa.

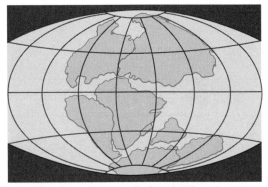

180 million years ago Pangaea splits, Laurasia drifts north. Gondwanaland breaks into South America/Africa, India, and Australia/Antarctica.

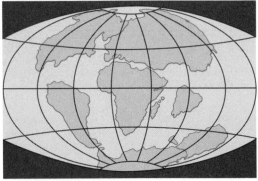

65 million years ago ocean basins take shape as South America and India move from Africa and the Tethys Sea closes to form the Mediterranean Sea.

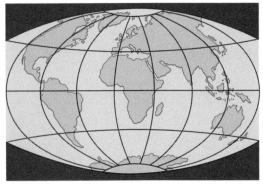

The present day: India has merged with Asia, Australia is free of Antarctica, and North America is free of Eurasia.

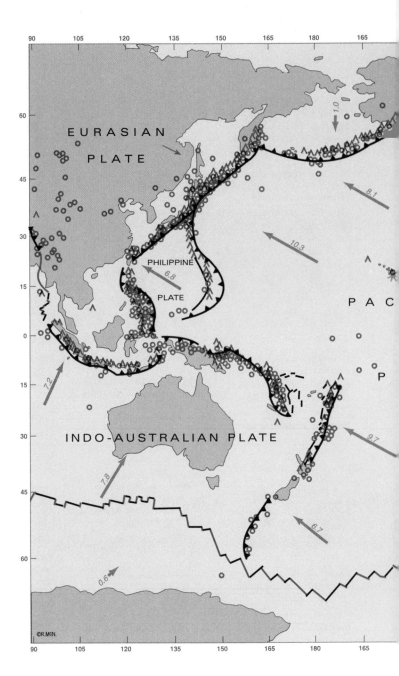

PLATE TECTONICS

Types of plate boundaries

——— **Divergent:** magma emerges from the earth's mantle at the mid-ocean ridges forming new crust and forcing the plates to spread apart at the ridges.

▲▲▲ **Convergent:** plates collide at subduction zones where the denser plate is forced back into the earth's mantle forming deep ocean trenches.

——— **Transform:** plates slide past one another producing faults and fracture zones.

Other map symbols

→ Direction of plate movement

6.7 Length of arrow is proportional to the amount of plate movement (number indicates centimeters of movement per year)

○ Earthquake of magnitude 7.5 and above (from 10 A.D. to the present)

∧ Volcano (eruption since 1900)

✳ Selected hot spots

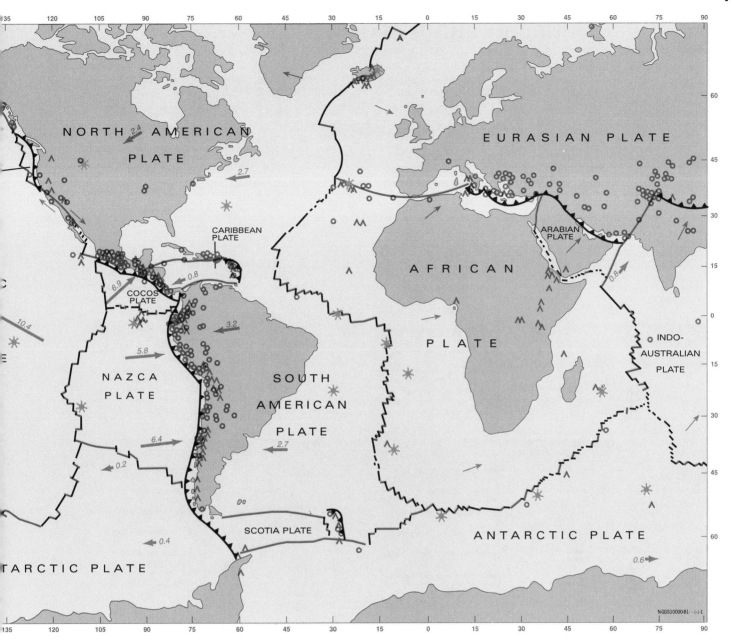

According to plate tectonic theory, Earth's lithosphere—the crust and uppermost rigid part of the mantle—is divided into plates that move relative to one another. The map above shows the locations and names of the major plates.

These rigid plates move on a molten layer of Earth's mantle called the asthenosphere. The moving plates meet at three different types of boundaries—divergent, convergent, and transform. (See map legend at the left.)

Divergent Boundaries

At divergent boundaries, plates are pushed apart by currents in the asthenosphere in a process called rifting. Most rifting occurs on the ocean floors. In ocean floor rifting, molten material from the asthenosphere wells up between the separated plates, hardens, and forms ridges. (See World Physical Map and Ocean Depths Profile, pages 54 and 55.) This process of adding to the Earth's crust is called seafloor spreading.

Convergent Boundaries

At convergent boundaries, the moving plates collide with one another. The edge of the heavier plate sinks under the crust of the lighter plate, and is consumed back into Earth's mantle in a process called subduction. Subduction can create deep ocean trenches as the crust

of the lighter plate sinks into the mantle. (See World Physical Map, pages 54 and 55.) The colliding plates also create mountain chains as the lighter plate is pushed up over the heavier plate.

Transform Boundaries

When plates meet at transform boundaries or faults, they grind past each other. This movement neither increases nor destroys Earth's crust. The San Andreas Fault, north of San Francisco, is a famous example of a transform boundary.

Earthquakes and Volcanoes

Most of Earth's volcanoes and earthquakes occur along plate boundaries. The ring of volcanic and seismic activity along the west coasts of North and South America and the east coast of Asia, known as the Ring of Fire, follows plate boundaries. Volcanoes and earthquakes also occur at locations known as hot spots, where hot rock from deep in the mantle rises to the surface, creating some of Earth's tallest mountains.

Continental Drift

Plate tectonic theory assumes that the rigid plates have moved slowly through the millennia, carrying the continents with them. The history of this continental drifting is illustrated by the four maps to the left.

Continents and Islands

The word "continents" designates the largest continuous masses of land in the world.

For reasons that are mainly historical, seven continents are generally recognized: Africa, Antarctica, Asia, Australia, Europe, North America, and South America. Since Asia and Europe actually share the same land mass, they are sometimes identified as a single continent, Eurasia.

The lands of the central and south Pacific, including Australia, New Zealand, Micronesia, Melanesia, and Polynesia, are sometimes grouped together as Oceania.

The Continents

Africa

Area in square miles (sq km):
11,700,000 (30,300,000)
Estimated population:
832,590,000
Population per square mile (sq km):
71 (27)
Mean elevation in feet (meters):
1,900 (580)
Highest elevation in feet (meters):
Kilimanjaro, Tanzania, 19,340 (5,895)
Lowest elevation in feet (meters):
Lac Assal, Djibouti, 515 (157) below sea level

Antarctica

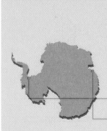

Area in square miles (sq km):
5,400,000 (14,000,000)
Estimated population:
Uninhabited
Population per square mile (sq km):
0 (0)
Mean elevation in feet (meters):
6,000 (1,830)
Highest elevation in feet (meters):
Vinson Massif, 16,066 (4,897)
Lowest elevation in feet (meters):
Deep Lake, 184 (56) below sea level

Asia

Area in square miles (sq km):
17,300,000 (44,900,000)
Estimated population:
3,761,165,000
Population per square mile (sq km):
217 (84)
Mean elevation in feet (meters):
3,000 (910)
Highest elevation in feet (meters):
Mt. Everest, China (Tibet)–Nepal, 29,028 (8,848)
Lowest elevation in feet (meters):
Dead Sea, Israel–Jordan, 1,339 (408) below sea level

Australia

Area in square miles (sq km):
2,966,155 (7,682,300)
Estimated population:
19,455,000
Population per square mile (sq km):
6.6 (2.5)
Mean elevation in feet (meters):
1,000 (305)
Highest elevation in feet (meters):
Mt. Kosciuszko, New South Wales, 7,313 (2,229)
Lake Eyre, South Australia, 52 (16) below sea level

Europe

Area in square miles (sq km):
3,800,000 (9,900,000)
Estimated population:
728,975,000
Population per square mile (sq km):
192 (74)
Mean elevation in feet (meters):
980 (300)
Highest elevation in feet (meters):
Gora El'brus, Russia, 18,510 (5,642)
Lowest elevation in feet (meters):
Caspian Sea, Asia-Europe, 92 (28) below sea level

North America

Area in square miles (sq km):
9,500,000 (24,700,000)
Estimated population:
488,780,000
Population per square mile (sq km):
51 (20)
Mean elevation in feet (meters):
2,000 (610)
Highest elevation in feet (meters):
Mt. McKinley, Alaska, U.S., 20,320 (6,194)
Lowest elevation in feet (meters):
Death Valley, California, U.S.,
282 (86) below sea level

Oceania *(incl. Australia)*

Area in square miles (sq km):
3,300,000 (8,500,000)
Estimated population:
31,415,000
Population per square mile (sq km):
9.5 (3.7)
Mean elevation in feet (meters):
0 (0)
Highest elevation in feet (meters):
Mt. Wilhelm, Papua New Guinea, 14,793 (4,509)
Lowest elevation in feet (meters):
Lake Eyre, South Australia, 52 (16) below sea level

South America

Area in square miles (sq km):
6,900,000 (17,800,000)
Estimated population:
352,960,000
Population per square mile (sq km):
51 (20)
Mean elevation in feet (meters):
1,800 (550)
Highest elevation in feet (meters):
Cerro Aconcagua, Argentina, 22,831 (6,959)
Lowest elevation in feet (meters):
Salinas Chicas, Argentina, 138 (42) below sea level

World

Area in square miles (sq km):
57,900,000 (150,100,000)
Estimated population:
6,195,885,000
Population per square mile (sq km):
107 (41)
Mean elevation in feet (meters):
0 (0)
Highest elevation in feet (meters):
Mt. Everest, China (Tibet)–Nepal, 29,028 (8,848)
Lowest elevation in feet (meters):
Dead Sea, Israel–Jordan,
1,339 (408) below sea level

Largest Islands

Rank	Name	Area square miles	Area square km
1	Greenland, North America	840,000	2,175,600
2	New Guinea, Asia-Oceania	309,000	800,000
3	Borneo (Kalimantan), Asia	287,300	744,100
4	Madagascar, Africa	226,500	587,000
5	Baffin Island, Canada	195,928	507,451
6	Sumatra (Sumatera), Indonesia	182,860	473,606
7	Honshū, Japan	89,176	230,966
8	Great Britain, United Kingdom	88,795	229,978
9	Victoria Island, Canada	83,897	217,291
10	Ellesmere Island, Canada	75,767	196,236
11	Celebes (Sulawesi), Indonesia	73,057	189,216
12	South Island, New Zealand	57,708	149,463
13	Java (Jawa), Indonesia	51,038	132,187
14	North Island, New Zealand	44,332	114,821
15	Cuba, North America	42,800	110,800
16	Newfoundland, Canada	42,031	108,860
17	Luzon, Philippines	40,420	104,688
18	Iceland, Europe	39,800	103,000
19	Mindanao, Philippines	36,537	94,630
20	Ireland, Europe	32,600	84,400
21	Hokkaidō, Japan	32,245	83,515
22	Sakhalin, Russia	29,500	76,400
23	Hispaniola, North America	29,400	76,200
24	Banks Island, Canada	27,038	70,028
25	Tasmania, Australia	26,200	67,800
26	Sri Lanka, Asia	24,900	64,600
27	Devon Island, Canada	21,331	55,247
28	Berkner Island, Antarctica	20,005	51,829
29	Alexander Island, Antarctica	19,165	49,652
30	Tierra del Fuego, South America	18,600	48,200
31	Novaya Zemlya, north island, Russia	18,436	47,764
32	Kyūshū, Japan	17,129	44,363
33	Melville Island, Canada	16,274	42,149
34	Southampton Island, Canada	15,913	41,214
35	Axel Heiberg, Canada	15,498	40,151
36	Spitsbergen, Norway	15,260	39,523
37	New Britain, Papua New Guinea	14,093	36,500
38	Taiwan, Asia	13,900	36,000
39	Hainan Dao, China	13,100	34,000
40	Prince of Wales Island, Canada	12,872	33,339
41	Novaya Zemlya, south island, Russia	12,633	32,730
42	Vancouver Island, Canada	12,079	31,285
43	Sicily, Italy	9,926	25,709
44	Somerset Island, Canada	9,570	24,786
45	Sardinia, Italy	9,301	24,090
46	Bathurst Island, Canada	7,600	19,684
47	Shikoku, Japan	7,258	18,799
48	Ceram (Seram), Indonesia	7,191	18,625
49	North East Land, Norway	6,350	16,446
50	New Caledonia, Oceania	6,252	16,192
51	Prince Patrick Island, Canada	5,986	15,509
52	Timor, Asia	5,743	14,874
53	Sumbawa, Indonesia	5,549	14,377
54	Ostrov Oktyabr'skoy Revolyutsii, Russia	5,511	14,279
55	Flores, Indonesia	5,502	14,250
56	Samar, Philippines	5,100	13,080
57	King William Island, Canada	4,961	12,853
58	Negros, Philippines	4,907	12,710
59	Thurston Island, Antarctica	4,854	12,576
60	Palawan, Philippines	4,550	11,785

Islands, Islands, Everywhere

Four islands—Hokkaidō, Honshū, Kyūshū, and Shikoku—
constitute 98% of Japan's total land area, but the country is actually
comprised of more than 3,000 islands. Similarly, two islands—Great
Britain and Ireland—make up 93% of the total land area of the British
Isles, but the island group also includes more than 5,000 smaller
islands.

Greenland

New Guinea

Borneo

Madagascar

Baffin Island

Sumatra

Honshū

Great Britain

Victoria Island

Ellesmere Island

Major World Island Groups

Aleutian Islands (Pacific Ocean)

Alexander Archipelago
(Pacific Ocean)

Azores (Atlantic Ocean)

Bahamas (Atlantic Ocean)

Balearic Islands
(Mediterranean Sea)

Bismarck Archipelago
(Pacific Ocean)

British Isles (Atlantic Ocean)

Cape Verde Islands
(Atlantic Ocean)

Dodecanese (Mediterranean Sea)

Faroe Islands (Atlantic Ocean)

Falkland Islands (Atlantic Ocean)

Fiji Islands (Pacific Ocean)

Galapagos Islands (Pacific Ocean)

Greater Sunda Islands
(Indian/Pacific Oceans)

Hawai'ian Islands (Pacific Ocean)

Ionian Islands
(Mediterranean Sea)

Islas Canarias (Atlantic Ocean)

Japan (Pacific Ocean)

Kikládhes (Mediterranean Sea)

Kuril Islands (Pacific Ocean)

Lesser Sunda Islands
(Indian Ocean)

Moluccas (Pacific Ocean)

Nansei Shotō (Pacific Ocean)

New Hebrides (Atlantic Ocean)

New Siberian Islands
(Arctic Ocean)

Novaya Zemlya (Arctic Ocean)

Philippine Islands (Pacific Ocean)

Severnaya Zemlya (Arctic Ocean)

Solomon Islands (Pacific Ocean)

Spitsbergen (Arctic Ocean)

West Indies (Atlantic Ocean)

Contrasting Population Densities

Some islands are among
the most densely populated
places on Earth, while
others are among the least
densely populated. This
fact is dramatically
illustrated by
the following
comparison of
five islands:

Manhattan, N.Y., U.S., (pop. 1,537,000) — 69,864/ sq mile (26,965/ sq km)

Singapore Island, Singapore (pop. 4,375,000) — 17,785/ sq mile (6,879/ sq km)

Long Island, N.Y., U.S. (pop. 7,449,000) — 5,410/ sq mile (2,089/ sq km)

Population per square mile (sq km)

Baffin Island, Canada (pop. 11,700) — 0.06/ sq mile (0.02/ sq km)

Greenland (pop. 56,000) — 0.07/ sq mile (0.03/ sq km)

Mountains, Volcanoes, and Earthquakes

The Tallest Mountain in the World

With its peak reaching 29,028 feet (8,848 m) above sea level, Mt. Everest ranks as the *highest* mountain in the world, but not the *tallest*. That title goes to Mauna Kea, one of the five volcanic mountains that make up the island of Hawai'i. From its base on the floor of the Pacific Ocean, Mauna Kea rises 33,476 feet (10,210 m)—more than six miles—although only the top 13,796 feet (4,205 m) are above sea level.

Seafloor Atop Mt. Everest

When Sir Edmund Percival Hillary and Tenzing Norgay reached the summit of Mt. Everest in 1953, they probably did not realize they were standing on the seafloor.

The Himalayan mountain system was formed through the process of plate tectonics. Ocean once separated India and Asia, but 180 million years ago the Indo-Australian crustal plate, on which India sits, began a northward migration and eventually collided with the Eurasian plate. The seafloor between the two landmasses crumpled and was slowly thrust upward. Rock layers that once lay at the bottom of the ocean now crown the peaks of the highest mountains in the world.

Principal Mountains of the World
Δ = *Highest mountain in range, region, country, or state named*

Location	Height Feet	Meters
Africa		
Kilimanjaro, Δ Tanzania (Δ Africa)	19,340	5,895
Kirinyaga (Mount Kenya), Δ Kenya	17,058	5,199
Margherita Peak, Δ Uganda–Δ Dem. Rep. of the Congo	16,763	5,109
Ras Dashen Terara, Δ Ethiopia	15,158	4,620
Meru, Mount, Tanzania	14,978	4,565
Karisimbi, Volcan, Δ Rwanda-Dem. Rep. of the Congo	14,787	4,507
Elgon, Mount, Kenya-Uganda	14,178	4,321
Toubkal, Jebel, Δ Morocco (Δ Atlas Mts.)	13,665	4,165
Cameroon Mountain, Δ Cameroon	13,451	4,100
Antarctica		
Vinson Massif, Δ Antarctica	16,066	4,897
Kirkpatrick, Mount	14,856	4,528
Markham, Mount	14,049	4,282
Jackson, Mount	13,747	4,190
Sidley, Mount	13,717	4,181
Wade, Mount	13,396	4,083
Asia		
Everest, Mount, Δ China-Δ Nepal (Δ Tibet; Δ Himalayas; Δ Asia; Δ World)	29,028	8,848
K2 (Qogir Feng), China-Δ Pakistan (Δ Kashmir; Δ Karakoram Range)	28,250	8,611
Kanchenjunga, Δ India-Nepal	28,208	8,598
Makalu, China-Nepal	27,825	8,481
Dhawalāgiri, Nepal	26,810	8,172
Nanga Parbat, Pakistan	26,660	8,126
Annapurna, Nepal	26,504	8,078
Gasherbrum, China-Pakistan	26,470	8,068
Xixabangma Feng, China	26,286	8,012
Nanda Devi, India	25,645	7,817
Kamet, China-India	25,447	7,756
Namjagbarwa Feng, China	25,446	7,756
Muztag, China (Δ Kunlun Shan)	25,338	7,723
Tirich Mir, Pakistan (Δ Hindu Kush)	25,230	7,690
Gongga Shan, China	24,790	7,556
Kula Kangri, Δ Bhutan	24,784	7,554
Ismail Samani, pik, Δ Tajikistan (Δ Pamir)	24,590	7,495
Nowshak, Δ Afghanistan-Pakistan	24,557	7,485
Pobedy, Pik, China-Russia	24,406	7,439
Chomo Lhari, Bhutan-China	23,997	7,314
Muztag, China	23,891	7,282
Lenina, Pik, Δ Kyrgyzstan-Tajikistan	23,406	7,134
Api, Nepal	23,399	7,132
Kangrinboqê Feng, China	22,028	6,714
Hkakabo Razi, Δ Myanmar	19,296	5,881
Damavand, Qolleh-ye, Δ Iran	18,386	5,604
Agri Dagi (Mount Ararat), Δ Turkey	16,854	5,137
Fuladi, Kuh-e, Afghanistan	16,847	5,135
Jaya, Puncak, Δ Indonesia (Δ New Guinea)	16,503	5,030
Klyuchevskaya, Vulkan, Russia (Δ Poluostrov Kamchatka)	15,584	4,750
Trikora, Puncak, Indonesia	15,584	4,750
Belukha, Gora, Kazakhstan-Russia	14,783	4,506
Turgen, Mount, Mongolia	14,311	4,362
Kinabalu, Gunong, Δ Malaysia (Δ Borneo)	13,455	4,101
Yü Shan, Δ Taiwan	13,114	3,997
Erciyes Dagı, Turkey	12,851	3,917
Kerinci, Gunung, Indonesia (Δ Sumatra)	12,467	3,800
Fuji San, Δ Japan (Δ Honshu)	12,388	3,776
Rinjani, Gunung, Indonesia (Δ Lombok)	12,224	3,726
Semeru, Gunung, Indonesia (Δ Java)	12,060	3,676
Hadūr Shu'ayb, Jabal an-, Δ Yemen (Δ Arabian Peninsula)	12,008	3,660
Australia / Oceania		
Wilhelm, Mt., Δ Papua New Guinea	14,793	4,509
Giluwe, Mt., Papua New Guinea	14,330	4,368
Bangeta, Mt., Papua New Guinea	13,520	4,121
Victoria, Mt., Papua New Guinea (Δ Owen Stanley Range)	13,238	4,035
Aoraki (Mt. Cook), Δ New Zealand (Δ South Island)	12,316	3,754
Europe		
El'brus, Gora, Δ Russia (Δ Caucasus; Δ Europe)	18,510	5,642
Dykhtau, Mt., Russia	17,073	5,204
Blanc, Mont (Monte Bianco) Δ France-Δ Italy (Δ Alps)	15,771	4,807

Location	Height Feet	Meters
Dufourspitze, Italy-Δ Switzerland	15,203	4,634
Weisshorn, Switzerland	14,783	4,506
Matterhorn, Italy-Switzerland	14,692	4,478
Finsteraarhorn, Switzerland	14,022	4,274
Jungfrau, Switzerland	13,642	4,158
Écrins, Barre des, France	13,458	4,102
Viso, Monte, Italy (Δ Cottian Alps)	12,602	3,841
Grossglockner, Δ Austria	12,461	3,798
Teide, Pico de, Δ Spain (Δ Canary Is.)	12,188	3,715
North America		
McKinley, Mt., Δ Alaska (Δ United States; Δ North America)	20,320	6,194
Logan, Mt., Δ Canada (Δ Yukon; Δ St. Elias Mts.)	19,551	5,959
Orizaba, Pico de, Δ Mexico	18,406	5,610
St. Elias, Mt., Alaska-Canada	18,008	5,489
Popocatépetl, Volcán, Mexico	17,930	5,465
Foraker, Mt., Alaska	17,400	5,304
Iztaccíhuatl, Mexico	17,159	5,230
Lucania, Mt., Canada	17,147	5,226
Fairweather, Mt., Alaska-Canada (Δ British Columbia)	15,300	4,663
Whitney, Mt., Δ California	14,494	4,418
Elbert, Mt., Δ Colorado (Δ Rocky Mts.)	14,433	4,399
Massive, Mt., Colorado	14,421	4,396
Harvard, Mt., Colorado	14,420	4,395
Rainier, Mt., Δ Washington (Δ Cascade Range)	14,410	4,392
Williamson, Mt., California	14,370	4,380
La Plata Pk., Colorado	14,361	4,377
Blanca Pk., Colorado (Δ Sangre de Cristo Mts.)	14,345	4,372
Uncompahgre Pk., Colorado (Δ San Juan Mts.)	14,309	4,361
Grays Pk., Colorado (Δ Front Range)	14,270	4,349
Evans, Mt., Colorado	14,264	4,348
Longs Pk., Colorado	14,255	4,345
Wrangell, Mt., Alaska	14,163	4,317
Shasta, Mt., California	14,162	4,317
Pikes Pk., Colorado	14,110	4,301
Colima, Nevado de, Mexico	13,991	4,240
Tajumulco, Volcán, Δ Guatemala (Δ Central America)	13,845	4,220
Gannett Pk., Δ Wyoming	13,804	4,207
Mauna Kea, Δ Hawaii	13,796	4,205
Grand Teton, Wyoming	13,770	4,197
Mauna Loa, Hawaii	13,679	4,169
Kings Pk., Δ Utah	13,528	4,123
Cloud Pk., Wyoming (Δ Bighorn Mts.)	13,167	4,013
Waddington, Mt., Canada (Δ Coast Mts.)	13,163	4,012
Wheeler Pk., Δ New Mexico	13,161	4,011
Boundary Pk., Δ Nevada	13,140	4,005
Robson, Mt., Canada (Δ Canadian Rockies)	12,972	3,954
Granite Pk., Δ Montana	12,799	3,901
Borah Pk., Δ Idaho	12,662	3,859
Humphreys Pk., Δ Arizona	12,633	3,851
Chirripó, Volcán, Δ Costa Rica	12,530	3,819
Columbia, Mt., Canada (Δ Alberta)	12,294	3,747
Adams, Mt., Washington	12,276	3,742
Gunnbjørn Fjeld, Δ Greenland	12,139	3,700
South America		
Aconcagua, Cerro, Δ Argentina (Δ Andes; Δ South America)	22,831	6,959
Ojos del Salado, Nevado, Argentina-Δ Chile	22,615	6,893
Bonete, Cerro, Argentina	22,546	6,872
Huascarán, Nevado, Δ Peru	22,133	6,746
Llullaillaco, Volcán, Argentina-Chile	22,110	6,739
Yerupaja, Nevado, Peru	21,765	6,634
Tupungato, Cerro, Argentina-Chile	21,555	6,570
Sajama, Nevado, Bolivia	21,463	6,542
Illampu, Nevado, Bolivia	21,066	6,421
Illimani, Nevado, Bolivia	20,741	6,322
Chimborazo, Δ Ecuador	20,702	6,310
Antofalla, Volcán, Argentina	20,013	6,100
Cotopaxi, Ecuador	19,347	5,897
Misti, Volcán, Peru	19,101	5,822
Huila, Nevado de, Colombia (Δ Cordillera Central)	18,865	5,750
Bolívar, Pico, Δ Venezuela	16,427	5,007

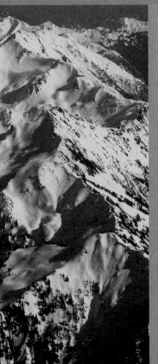

Principal Mountain Systems and Ranges of the World

Alaska Range (North America)
Alps (Europe)
Altai (Asia)
Andes (South America)
Appennino (Europe)
Atlas Mountains (Africa)
Appalachian Mountains (North America)
Brooks Range (North America)
Carpathian Mountains (Europe)
Cascade Range (North America)
Caucasus (Europe/Asia)
Coast Mountains (North America)
Coast Ranges (North America)
Great Dividing Range (Australia)
Greater Khingan Range (Asia)
Himalayas (Asia)
Hindu Kush (Asia)
Karakoram Range (Asia)
Kunlun Shan (Asia)
Madre Occidental, Sierra (North America)
Madre Oriental, Sierra (North America)
Nevada, Sierra (North America)
Pamirs (Asia)
Pyrenees (Europe)
Rocky Mountains (North America)
Sayan Khrebet (Asia)
Southern Alps (New Zealand)
Tien Shan (Asia)
Urals (Europe)
Zagros Mountains (Asia)

Notable Volcanic Eruptions

Year	Volcano Name, Location	Comments
ca. 4895 B.C.	Crater Lake, Oregon, U.S.	Collapse forms caldera that now contains Crater Lake.
ca. 4350 B.C.	Kikai, Ryukyu Islands, Japan	Japan's largest known eruption.
ca. 1628 B.C.	Santorini (Thira), Greece	Eruption devastates late Minoan civilization.
79 A.D.	Vesuvius (Vesuvio), Italy	Roman towns of Pompeii and Herculaneum are buried.
ca. 180	Taupo, New Zealand	Area measuring 6,200 square miles (16,000 sq km) is devastated.
ca. 260	Ilopango, El Salvador	Thousands killed, with major impact on Mayan civilization.
915	Towada, Honshu, Japan	Japan's largest historic eruption.
ca. 1000	Baitoushan, China/Korea	Largest known eruption on Asian mainland.
1259	Unknown	Evidence from polar ice cores suggests that a huge eruption, possibly the largest of the millennium, occurred in this year.
1586	Kelut, Java	Explosions in crater lake; mudflows kill 10,000.
1631	Vesuvius (Vesuvio), Italy	Eruption kills 4,000.
ca. 1660	Long Island, Papua New Guinea	"The time of darkness" in tribal legends on Papua New Guinea.
1672	Merapi, Java	Pyroclastic flows and mudflows kill 3,000.
1711	Awu, Sangihe Islands, Indonesia	Pyroclastic flows kill 3,000.
1760	Makian, Halmahera, Indonesia	Eruption kills 2,000; island evacuated for seven years.
1772	Papandayan, Java	Debris avalanche causes 2,957 fatalities.
1783	Lakagigar, Iceland	Largest historic lava flows; 9,350 deaths.
1790	Kīlauea, Hawai'i	Hawai'i's last large explosive eruption.
1792	Unzen, Kyushu, Japan	Tsunami and debris avalanche kill 14,500.
1815	Tambora, Indonesia	History's most explosive eruption; 92,000 deaths.
1822	Galunggung, Java	Pyroclastic flows and mudflows kill 4,011.
1856	Awu, Sangihe Islands, Indonesia	Pyroclastic flows kill 2,806.
1883	Krakatau, Indonesia	Caldera collapse; 36,417 people killed, most by tsunami.
1888	Ritter Island, Papua New Guinea	3,000 killed, most by tsunami created by debris avalanche.
1902	Mont Pelee, West Indies	Town of St. Pierre destroyed; 28,000 people killed.
1902	Santa Maria, Guatemala	5,000 killed as 10 villages are buried by volcanic debris.
1912	Novarupta (Katmai), Alaska	Largest 20th-century eruption.
1914	Lassen, California, U.S.	California's last historic eruption.
1919	Kelut, Java	Mudflows devastate 104 villages and kill 5,110 people.
1930	Merapi, Java	1,369 people are killed as 42 villages are totally or partially destroyed.
1943	Parícutin, Mexico	Fissure in cornfield erupts, building cinder cone 1,500 feet (460 m) high within two years. One of the few volcano births ever witnessed.
1951	Lamington, Papua New Guinea	Pyroclastic flows kill 2,942.
1963	Surtsey, Iceland	Submarine eruption builds new island.
1977	Nyiragongo, Dem. Rep. of the Congo	One of the shortest major eruptions and fastest lava flows ever recorded.
1980	St. Helens, Washington, U.S.	Lateral blast; 230-square-mile (600 sq km) area devastated.
1982	El Chichón, Mexico	Pyroclastic surges kill 1,877.
1985	Ruiz, Colombia	Mudflows kill 23,080.
1991	Pinatubo, Luzon, Philippines	Major eruption in densely populated area prompts evacuation of 250,000 people; fatalities number fewer than 800. Enormous amount of gas released into stratosphere lowers global temperatures for more than a year.
1995	Soufriere Hills Volcano, Montserrat Island	Forced evacuation of the southern half of the island, destroyed capital city of Plymouth.

Sources: Smithsonian Institution Global Volcanism Program; Volcanoes of the World, Second Edition, by Tom Simkin and Lee Siebert, Geoscience Press and Smithsonian Institution, 1994. USGS National Earthquake Information Center.

Eruption of Mt. St. Helens in 1980

Significant Earthquakes through History

Year	Estimated Magnitude	Number of Deaths	Place
365		50,000	Knossos, Crete
844		50,000	Damascus, Syria; Antioch, Turkey
856		150,000	Dämghän, Kashan, Qumis, Iran
893		150,000	Caucasus region
894		180,000	western India
1042		50,000	Palmyra, Baalbek, Syria
1138		230,000	Aleppo, Gansana, Syria
1139	6.8	300,000	Gäncä, Kiapas, Azerbaijan
1201		50,000	upper Egypt to Syria
1290	6.7	100,000	eastern China
1556		820,000	Shanxi Province, China
1662		300,000	China
1667	6.9	80,000	Caucusus region, northern Iran
1668		50,000	Shandong Province, China
1693		93,000	Sicily, Italy
1727		77,000	Tabrīz, Iran
1731		100,000	Beijing, China
1739		50,000	China
1755		62,000	Morocco, Portugal, Spain
1780	6.7	100,000	Tabrīz, Iran
1868	7.7	70,000	Ecuador, Colombia
1908	7.5	83,000	Calabria, Messina, Italy
1920	8.5	200,000	Gansu and Shanxi provinces, China
1923	8.2	142,807	Tokyo, Yokohama, Japan
1927	8.3	200,000	Gansu and Qinghai provinces, China
1932	7.6	70,000	Gansu Province, China
1970	7.8	66,794	northern Peru
1976	7.8	242,000	Tangshan, China
1990	7.7	50,000	northwestern Iran

Some Significant U.S. Earthquakes

Year	Estimated Magnitude	Number of Deaths	Place
1811–12	8.6, 8.4, 8.7	<10	New Madrid, Missouri (series)
1886	7.0	60	Charleston, South Carolina
1906	8.3	3,000	San Francisco, California
1933	6.3	115	Long Beach, California
1946	7.4	5 ‡	Alaska
1964	8.4	125	Anchorage, Alaska
1971	6.8	65	San Fernando, California
1989	7.1	62	San Francisco Bay Area, California
1994	6.8	58	Northridge, California

‡ A tsunami generated by this earthquake struck Hilo, Hawaii, killing 159 people.

Oceans and Lakes

Oceans, Seas, Gulfs, and Bays

	Area sq. miles	Area sq. km.	Volume of water cubic miles	Volume of water cubic km.	Mean depth feet	Mean depth meters	Greatest known depth feet	Greatest known depth meters	
Pacific Ocean	63,800,000	165,200,000	169,650,000	707,100,000	12,987	3,957	35,810	10,922	Mariana Trench
Atlantic Ocean	31,800,000	82,400,000	79,199,000	330,100,000	11,821	3,602	28,232	8,611	Puerto Rico Trench
Indian Ocean	28,900,000	74,900,000	68,282,000	284,600,000	12,261	3,736	23,812	7,258	Weber Basin
Arctic Ocean	5,400,000	14,000,000	4,007,000	16,700,000	3,712	1,131	17,897	5,453	Lat. 77° 45'N, long. 175°W
Coral Sea	1,850,000	4,791,000	2,752,000	11,470,000	7,857	2,394	30,079	9,165	
Arabian Sea	1,492,000	3,864,000	2,416,000	10,070,000	8,973	2,734	19,029	5,803	
South China Sea	1,331,000	3,447,000	943,000	3,929,000	3,741	1,140	18,241	5,563	
Caribbean Sea	1,063,000	2,753,000	1,646,000	6,860,000	8,175	2,491	25,197	7,685	Off Cayman Islands
Mediterranean Sea	967,000	2,505,000	901,000	3,754,000	4,916	1,498	16,470	5,023	Off Cape Matapan, Greece
Bering Sea	876,000	2,269,000	911,000	3,796,000	5,382	1,640	25,194	7,684	Off Buldir Island
Bengal, Bay of	839,000	2,173,000	1,357,000	5,616,000	8,484	2,585	17,251	5,261	
Okhotsk, Sea of	619,000	1,603,000	316,000	1,317,000	2,694	821	1,029	3,374	Lat. 146° 10'E, long. 46° 50'N
Norwegian Sea	597,000	1,546,000	578,000	2,408,000	5,717	1,742	13,189	4,022	
Mexico, Gulf of	596,000	1,544,000	560,000	2,332,000	8,205	2,500	14,370	4,382	Sigsbee Deep
Hudson Bay	475,000	1,230,000	22,000	92,000	328	100	850	259	Near entrance
Greenland Sea	465,000	1,204,000	417,000	1,740,000	4,739	1,444	15,899	4,849	
Japan, Sea of	413,000	1,070,000	391,000	1,630,000	5,037	1,535	12,041	3,669	
Arafura Sea	400,000	1,037,000	49,000	204,000	646	197	12,077	3,680	
East Siberian Sea	357,000	926,000	14,000	61,000	216	66	508	155	
Kara Sea	349,000	903,000	24,000	101,000	371	113	2,034	620	
East China Sea	290,000	752,000	63,000	263,000	1,145	349	7,778	2,370	
Banda Sea	268,000	695,000	511,000	2,129,000	10,056	3,064	24,418	7,440	
Baffin Bay	263,000	681,000	142,000	593,000	2,825	861	7,010	2,136	
Laptev Sea	262,000	678,000	87,000	363,000	1,772	540	9,780	2,980	
Timor Sea	237,000	615,000	60,000	250,000	1,332	406	10,863	3,310	
Andaman Sea	232,000	602,000	158,000	660,000	3,597	1,096	13,777	4,198	
Chukchi Sea	228,000	590,000	11,000	45,000	252	77	525	160	
North Sea	214,000	554,000	12,000	52,000	315	96	2,655	809	
Java Sea	185,000	480,000	5,000	22,000	147	45	292	89	
Beaufort Sea	184,000	476,000	115,000	478,000	3,295	1,004	12,245	3,731	
Red Sea	174,000	450,000	60,000	251,000	1,831	558	8,648	2,635	
Baltic Sea	173,000	448,000	5,000	20,000	157	48	1,506	459	
Celebes Sea	168,000	435,000	380,000	1,586,000	11,962	3,645	19,173	5,842	
Black Sea	166,000	431,000	133,000	555,000	3,839	1,170	7,256	2,211	
Yellow Sea	161,000	417,000	4,000	17,000	131	40	344	105	
Sulu Sea	134,000	348,000	133,000	553,000	5,221	1,591	18,300	5,576	
Molucca Sea	112,000	291,000	133,000	554,000	6,242	1,902	16,311	4,970	
Ceram Sea	72,000	187,000	54,000	227,000	3,968	1,209	17,456	5,319	
Flores Sea	47,000	121,000	53,000	222,000	6,003	1,829	16,813	5,123	
Bali Sea	46,000	119,000	12,000	49,000	1,349	411	4,253	1,296	
Savu Sea	41,000	105,000	43,000	178,000	5,582	1,701	11,060	3,370	
White Sea	35,000	91,000	1,000	4,400	161	49	1,083	330	
Azov, Sea of	15,000	40,000	100	400	29	9	46	14	
Marmara, Sea of	4,000	11,000	1,000	4,000	1,171	357	4,138	1,261	

Source: *Atlas of World Water Balance, USSR National Committee for the International Water Decade and UNESCO, 1977.*

Note: In 2000, the International Hydrographic Organization delimited a fifth world ocean: the Southern Ocean. This ocean, which encircles Antarctica, is not included in this chart.

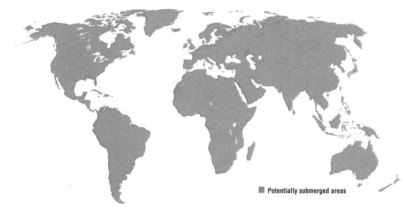

■ Potentially submerged areas

Fluctuating Sea Level

Changes in the Earth's climate have a dramatic effect on the sea level. Only 20,000 years ago, at the height of the most recent ice age, a vast amount of the Earth's water was locked up in ice sheets and glaciers, and the sea level was 330 feet (100 meters) lower than it is today. As the climate warmed slowly, the ice began to melt and the oceans began to rise.

Today there is still a tremendous amount of ice on the Earth. More than nine-tenths of it resides in the enormous ice cap which covers Antarctica. Measuring about 5.4 million square miles (14 million sq km) in surface area, the ice cap is on average one mile (1.6 km) thick but in some places is nearly three miles (4.8 km) thick. If it were to melt, the oceans would rise another 200 feet (60 m), and more than half of the world's population would have to relocate.

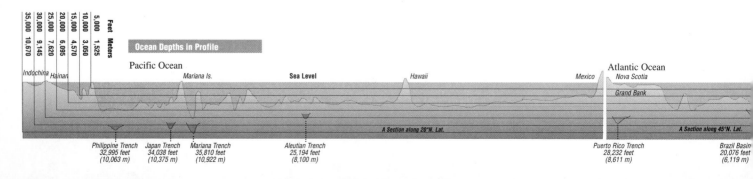

Ocean Depths in Profile

Deepest Lakes

	Lake	Greatest depth feet	meters
1	Baikal, Lake, Russia	5,315	1,621
2	Tanganyika, Lake, Africa	4,800	1,464
3	Caspian Sea, Asia-Europe	3,363	1,025
4	Nyasa, Lake (Lake Malawi), Malawi-Mozambique-Tanzania	2,317	706
5	Issyk-Kul', Lake, Kyrgyzstan	2,303	702
6	Great Slave Lake, NWT, Canada	2,015	614
7	Matana, Lake, Indonesia	1,936	590
8	Crater Lake, Oregon, U.S.	1,932	589
9	Toba, Lake (Danau Toba), Indonesia	1,736	529
10	Sarez, Lake, Tajikistan	1,657	505
11	Tahoe, Lake, California-Nevada, U.S.	1,645	502
12	Kivu, Lake, Rwanda-Dem. Rep. of the Congo	1,628	496
13	Chelan, Lake, Washington, U.S.	1,605	489
14	Quesnel Lake, BC, Canada	1,560	476
15	Adams Lake, BC, Canada	1,500	457

Lakes with the Greatest Volume of Water

	Lake	Volume of water cubic mi	cubic km
1	Caspian Sea, Asia-Europe	18,900	78,200
2	Baikal, Lake, Russia	5,500	23,000
3	Tanganyika, Lake, Africa	4,500	18,900
4	Superior, Lake, Canada-U.S.	2,900	12,200
5	Nyasa, Lake (Lake Malawi), Malawi-Mozambique-Tanzania	1,900	7,725
6	Michigan, Lake, U.S.	1,200	4,910
7	Huron, Lake, Canada-U.S.	860	3,580
8	Victoria, Lake, Kenya-Tanzania-Uganda	650	2,700
9	Issyk-Kul', Lake, Kyrgyzstan	415	1,730
10	Ontario, Lake, Canada-U.S.	410	1,710
11	Great Slave Lake, Canada	260	1,070
12	Great Bear Lake, Canada	240	1,010
13	Ladozhskoye, Ozero, Russia	220	908
14	Titicaca, Lago, Bolivia-Peru	170	710

Sources for volume and depth information: Atlas of World Water Balance, USSR National Committee for the International Water Decade and UNESCO, 1977; Principal Rivers and Lakes of the World, National Oceanic and Atmospheric Administration, 1982.

Principal Lakes

	Lake	Area sq mi	sq km
1	Caspian Sea, Asia-Europe	143,240	370,990
2	Superior, Lake, Canada-U.S.	31,700	82,100
3	Victoria, Lake, Kenya-Tanzania-Uganda	26,820	69,463
4	Huron, Lake, Canada-U.S.	23,000	60,000
5	Michigan, Lake, U.S.	22,300	57,800
6	Tanganyika, Lake, Africa	12,350	31,986
7	Baikal, Lake, Russia	12,200	31,500
8	Great Bear Lake, Canada	12,095	31,326
9	Nyasa, Lake (Lake Malawi), Malawi-Mozambique-Tanzania	11,150	28,878
10	Aral Sea, Kazakhstan-Uzbekistan	11,100	28,700
11	Great Slave Lake, Canada	11,030	28,568
12	Erie, Lake, Canada-U.S.	9,910	25,667
13	Winnipeg, Lake, Canada	9,416	24,387
14	Ontario, Lake, Canada-U.S.	7,540	19,529
15	Balqash koli (Lake Balkhash), Kazakhstan	7,100	18,300
16	Ladozhskoye, Ozero, Russia	6,833	17,700
17	Chad, Lake (Lac Tchad), Cameroon-Chad-Nigeria	6,300	16,300
18	Onezhskoye, Ozero, Russia	3,753	9,720
19	Eyre, Lake, Australia	3,700	9,500
20	Titicaca, Lago, Bolivia-Peru	3,200	8,300
21	Nicaragua, Lago de, Nicaragua	3,150	8,158
22	Mai-Ndombe, Lac, Dem. Rep. of the Congo	3,100	8,000
23	Athabasca, Lake, Canada	3,064	7,935
24	Reindeer Lake, Canada	2,568	6,650
25	Tônlé Sap, Cambodia	2,500	6,500
26	Rudolf, Lake, Ethiopia-Kenya	2,473	6,405
27	Issyk-Kul', Ozero, Kyrgyzstan	2,425	6,280
28	Torrens, Lake, Australia	2,300	5,900
29	Albert, Lake, Uganda-Dem. Rep. of the Congo	2,160	5,594
30	Vänern, Sweden	2,156	5,584
31	Nettilling Lake, Canada	2,140	5,542
32	Winnipegosis, Lake, Canada	2,075	5,374
33	Bangweulu, Lake, Zambia	1,930	4,999
34	Nipigon, Lake, Canada	1,872	4,848
35	Orumiyeh, Daryacheh-ye, Iran	1,815	4,701
36	Manitoba, Lake, Canada	1,785	4,624
37	Woods, Lake of the, Canada-U.S.	1,727	4,472
38	Kyoga, Lake, Uganda	1,710	4,429

Lake Baikal

Russia's Great Lake

On a map of the world, Lake Baikal is easy to overlook — a thin blue crescent adrift in the vastness of Siberia. But its inconspicuousness is deceptive, for Baikal is one of the greatest bodies of fresh water on Earth.

Although lakes generally have a life span of less than one million years, Baikal has existed for perhaps as long as 25 million years, which makes it the world's oldest body of fresh water. It formed in a rift that tectonic forces had begun to tear open in the Earth's crust. As the rift grew, so did Baikal. Today the lake is 395 miles (636 km) long and an average of 30 miles (48 km) wide. Only seven lakes in the world have a greater surface area.

Baikal is the world's deepest lake. Its maximum depth is 5,315 feet (1,621 m) — slightly over a mile, and roughly equal to the greatest depth of the Grand Canyon. The lake bottom lies 4,250 feet (1,295 m) below sea level and two-and-a-third miles (3.75 km) below the peaks of the surrounding mountains. The crustal rift which Baikal occupies is the planet's deepest land depression, extending to a depth of more than five-and-a-half miles (9 km). The lake sits atop at least four miles (6.4 km) of sediment, the accumulation of 25 million years.

More than 300 rivers empty into Baikal, but only one, the Angara, flows out of it. Despite having only 38% of the surface area of North America's Lake Superior, Baikal contains more water than all five of the Great Lakes combined. Its volume of 5,500 cubic miles (23,000 cubic km) is greater than that of any other freshwater lake in the world and represents approximately one-fifth of all of the Earth's unfrozen fresh water.

Caspian Sea Lake Superior Lake Victoria Aral Sea

Lake Huron Lake Michigan Lake Tanganyika

Lake Baikal Great Bear Lake Lake Nyasa (Malawi)

Mediterranean Sea Indian Ocean Arctic Ocean Pacific Ocean

France Gibraltar Malta Israel Sea Level Sumba North Pole 65°N 65°S South Pole

A Section along 10°N. Lat.

Rivers

World's Longest Rivers

Rank	River	Length Miles	Length Kilometers	Rank	River	Length Miles	Length Kilometers
1	Nile, Africa	4,145	6,671	36	Murray, Australia	1,566	2,520
2	Amazon (Amazonas)-Ucayali, South America	4,000	6,400	37	Ganges, Asia	1,560	2,511
3	Yangtze (Chang), Asia	3,900	6,300	38	Pilcomayo, South America	1,550	2,494
4	Mississippi-Missouri, North America	3,740	6,019	39	Euphrates, Asia	1,510	2,430
5	Huang (Yellow), Asia	3,395	5,464	40	Ural, Asia	1,509	2,428
6	Ob'-Irtysh, Asia	3,362	5,410	41	Arkansas, North America	1,459	2,348
7	Río de la Plata-Paraná, South America	3,030	4,876	42	Colorado, North America (U.S.-Mexico)	1,450	2,334
8	Congo, Africa	2,900	4,700	43	Aldan, Asia	1,412	2,273
9	Paraná, South America	2,800	4,500	44	Syr Darya, Asia	1,370	2,205
10	Amur-Argun, Asia	2,761	4,444	45	Dnieper, Europe	1,350	2,200
11	Lena, Asia	2,700	4,400	46	Araguaia, South America	1,350	2,200
12	Mackenzie, North America	2,635	4,241	47	Cassai (Kasai), Africa	1,338	2,153
13	Mekong, Asia	2,600	4,200	48	Tarim, Asia	1,328	2,137
14	Niger, Africa	2,600	4,200	49	Kolyma, Asia	1,323	2,129
15	Yenisey, Asia	2,543	4,092	50	Orange, Africa	1,300	2,100
16	Missouri-Red Rock, North America	2,533	4,076	51	Negro, South America	1,300	2,100
17	Mississippi, North America	2,348	3,779	52	Ayeyarwady (Irrawaddy), Asia	1,300	2,100
18	Murray-Darling, Australia	2,330	3,750	53	Red, North America	1,270	2,044
19	Missouri, North America	2,315	3,726	54	Juruá, South America	1,250	2,012
20	Volga, Europe	2,194	3,531	55	Columbia, North America	1,240	2,000
21	Madeira, South America	2,013	3,240	56	Xingu, South America	1,230	1,979
22	São Francisco, South America	1,988	3,199	57	Ucayali, South America	1,220	1,963
23	Grande, Rio (Río Bravo), North America	1,885	3,034	58	Saskatchewan-Bow, North America	1,205	1,939
24	Purús, South America	1,860	2,993	59	Peace, North America	1,195	1,923
25	Indus, Asia	1,800	2,900	60	Tigris, Asia	1,180	1,899
26	Danube, Europe	1,776	2,858	61	Don, Europe	1,162	1,870
27	Brahmaputra, Asia	1,770	2,849	62	Songhua, Asia	1,140	1,835
28	Yukon, North America	1,770	2,849	63	Pechora, Europe	1,124	1,809
29	Salween (Nu), Asia	1,750	2,816	64	Kama, Europe	1,122	1,805
30	Zambezi, Africa	1,700	2,700	65	Limpopo, Africa	1,120	1,800
31	Vilyuy, Asia	1,647	2,650	66	Angara, Asia	1,105	1,779
32	Tocantins, South America	1,640	2,639	67	Snake, North America	1,038	1,670
33	Orinoco, South America	1,615	2,600	68	Uruguay, South America	1,025	1,650
34	Paraguay, South America	1,610	2,591	69	Churchill, North America	1,000	1,600
35	Amu Darya, Asia	1,578	2,540	70	Marañón, South America	995	1,592

The World's Greatest River

Although the Nile is slightly longer, the Amazon surpasses all other rivers in volume, size of drainage basin, and in nearly every other important category. If any river is to be called the greatest in the world, surely it is the Amazon.

It has been estimated that one-fifth of all of the flowing water on Earth is carried by the Amazon. From its 150-mile (240-km)-wide mouth, the river discharges 6,180,000 cubic feet (174,900 cubic m) of water per second — four-and-a-half times as much as the Congo, ten times as much as the Mississippi, and fifty-six times as much as the Nile. The Amazon's tremendous outflow turns the waters of the Atlantic from salty to brackish for more than 100 miles (160 km) offshore.

Drainage basin of the Amazon River

Covering more than one-third of the entire continent of South America, the Amazon's vast drainage basin measures 2,669,000 square miles (6,915,000 sq km) and is nearly twice as large as that of the second-ranked Congo. The Amazon begins its 4,000-mile (6,400-km) journey to the Atlantic from high up in the Andes, only 100 miles (160 km) from the Pacific. Along its course it receives the waters of more than 1,000 tributaries, which rise principally from the Andes, the Guiana Highlands, and the Brazilian Highlands. Seven of the tributaries are more than 1,000 miles (1,600 km) long, and one, the Madeira, is more than 2,000 miles (3,200 km) long.

The depth of the Amazon throughout most of its Brazilian segment exceeds 150 feet (45 m). Depths of more than 300 feet (90 m) have been recorded at points near the mouth. The largest ocean-going vessels can sail as far inland as Manaus, 1,000 miles (1,600 km) from the mouth. Freighters and small passenger vessels can navigate to Iquitos, 2,300 miles (3,700 km) from the mouth, even during times of low water.

Rivers with the Greatest Volume of Water

Rank	River Name	Flow of water per second at mouth		Rank	River Name	Flow of water per second at mouth	
		cubic feet	cubic meters			cubic feet	cubic meters
1	Amazon (Amazonas), South America	6,180,000	174,900	18	Para-Tocantins, South America (joins Amazon at mouth)	360,000	10,200
2	Congo, Africa	1,377,000	39,000	19	Salween, Asia	353,000	10,000
3	Negro, South America (tributary of Amazon)	1,236,000	35,000	20	Cassai (Kasai), Africa (trib. of Congo)	351,000	9,900
4	Orinoco, South America	890,000	25,200	21	Mackenzie, North America	343,000	9,700
5	Río de la Plata-Paraná, South America	809,000	22,900	22	Volga, Europe	271,000	7,700
6	Yangtze (Chang), Asia;	770,000	21,800	23	Ohio, North America (trib. of Mississippi)	257,000	7,300
	Madeira, South America (trib. of Amazon)	770,000	21,800	24	Yukon, North America	240,000	6,800
7	Missouri, North America (trib. of Mississippi)	763,000	21,600	25	Indus, Asia	235,000	6,600
8	Mississippi, North America*	640,300	18,100	26	Danube, Europe	227,000	6,400
9	Yenisey, Asia	636,000	18,000	27	Niger, Africa	215,000	6,100
10	Brahmaputra, Asia	575,000	16,300	28	Atchafalaya, North America	181,000	5,100
11	Lena, Asia	569,000	16,100	29	Paraguay, South America	155,000	4,400
12	Zambezi, Africa	565,000	16,000	30	Ob'-Katun, Asia	147,000	4,200
13	Mekong, Asia	500,000	14,100	31	São Francisco, South America	120,000	3,400
14	Saint Lawrence, North America	460,000	13,000	32	Tunguska, Asia	118,000	3,350
15	Ayeyarwady (Irrawaddy), Asia	447,000	12,600	33	Huang (Yellow), Asia	116,000	3,300
16	Ob'-Irtysh, Asia; Ganges, Asia	441,000	12,500	34	Nile, Africa	110,000	3,100
17	Amur, Asia	390,000	11,000				

*Approximately one-third of the Mississippi's water is diverted above Baton Rouge, Louisiana, and reaches the Gulf of Mexico via the Atchafalaya River.

Principal Rivers of the Continents

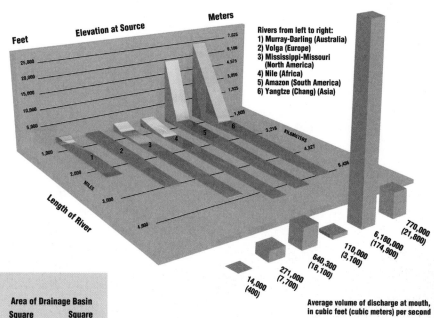

Rivers from left to right:
1) Murray-Darling (Australia)
2) Volga (Europe)
3) Mississippi-Missouri (North America)
4) Nile (Africa)
5) Amazon (South America)
6) Yangtze (Chang) (Asia)

Elevation at Source

Feet — Meters

Length of River

Average volume of discharge at mouth, in cubic feet (cubic meters) per second

14,000 (400)
271,000 (7,700)
110,000 (3,100)
640,300 (18,100)
6,180,000 (174,900)
770,000 (21,800)

Rivers with the Largest Drainage Basins

Rank	River	Area of Drainage Basin	
		Square Miles	Square Kilometers
1	Amazon (Amazonas), South America	2,669,000	6,915,000
2	Congo, Africa	1,474,500	3,820,000
3	Mississippi-Missouri, North America	1,243,000	3,220,000
4	Río de la Plata-Paraná, South America	1,197,000	3,100,000
5	Ob'-Irtysh, Asia	1,154,000	2,990,000
6	Nile, Africa	1,108,000	2,870,000
7	Yenisey-Angara, Asia	1,011,000	2,618,500
8	Lena, Asia	961,000	2,490,000
9	Niger, Africa	807,000	2,090,000
10	Amur-Argun, Asia	792,000	2,051,300
11	Yangtze (Chang), Asia	705,000	1,826,000
12	Volga, Europe	525,000	1,360,000
13	Zambezi, Africa	513,500	1,330,000
14	St. Lawrence, North America	503,000	1,302,800
15	Huang (Yellow), Asia	486,000	1,258,700

Sources for volume and drainage basin information: Atlas of World Water Balance, USSR National Committee for the International Hydrological Decade and UNESCO, 1977; Principal Rivers and Lakes of the World, National Oceanic and Atmospheric Administration, 1982.

Climate and Weather

Temperature Extremes by Continent

Africa

Highest recorded temperature
Al 'Azīzīyah, Libya, September 13, 1922:
136° F (58° C),
Lowest recorded temperature
Ifrane, Morocco, February 11, 1935:
-11° F (-24° C)

Antarctica

Highest recorded temperature
Vanda Station, January 5, 1974:
59° F (15° C)
Lowest recorded temperature
Vostok, July 21, 1983:
-129° F (-89° C)

Asia

Highest recorded temperature
Tirat Zevi, Israel, June 21, 1942:
129° F (54° C)
Lowest recorded temperature
Oymyakon, Russia, February 6, 1933,
and Verkhoyansk, Russia, February 7, 1892:
-90° F (-68° C)

Australia / Oceania

Highest recorded temperature
Cloncurry, Queensland, Australia,
January 16, 1889: 128° F (53° C)
Lowest recorded temperature
Charlotte Pass, New South Wales, Australia,
June 29, 1994: -9.4° F (-22° C)

Europe

Highest recorded temperature
Sevilla, Spain, August 4, 1881:
122° F (50° C)
Lowest recorded temperature
Ust' Ščugor, Russia, (date not known):
-67° F (-55° C)

North America

Highest recorded temperature
Death Valley, California, United States,
July 10, 1913: 134° F (57° C)
Lowest recorded temperature
Northice, Greenland, January 9, 1954:
-87° F (-66° C)

South America

Highest recorded temperature
Rivadavia, Argentina, December 11, 1905:
120° F (49° C)
Lowest recorded temperature
Sarmiento, Argentina, June 1, 1907:
-27° F (-33° C)

World

Highest recorded temperature
Al 'Azīzīyah, Libya, September 13, 1922:
136° F (58° C)
Lowest recorded temperature
Vostok, Antarctica, July 21, 1983:
-129° F (-89° C)

World Temperature Extremes

Highest mean annual temperature Dalol, Ethiopia, 94° F (34° C)
Lowest mean annual temperature Plateau Station, Antarctica: -70° F (-57° C)

Greatest difference between highest and lowest recorded temperatures
Verkhoyansk, Russia. The highest temperature ever recorded there is 93.5° F (34.2° C); the lowest is -89.7° F (−67.6° C)
— a difference of 183° F (102° C).

Highest temperature ever recorded at the South Pole 7.5° F (-14° C) on December 27, 1978

Most consecutive days with temperatures of 100° F (38° C) or above Marble Bar, Australia, 162 days: October 30, 1923 to April 7, 1924

Greatest rise in temperature within a 12-hour period
Granville, North Dakota, on February 21, 1918. The temperature rose 83° F (46° C), from -33° F (-36° C)
in early morning to +50° F (10° C) in late afternoon

Greatest drop in temperature within a 12-hour period
Fairfield, Montana, on December 24, 1924. The temperature dropped 84° F (46° C), from 63° F (17° C)
at noon to -21° F (-29° C) by midnight

Temperature Ranges for 14 Major Cities around the World

City	Mean Temperature — Coldest Winter Month	Mean Temperature — Hottest Summer Month	City	Mean Temperature — Coldest Winter Month	Mean Temperature — Hottest Summer Month
Buenos Aires, Argentina	Aug: 51.3° F (10.7° C)	Jan: 75.0° F (23.9° C)	Mumbai (Bombay), India	Jan: 74.3° F (23.5° C)	May: 85.5° F (29.7° C)
Kolkata (Calcutta), India	Jan: 67.5° F (19.7° C)	May: 88.5° F (31.4° C)	New York City, U.S.	Jan: 32.9° F (0.5° C)	Jul: 77.0° F (25.0° C)
London, England	Feb: 39.4° F (4.1° C)	Jul: 63.9° F (17.7° C)	Osaka, Japan	Jan: 40.6° F (4.8° C)	Aug: 82.2° F (27.9° C)
Los Angeles, U.S.	Jan: 56.3° F (13.5° C)	Jul: 74.1° F (23.4° C)	Rio de Janeiro, Brazil	Jul: 70.2° F (21.2° C)	Jan: 79.9° F (26.6° C)
Manila, Philippines	Jan: 77.7° F (25.4° C)	May: 84.9° F (29.4° C)	São Paulo, Brazil	Jul: 58.8° F (14.9° C)	Jan: 71.1° F (21.7° C)
Mexico City, Mexico	Jan: 54.1° F (12.3° C)	May: 64.9° F (18.3° C)	Seoul, South Korea	Jan: 23.2° F (-4.9° C)	Aug: 77.7° F (25.4° C)
Moscow, Russia	Feb: 14.5° F (-9.7° C)	Jul: 65.8° F (18.8° C)	Tokyo, Japan	Jan: 39.6° F (4.2° C)	Aug: 79.3° F (26.3° C)

Precipitation

Greatest local average annual rainfall
Mt. Waialeale, Kaua'i, Hawaii,
460 inches (1,168 cm)

Lowest local average annual rainfall
Arica, Chile, .03 inches (.08 cm)

Greatest rainfall in 12 months
Cherrapunji, India, August 1860 to August 1861:
1,042 inches (2,646 cm)

Greatest rainfall in one month
Cherrapunji, India, July 1861: 366 inches (930 cm)

Greatest rainfall in 24 hours
Cilaos, Reunion, March 15 and 16, 1952:
74 inches (187 cm)

Greatest rainfall in 12 hours
Belouve, Reunion, February 28 and 29, 1964:
53 inches (135 cm)

Most thunderstorms annually
Kampala, Uganda, averages 242 days per
year with thunderstorms

Between 1916 and 1920, Bogor, Indonesia,
averaged 322 days per year with thunderstorms

Longest dry period
Arica, Chile, October, 1903
to January, 1918 — over 14 years

Largest hailstone ever recorded
Aurora, Nebraska, U.S., June 22, 1993:
circumference 18.75 inches (47.6 cm),
diameter 7 inches (17.8 cm)

Heaviest hailstone ever recorded
Kazakhstan, 1959: 4.18 pounds (1.9 kilograms)

North America's greatest snowfall in one season
Rainier Paradise Ranger Station, Washington,
U.S., 1971–1972: 1,122 inches (2,850 cm)

North America's greatest snowfall in one storm
Mt. Shasta Ski Bowl, California, U.S.,
February 13 to 19, 1959: 189 inches (480 cm)

North America's greatest snowfall in 24 hours
Silver Lake, Colorado, U.S., April 14 and 15, 1921:
76 inches (1 92.5 cm)

N. America's greatest depth of snowfall on the ground
Tamarack, California, U.S., March 11, 1911:
451 inches (1,145.5 cm)

Foggiest place on the U.S. West Coast
Cape Disappointment, Washington,
averages 2,552 hours of fog per year

Foggiest place on the U.S. East Coast
Mistake Island, Maine, averages
1,580 hours of fog per year

Wind

Highest 24-hour mean surface wind speed
Mt. Washington, New Hampshire, U.S.,
April 11 and 12, 1934: 128 mph (206 kph)

Highest 5-minute mean surface wind speed
Mt. Washington, New Hampshire, U.S.,
April 12, 1934: 188 mph (303 kph)

Highest surface wind peak gust:
Mt. Washington, New Hampshire, U.S.,
April 12, 1934: 231 mph (372 kph)

Windiest U.S. Cities

Chicago is sometimes called "The Windy City."
It earned this nickname because of long-winded politicians,
not because it has the strongest gales.

The windiest cities in the U.S. are as follows:

Cities	Average wind speed	
	mph	kph
Dodge City, Kansas	13.9	22.4
Amarillo, Texas	13.5	21.7
Cheyenne, Wyoming	12.9	20.8
Rochester, Minnesota	12.9	20.8
Casper, Wyoming	12.7	20.4

Chicago has an average wind speed of 10.3 mph (16.6 kph).

Deadliest Hurricanes in the U.S. since 1890

Rank	Place	Year	Number of Deaths
1	Texas (Galveston)	1900	8,000
2	Louisiana	1893	2,000
3	Florida (Lake Okeechobee)	1928	1,836
4	South Carolina, Georgia	1893	>1,000
5	Florida (Keys)	1919	>600
6	New England	1938	600
7	Florida (Keys)	1935	408
8	Southwest Louisiana, north Texas—"Hurricane Audrey"	1957	390
	Northeast U.S.	1944	390
9	Louisiana (Grand Isle)	1909	350
10	Louisana (New Orleans)	1915	275

Tornadoes in the U.S., 1950—2003

Rank	State	Total Number of Tornadoes	Yearly Average	Total Number of Deaths
1	Texas	7,411	137	527
2	Florida	4,268	79	159
3	Oklahoma	3,183	59	263
4	Kansas	3,047	56	214
5	Nebraska	2,386	44	575
	U.S. Total	53,052	982	5,186

Deadliest Floods in the U.S. since 1900

Rank	Place	Year	Number of Deaths
1	Ohio River and tributaries	1913	467
2	Mississippi Valley	1927	246
3	Black Hills, South Dakota	1972	237
4	Willow Creek, Oregon	1903	225
5	Texas rivers	1921	215
6	Texas rivers	1913	180
7	Northeastern U.S., following Hurricane Diane	1955	180
8	New England	1936	150+
9	Big Thompson Canyon, Colorado	1976	144
10	Ohio and Lower Mississippi river basins	1937	137
11	Buffalo Creek, West Virginia	1972	125
12	James River basin, Virginia, following Hurricane Camille	1969	117

Population

During the first two million years of our species' existence, human population grew at a very slow rate, and probably never exceeded 10 million. With the development of agriculture circa 8000 B.C., the growth rate began to rise sharply: by the year A.D. 1, the world population stood at approximately 250 million.

By 1650 the population had doubled to 550 million, and within only 200 years it doubled again, reaching almost 1.2 billion by 1850. Each subsequent doubling has taken only about half as long as the previous one: it took just 100 years to reach 2.5 billion, and 40 years to reach 5.2 billion.

World Population

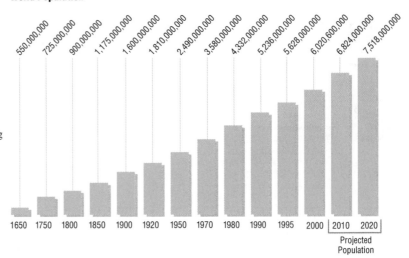

Year	Value
1650	550,000,000
1750	725,000,000
1800	900,000,000
1850	1,175,000,000
1900	1,600,000,000
1920	1,810,000,000
1950	2,490,000,000
1970	3,580,000,000
1980	4,332,000,000
1990	5,236,000,000
1995	5,628,000,000
2000	6,020,600,000
2010	6,824,000,000
2020	7,518,000,000

Projected Population

Historical Populations of the Continents and the World

Year	Africa	Asia	Australia	Europe	North America	Oceania, incl. Australia	South America	World
1650	*100,000,000*	335,000,000	*<1,000,000*	*100,000,000*	*5,000,000*	*2,000,000*	*8,000,000*	*550,000,000*
1750	*95,000,000*	476,000,000	*<1,000,000*	*140,000,000*	*5,000,000*	*2,000,000*	*7,000,000*	*725,000,000*
1800	*90,000,000*	593,000,000	*<1,000,000*	*190,000,000*	*13,000,000*	*2,000,000*	*12,000,000*	*900,000,000*
1850	*95,000,000*	754,000,000	*<1,000,000*	*265,000,000*	*39,000,000*	*2,000,000*	*20,000,000*	*1,175,000,000*
1900	*118,000,000*	932,000,000	4,000,000	400,000,000	106,000,000	6,000,000	38,000,000	*1,600,000,000*
1920	*140,000,000*	1,000,000,000	6,000,000	453,000,000	147,000,000	9,000,000	61,000,000	*1,810,000,000*
1950	199,000,000	1,418,000,000	8,000,000	530,000,000	219,000,000	13,000,000	111,000,000	*2,490,000,000*
1970	346,900,000	2,086,200,000	12,460,000	623,700,000	316,600,000	19,200,000	187,400,000	3,580,000,000
1980	463,800,000	2,581,000,000	14,510,000	660,000,000	365,000,000	22,700,000	239,000,000	4,332,000,000
1990	648,300,000	3,156,100,000	16,950,000	688,000,000	423,600,000	26,300,000	293,700,000	5,236,000,000
2000	781,300,000	3,676,700,000	19,050,000	709,500,000	478,200,000	30,500,000	344,400,000	6,020,600,000

Figures for years prior to 1970 are rounded to the nearest million. Figures in italics represent rough estimates.

The Most Populous City in the World, through History

With more than 30 million people, Japan's Tokyo-Yokohama agglomeration ranks as the most populous metropolitan area in the world today. New York City held this title from the mid-1920's through the mid-1960's. But what city was the most populous in the world five hundred years ago? Five *thousand* years ago?

The following time line represents one expert's attempt to name the cities that have reigned as the most populous in the world since 3200 B.C. The time line begins with Memphis, the capital of ancient Egypt, which was possibly the first city in the world to attain a population of 20,000.

Listed after each city name is the name of the political entity to which the city belonged during the time that it was the most populous city in the world. The name of the modern political entity in which the city, its ruins, or its site is located, where this entity differs from the historic political entity, is listed in parentheses.

For the purpose of this time line, the word "city" is used in the general sense to denote a city, metropolitan area, or urban agglomeration.

It is important to note that reliable census figures are not available for most of the 5,200 years covered by this time line. Therefore the time line is somewhat subjective and conjectural.

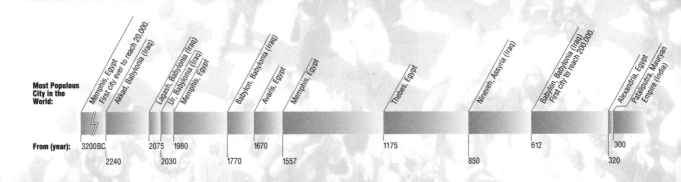

Most Populous City in the World:

- Memphis, Egypt. First city ever to reach 20,000.
- Akkad, Babylonia (Iraq)
- Lagash, Babylonia (Iraq)
- Ur, Babylonia (Iraq)
- Memphis, Egypt
- Babylon, Babylonia (Iraq)
- Avaris, Egypt
- Memphis, Egypt
- Thebes, Egypt
- Nineveh, Assyria (Iraq)
- Babylon, Babylonia (Iraq). First city to reach 200,000.
- Alexandria, Egypt
- Pataliputra, Mauryan Empire (India)

From (year): 3200 B.C. | 2240 | 2075 | 1980 | 2030 | 1670 | 1770 | 1557 | 1175 | 850 | 612 | 300 | 320

Most Densely Populated Countries

Rank	Country (Population)	Population per Square Mile	Kilometer
1	Monaco (32,000)	45,489	16,759
2	Singapore (4,375,000)	17,481	6,762
3	Vatican City (1,000)	5,000	2,500
4	Malta (395,000)	3,234	1,249
5	Maldives (315,000)	2,702	1,043
6	Bahrain (650,000)	2,417	934
7	Bangladesh (132,315,000)	2,361	912
8	Guernsey (64,000)	2,144	825
9	Jersey (89,000)	1,986	770
10	Barbados (275,000)	1,659	640
11	Taiwan (22,460,000)	1,609	621
12	Mauritius (1,195,000)	1,510	583
13	Nauru (12,000)	1,492	576
14	Korea, South (48,120,000)	1,253	484
15	San Marino (28,000)	1,136	448

Least Densely Populated Countries

Rank	Country (Population)	Population per Square Mile	Kilometer
1	Greenland (56,000)	0.07	0.03
2	Mongolia (2,675,000)	4.4	1.7
3	Namibia (1,810,000)	5.6	2.2
4	Australia (19,455,000)	6.5	2.5
5	Mauritania (2,790,000)	6.9	2.6
6	Suriname (435,000)	6.9	2.6
7	Iceland (280,000)	7.0	2.7
8	Botswana (1,590,000)	7.1	2.7
9	Libya (5,305,000)	7.7	3.0
10	Canada (31,750,000)	8.2	3.2
11	Guyana (695,000)	8.4	3.2
12	Gabon (1,225,000)	11.8	4.6
13	Central African Republic (3,610,000)	14.9	5.7
14	Kazakhstan (16,735,000)	15.9	6.2
15	Chad (8,850,000)	17.6	6.8

Most Highly Urbanized Countries

Country	Urban pop. as a % of total pop.
Vatican City	100%
Singapore	100%
Monaco	100%
Belgium	96%
Kuwait	96%
Iceland	92%
Uruguay	91%
Israel (excl. Occupied Areas)	90%
Qatar	90%
Andorra	89%
Argentina	89%
San Marino	89%
United Kingdom	89%
Bahrain	88%
Malta	87%

Least Urbanized Countries

Country	Urban pop. as a % of total pop.
Bhutan	5%
Burundi	5%
Rwanda	5%
Nepal	9%
Oman	11%
Cambodia (Kampuchea)	14%
Bangladesh	14%
Uganda	15%
Burkina Faso	15%
Eritrea	15%
Grenada	15%
Solomon Islands	15%
Niger	15%
Ethiopia	16%
Nigeria	16%

World's Largest Metropolitan Areas

Rank	Name	Population
1	Tōkyō-Yokohama, Japan	31,915,000
2	Seoul, South Korea	21,450,000
3	Mexico City, Mexico	20,150,000
4	New York City, U.S.	19,500,000
5	Jakarta, Indonesia	17,600,000
6	São Paulo, Brazil	17,480,000
7	Ōsaka-Kōbe-Kyōto, Japan	17,350,000
8	Mumbai (Bombay), India	16,600,000
9	Delhi-New Delhi, India	16,000,000
10	Los Angeles, U.S.	15,200,000
11	Kolkata (Calcutta), India	14,000,000
12	Buenos Aires, Argentina	13,900,000
13	Cairo, Egypt	13,300,000
14	Moscow, Russia	12,800,000
15	London, England	12,700,000

The 50 Most Populous Countries

Rank	Country	Population	Rank	Country	Population	Rank	Country	Population
1	China	1,278,720,000	18	Iran	66,365,000	35	Canada	31,750,000
2	India	1,037,955,000	19	Thailand	62,080,000	36	Kenya	30,960,000
3	United States	279,310,000	20	United Kingdom	59,715,000	37	Morocco	30,905,000
4	Indonesia	230,260,000	21	France	59,660,000	38	Peru	27,720,000
5	Brazil	175,260,000	22	Italy	57,700,000	39	Afghanistan	27,280,000
6	Pakistan	146,145,000	23	Dem. Rep. of the Congo	54,455,000	40	Nepal	25,580,000
7	Russia	145,215,000	24	Ukraine	48,570,000	41	Uzbekistan	25,355,000
8	Bangladesh	132,315,000	25	Korea, South	48,120,000	42	Uganda	24,335,000
9	Nigeria	128,285,000	26	South Africa	43,645,000	43	Venezuela	24,105,000
10	Japan	126,880,000	27	Myanmar	42,120,000	44	Iraq	23,665,000
11	Mexico	102,640,000	28	Colombia	40,680,000	45	Saudi Arabia	23,130,000
12	Philippines	83,685,000	29	Spain	40,060,000	46	Taiwan	22,460,000
13	Germany	83,145,000	30	Poland	38,630,000	47	Malaysia	22,445,000
14	Vietnam	80,520,000	31	Argentina	37,600,000	48	Romania	22,340,000
15	Egypt	70,125,000	32	Tanzania	36,705,000	49	Korea, North	22,100,000
16	Turkey	66,905,000	33	Sudan	36,585,000	50	Ghana	20,070,000
17	Ethiopia	66,780,000	34	Algeria	32,005,000			

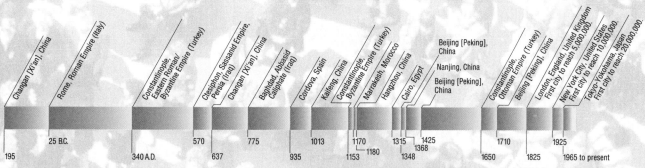

Source: Four Thousand Years of Urban Growth *by Tertius Chandler, Edwin Mellen Press, 1987.*

Economics and Energy

Annual World Production

Cattle

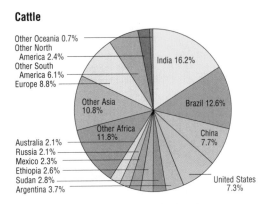

Other Oceania 0.7%
Other North America 2.4%
Other South America 6.1%
Europe 8.8%
Other Asia 10.8%
Other Africa 11.8%
Australia 2.1%
Russia 2.1%
Mexico 2.3%
Ethiopia 2.6%
Sudan 2.8%
Argentina 3.7%
India 16.2%
Brazil 12.6%
China 7.7%
United States 7.3%

Total annual world production: 1,346,583,000 head

Hogs

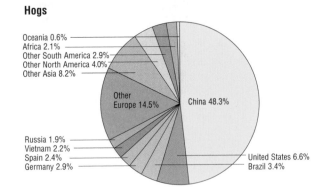

Oceania 0.6%
Africa 2.1%
Other South America 2.9%
Other North America 4.0%
Other Asia 8.2%
Other Europe 14.5%
Russia 1.9%
Vietnam 2.2%
Spain 2.4%
Germany 2.9%
China 48.3%
United States 6.6%
Brazil 3.4%

Total annual world production: 912,589,000 head

Corn

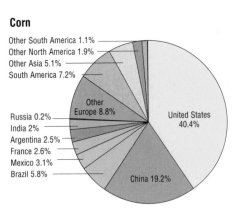

Other South America 1.1%
Other North America 1.9%
Other Asia 5.1%
South America 7.2%
Russia 0.2%
India 2%
Argentina 2.5%
France 2.6%
Mexico 3.1%
Brazil 5.8%
Other Europe 8.8%
United States 40.4%
China 19.2%

Total annual world production: 604,713,000 metric tons

Crude Steel

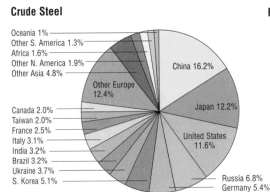

Oceania 1%
Other S. America 1.3%
Africa 1.6%
Other N. America 1.9%
Other Asia 4.8%
Canada 2.0%
Taiwan 2.0%
France 2.5%
Italy 3.1%
India 3.2%
Brazil 3.2%
Ukraine 3.7%
S. Korea 5.1%
Other Europe 12.4%
China 16.2%
Japan 12.2%
United States 11.6%
Russia 6.8%
Germany 5.4%

Total annual world production: 829,843,000 metric tons

Rice

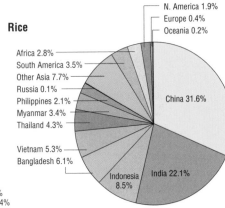

N. America 1.9%
Europe 0.4%
Oceania 0.2%
Africa 2.8%
South America 3.5%
Other Asia 7.7%
Russia 0.1%
Philippines 2.1%
Myanmar 3.4%
Thailand 4.3%
Vietnam 5.3%
Bangladesh 6.1%
China 31.6%
India 22.1%
Indonesia 8.5%

Total annual world production: 601,609,000 metric tons

Gross Domestic Product

Annual Gross Domestic Product (GDP) is the total market value of all the goods and services produced by a nation in a year. GDP is not an indicator of personal income; it is a measure of economic performance at the national level. Most governments carefully analyze changes in GDP from year to year. A GDP growth rate of about 2% per year is an indicator of a healthy national economy.

The most striking thing this bar graph shows is the economic power of the United States. With just 4.6% of the world's population, the United States accounts for 21.2% of the world's GDP. The ten countries with the highest GDPs account for nearly two-thirds of the world total. At the other end of the spectrum is the continent of Africa, which holds 13.3% of the world's people but represents just 3.7% of the GDP.

Annual Gross Domestic Product

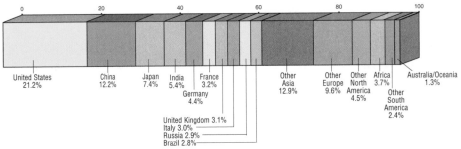

United States 21.2%
China 12.2%
Japan 7.4%
India 5.4%
Germany 4.4%
France 3.2%
United Kingdom 3.1%
Italy 3.0%
Russia 2.9%
Brazil 2.8%
Other Asia 12.9%
Other Europe 9.6%
Other North America 4.5%
Africa 3.7%
Other South America 2.4%
Australia/Oceania 1.3%

World Total=$49,000,000,000,000

Electricity

Hydroelectricity

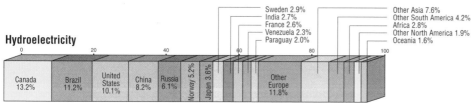

Total annual world production: 2,722,000 gigawatt hours

Nuclear Energy

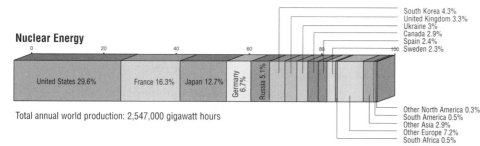

Total annual world production: 2,547,000 gigawatt hours

World Electricity Production

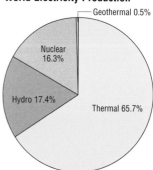

Total annual world electricity production:
15,614,000 gigawatt hours

Petroleum

Petroleum Production

Total annual world production: 24,606,731,000 barrels

Petroleum Reserves

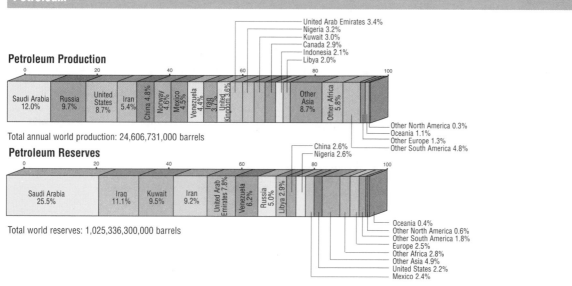

Total world reserves: 1,025,336,300,000 barrels

Commercial Energy

Commercial Energy Production

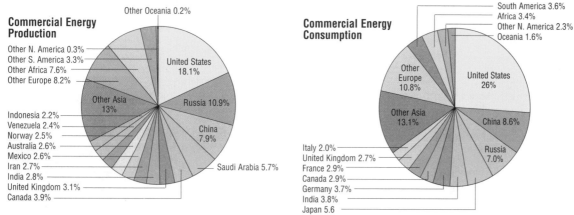

Total annual world production: equivalent of 12,941,675,000
metric tons of coal equivalent

Commercial Energy Consumption

Total annual world consumption: equivalent of 12,020,873,000
metric tons of coal equivalent

Questions and Answers

North America

What is the difference between "Central America" and "Middle America"?

The term "Central America" refers to the North American countries which lie south of Mexico and north of Colombia: Belize, Guatemala, Honduras, El Salvador, Nicaragua, Costa Rica, and Panama. The Caribbean islands are not considered part of Central America. "Middle America" is comprised of Central America as well as Mexico and all of the Caribbean islands.

What is the largest U.S. city east of Reno, Nevada and west of Chicago?

Los Angeles, California

Surprisingly, the answer is Los Angeles. Although Los Angeles is located on the Pacific Coast, it actually lies slightly farther east than Reno. The coast, which forms the western edge of the U.S., curves dramatically eastward below Cape Mendocino in northern California. San Diego, at the southern end of California's coast, is approximately as far east as the eastern borders of Washington and Oregon. *(Refer to map on pages 74-75.)*

Which is the southernmost U.S. state? The northernmost? The westernmost? The easternmost?

Hawaii is the southernmost state; Alaska is both the westernmost and the northernmost. The question of which state is the easternmost is a bit problematic. Generally, Maine is considered to be the easternmost, since it extends farther east than any other state along the Atlantic seaboard. However, Alaska is technically the easternmost state, since the Aleutian Islands cross the 180° longitude line which divides the globe into eastern and western hemispheres. These islands sit at the eastern edge of the eastern hemisphere.

How many national flags have flown over Texas?

Six. Spain (1682-1821), France (1685-1686), Mexico (1821-1836), the Republic of Texas (1836-1845), the United States (1845-1861), the Confederate States of America (from 1861 until the state was re-admitted to the Union in 1870), and the United States again (1870 through the present). Texas is the only U.S. state to have existed as an independent country.

What is the oldest city in the United States to be founded by Europeans?

St. Augustine, Florida. Spanish explorer Juan Ponce de León, searching for the Fountain of Youth, landed nearby and claimed the area for Spain in 1513. The French established a colony on the site in 1564, but it was destroyed in 1565 by the Spanish, who then founded the present city. The oldest U.S. state capital is Santa Fe, New Mexico, which was founded in 1609, also by the Spanish.

What is Papiamento?

Papiamento is a language which blends Dutch, Spanish, Portuguese, English, and Indian words. It is the principal language of Aruba and other islands in the Dutch Caribbean, and is spoken by an estimated 200,000 people.

If you were on a ship sailing from the Atlantic Ocean to the Pacific Ocean, in which direction would you be traveling as you passed through the Panama Canal?

Southeast. The Pacific lies west of the Atlantic, and it would seem that a ship passing through the canal from the Atlantic would be sailing west. However, because of the twisting shape of the Isthmus of Panama, the canal's Pacific end lies south and east of its Atlantic end. *(Refer to inset map on page 96.)*

Into what body of water does the Colorado River empty?

Currently, it doesn't empty into any body of water. Until recently, the river flowed into the Gulf of California. As the populations of water-poor Arizona and California have soared, more and more water has been drawn from the river for farms, industry, and homes. Today the Colorado is barely a trickle when it crosses the border into Mexico, and it disappears in the desert before it reaches the Gulf of California.

What is Canada's smallest province? Its largest?

Prince Edward Island is Canada's smallest province, at 2,185 square miles (5,660 sq km). Canada's largest province is Quebec, which covers 594,860 square miles (1,540,680 sq km). The territory of Nunavut represents the country's largest administrative division: It spreads over an area of 733,594 square miles (1,900,000 sq km), much of which lies within the Arctic Circle. If Nuvavut were an independent country, it would be larger than all but 15 of the world's countries.

What is the Continental Divide?

An imaginary line running down the backbone of North America. Except for those which empty into the Great Basin and other basins, rivers to the west of this line flow into the Pacific Ocean, including its bays and gulfs; rivers to the east flow into the Atlantic or Arctic oceans, including their bays and gulfs. From northwest Canada south to New Mexico, the Divide runs along the crest of the Rocky Mountains, and in northern Mexico it follows the ridge of the Sierra Madre Occidental. All continents except frozen Antarctica have "divides."

Is Niagara Falls the highest waterfall in the world?

Not even close. Niagara Falls' maximum drop of 167 feet (51 m) is surpassed by at least 22 waterfalls in North America alone. The highest waterfall in the world is Angel Falls in Venezuela, which spills 3,212 feet (979 m) from a flat mountain plateau. North America's highest waterfall is Yosemite National Park's Yosemite Falls, which drops 2,425 feet in two separate steps.

Niagara Falls actually consists of two separate waterfalls: American Falls, at left, and Canadian (Horseshoe) Falls.

Q What did ships do before the Panama Canal was built?

A Before the canal opened, ships traveling between New York and San Francisco would sail 13,000 miles (21,000 km) around the entire continent of South America. When the canal opened in 1914, this journey was shortened to 5,200 miles (8,400 km). However, the canal is now too narrow for many of today's largest ocean-going vessels, so they must once again sail around South America to reach their destination. A project to widen the canal began in 1992.

Gatun Lake, Panama Canal

Q What is the largest inland body of water in Central America?

A Lake Nicaragua, which has a surface area of 3,150 square miles (8,158 sq km). Its only outlet is the San Juan River, which flows into the Caribbean Sea. Lying in a lowland region called the Nicaragua Depression, the lake was once part of the sea but became separated when the land began to rise. The freshwater lake is home to many species of fish usually found only in salt water, including sharks, tuna, and swordfish.

Q Why does Minnesota have so many lakes?

A During the height of the most recent Ice Age, glaciers moved southward from the Arctic regions to cover Canada and much of the northern U.S., including Minnesota. As they advanced, the glaciers scoured the landscape, gouging out countless depressions. When the Earth's climate grew warmer, the glaciers began to melt and retreat, and the depressions filled with meltwater to become lakes. Although Minnesota bills itself as the "Land of 10,000 Lakes," it actually has more than 15,000 lakes. Other areas of the world which experienced extreme glaciation, including parts of Europe and Siberia, also contain many lakes.

Q What is the most popular U.S. national park?

A Great Smoky Mountains National Park. Covering over 521,500 acres (211,200 hectares) in eastern Tennessee, the park receives approximately 9.1 million visitors each year. Arizona's Grand Canyon National Park has the second-highest visitor count: it receives around 4.6 million people annually.

Q What two U.S. states share borders with the most other states?

A Missouri and Tennessee, which each border eight other states. Missouri borders Iowa, Illinois, Kentucky, Tennessee, Arkansas, Oklahoma, Kansas, and Nebraska. Tennessee borders Kentucky, Virginia, North Carolina, Georgia, Alabama, Mississippi, Arkansas, and Missouri.

Q How many U.S. states border only one other state?

A One: Maine, which borders only New Hampshire. Two states, Alaska and Hawaii, border no others.

Q What is the one place in North America where you can see both the Atlantic Ocean and the Pacific Ocean?

A Irazú, a volcano in central Costa Rica. From its summit, both the Atlantic and Pacific oceans can be seen on a clear day.

Q Where is the Yucatan Peninsula?

A This thumb of land juts off of southeastern Mexico, separating the Gulf of Mexico from the Caribbean Sea. Yucatan was the center of the Maya civilization from about the first century B.C. through the tenth century A.D. Extensive Mayan ruins can be found at Chichén Itzá, Cobá, Mayapán, Tulum, and Uxmal. Near the town of Chicxulub at the northern tip of the peninsula, there is evidence of an enormous crater which is thought to be the point of impact of a meteorite 65 million years ago. The impact would have sent so much dust into the atmosphere that the sun's rays would have been blocked for months or perhaps years, lowering temperatures globally and possibly causing the extinction of the dinosaurs.

Q What is the oldest capital city in the Americas?

A Mexico City. The city originated as Tenochtitlán, the capital of the Aztecs, founded in the mid-1300s. By the early 1500s, the city had a population of perhaps 150,000, which was not only greater than any other city in the Americas but also greater than any European city at the time. In 1521, after a three-month siege, Spanish invaders under Hernán Cortés captured Tenochtitlán, razed the entire city, and founded Mexico City upon its ruins.

Q What is the most densely populated country in North America?

A El Salvador, which has a density of 775 people per square mile (299 per sq km). The U.S. ranks eighth, with 75 people per square mile (29 per sq km). Canada, the continent's largest country, is by far the least densely populated: it averages only 8.2 people per square mile (3.2 per sq km).

Q What is the largest island in Caribbean Sea?

A Cuba, the world's 15th-largest island. It has a land area of 42,800 square miles (110,800 sq km). The second-largest Caribbean island is Hispaniola, which covers 29,400 square miles (76,200 sq km) and contains the countries of Haiti and the Dominican Republic. Jamaica, measuring 4,200 square miles (11,000 sq km), is the third-largest Caribbean island.

Q How many U.S. states have volcanoes that were active in the 20th century?

A Four. Alaska has the most: 34 of its volcanoes, most of which are located on the Alaska Peninsula and the Aleutian Islands, have erupted since 1900. The other states with documented eruptions in the 20th century are: Hawaii (3), Washington (1), and California (1).

Caldera and lava lake of Kīlauea, on the island of Hawaiʻi

Q What is the only Caribbean island with large oil reserves?

A Trinidad. The island's economy is based on oil, which accounts for about 80% of its exports. As a result of oil wealth, Trinidadians enjoy a higher standard of living than the people of most other Caribbean countries.

Q Which U.S. state has the highest average elevation?

A Colorado, with an average elevation of 6,800 feet (2,074 m) above sea level. However, the four highest peaks in the U.S. are found not in Colorado but in Alaska.

Questions and Answers

South America

Q What is Latin America?

A The term "Latin America" designates the parts of North and South America which were settled by Spanish and Portuguese colonists and still retain a Hispanic character. These include Mexico, Cuba, Puerto Rico, the Dominican Republic, some of the smaller islands in the West Indies, all of Central America except for Belize, and all of South America except for Guyana, Suriname, and French Guiana.

Q If you flew due south from Chicago, which South American country would you fly over first?

A You wouldn't fly over any South American countries. A straight line drawn south from Chicago passes through the Gulf of Mexico, Central America, and the Pacific Ocean. Point Parinas, Peru, the westernmost point of mainland South America, is about 500 miles (800 km) east of this line. The Galapagos Islands, which belong to Ecuador, lie about 75 miles (120 km) west of the line.

Q What percentage of the world's coffee beans come from South America?

A South America currently produces approximately 45% of the world's coffee beans. Brazil leads the continent, producing just under one-quarter of the world total. Another 16% are grown in Colombia. Coffee plants require hot, moist climates, and they yield the most flavorful beans when cultivated at elevations between 3,000 and 6,000 feet (900 and 1800 m). South America's principal coffee-growing regions are found in the Brazilian and Guiana Highlands, and in the valleys and foothills of the Andes.

Giant Galapagos turtle

Q What scientist made the Galapagos Islands famous?

A Charles Darwin, who visited the islands during his 1831-1836 expedition on the H.M.S. *Beagle*. Darwin's observations of how various animal species had adapted to life on the islands contributed to his ground-breaking theory of evolution, which he presented in the 1859 book *On the Origin of Species*.

Q Where are the Falkland Islands?

A In the Atlantic Ocean, about 275 miles (440 km) off the east coast of Argentina. The Falklands are a dependency of the United Kingdom, and nearly all of the residents are English-speakers of British descent. Argentina, which has asserted claims to the Falklands since 1816, invaded and occupied the islands in 1982. The U.K. sent a large task force that defeated the Argentineans in a war lasting less than a month.

Q What South American country is the longest when measured from north to south?

A Brazil. The country measures 2,725 miles (4,395 km) north to south, which is the approximate distance from New York City to Reno, Nevada. The second-longest country is Chile, with a length of 2,647 miles (4,270 km). In contrast to its great length, Chile measures only 235 miles (380 km) east to west at its widest point.

Q What was discovered in Venezuela's Lake Maracaibo in 1914?

A Oil. Maracaibo sits above one of the world's largest oil fields, and today the lake's surface is a thicket of oil derricks. Wealth from oil exportation has helped to make Venezuela one of the richest countries in Latin America.

Q What is Patagonia?

A Patagonia is a wind-swept plateau region occupying the southern third of South America, east of the Andes. The plateau receives little precipitation, and its only vegetation is scrubby grasses and thorny desert shrubs. The name "Patagonia" probably comes from the Grand Patagon, a dog-headed monster in a European romance called *Primaleon of Greece*. In 1592, the crew members of the ship *Desire* were attacked by a war-party of Tehuelche Indians wearing dog masks.

Q What South American city is the world's highest national capital?

A La Paz, Bolivia. The city sprawls across the floor of a deep canyon high in the Andes, at an elevation of 12,000 feet (19,350 km)—approximately the same height as the summit of Japan's Mt. Fuji. The canyon walls protect the city from the bitterly cold winds that whip across the surrounding plateau. Visitors from lower elevations often suffer from altitude sickness for several days until their bodies adjust to the thin, oxygen-poor air.

Q What is the southernmost city in the world?

A Ushuaia, Argentina, on the island of Tierra del Fuego. This city of 29,452 people lies at 54°48' south latitude, less than 700 miles (1,100 km) from Antarctica. The world's southernmost city with a population greater than 100,000 is Punta Arenas, Chile, located 150 miles (240 km) northwest of Ushuaia.

Q How many South American countries are named for famous people or cities?

A Three. Bolivia was named for Simón Bolívar, the revolutionary who helped to liberate much of northern South America from Spanish rule. Colombia takes its name from the explorer Christopher Columbus, who "discovered" South America in 1498 and sailed along the coast of present-day Colombia in 1502. The name "Venezuela" is Spanish for "Little Venice." When European explorers reached Lake Maracaibo in 1499, they found villages built on pilings over the shallow waters, which reminded them of Venice, Italy.

Q Why is South America sometimes referred to as "the hollow continent"?

A South America earned this nickname because most of its people live on or near the coasts; the interior is sparsely populated. Sixteen of the 20 largest metropolitan areas lie within 200 miles (320 km) of the coast. The continent's uneven population distribution has both a historical and a geographical explanation. Beginning in the 16th century, European colonists settled in the coastal regions from which raw materials were shipped back to Europe. The Amazon rain forest—hot, humid, and nearly impenetrable in places—has discouraged settlement of the northern half of the continent, and the Andes present a formidable barrier to eastward expansion from the Pacific coast. (Refer to population map on page 99.)

Q How many of South America's 20 longest rivers empty into the Pacific Ocean?

A None. South America's continental divide runs along the crest of the Andes at the continent's western edge. In most places the divide lies within 200 miles (320 km) of the Pacific coast. Rivers originating west of the divide have only a short distance to travel before reaching the Pacific. Rivers flowing east from the divide have nearly the whole expanse of the continent to cross before emptying into the Atlantic.

Q What South American city was the capital of the Inca empire?

A Cusco, Peru. The city was built by the Incas in the fourteenth century and served as their capital for 200 years until it was destroyed by Francisco Pizarro in 1533. Today, Cusco thrives as a major tourist attraction. Many of its houses and buildings are constructed on foundations of stone first cut by the Incas. Lying about 50 miles (80 km) northwest of Cusco is Machu Picchu, a well-preserved mountaintop Inca city, which was rediscovered in 1911.

Cathedral and rooftops in Cusco

Q What stretch of ocean off the South American coast is considered one of the most treacherous to ships?

A The Drake Passage. Approximately 500 miles (1,800 km) wide, this strait separates Cape Horn—at the southern tip of South America—from the South Shetland Islands which lie just north of Antarctica. First traversed in 1615, the passage was part of a major trade route between the Atlantic and Pacific oceans until 1914, when the Panama Canal opened. Frigid temperatures, rough waters, and high winds make the passage treacherous for all vessels but especially for the sailing ships of centuries past. Because the passage is so perilous, many ships avoid it by cutting through the Strait of Magellan to the north. However, this strait has its own dangers: it is narrow and twisting, and has been the site of numerous major shipwrecks.

Q Where is the Land of Fire?

A At the southern tip of South America. Tierra del Fuego, Spanish for "Land of Fire," is a group of islands lying south of the Strait of Magellan. When Portuguese explorer Ferdinand Magellan arrived in 1520, he named the islands after observing the native inhabitants carrying torches. The largest island, also called Tierra del Fuego, accounts for two-thirds of the land area of the island group. The eastern third of the islands belong to Argentina, and the rest belong to Chile.

Q What are the Nazca Lines?

A The Nazca Lines are gigantic drawings that were etched into Peru's desert floor by the Nazca people between 500 B.C. and A.D. 500. Scattered across 200 square miles (520 sq km), they form the world's largest display of art. The drawings fall into two categories: animal motifs and geometric patterns of crisscrossing straight lines. They were made by scraping away the top layer of red gravel to reveal the yellow sand below it. Archaeologists still disagree about the purpose of the Nazca Lines, but some theories hold that the lines formed ancient highways or were used as a giant calendar.

Q What is "El Niño"?

A El Niño is a seasonal ocean current that flows south along the Pacific coast of South America. The current takes its name—which is Spanish for "the Child"—from its usual arrival during the Christmas season. In normal years, when El Niño reaches northern Peru, southeasterly trade winds push its warm surface waters westward across the Pacific, away from the coast. Every four or five years, these trade winds weaken, allowing El Niño to travel farther south along the coast, raising local water temperatures by several degrees. This warmer water kills plankton and fish, crippling the fishing industry. Increased evaporation leads to excessive rainfall over parts of South America. The change in El Niño's normal flow pattern affects other ocean currents which often leads to dramatic climatic changes around the world.

Q How many of the Earth's species are found in the Amazon rain forest?

A Most of the Amazon basin has not been fully explored, and therefore most of its plant and animal species have not yet been catalogued. However, scientists estimate that the Amazon rain forest, which covers less than 5% of the Earth's total land area, contains almost one-half of the planet's animal and plant species. One in ten of the most common medicines we use today comes from rain forest plants, and scientists believe that cures for many diseases, such as cancer, might be derived from plant species not yet discovered.

Q Where in South America could you find places in which no rainfall has ever been recorded?

A The Atacama Desert in northern Chile. This barren land of sand, rocks, borax lakes and saline deposits is one of the driest regions in the world. In parts of the desert, no rainfall has ever been recorded, and the city of Arica, at the northern edge, endured more than 14 consecutive years of drought from October 1903 through January 1918.

Q What South American possession lies farthest from the mainland?

A Easter Island, situated 2,300 miles (3,700 km) west of Chile in the Pacific Ocean. This small volcanic island was discovered on Easter Sunday in 1722, and was annexed by Chile in 1888. Although it belongs to Chile, geographically Easter Island is considered to be part of Oceania, not South America. It is best known for its strange monuments: scattered over the island are more than 600 huge stone faces, the earliest dating back more than 1,500 years.

Ancient statues, Easter Island

Q Where are the pampas?

A These flat, grassy plains—which are much like the prairies of North America—are found in the temperate regions of southern South America, east of the Andes. The largest such plain, known simply as the Pampa, covers much of central and northern Argentina, and extends into Uruguay. Since the 1550s, when European colonists introduced cattle to the Pampa, livestock raising has been a thriving industry. For many people, gauchos, or Argentinean cowboys, are the enduring symbol of the Pampa, although in the last century farming has superseded cattle ranching in economic importance.

Questions and Answers

Europe

Q Where is the Black Forest?

A In southwestern Germany, between the Rhine and Neckar rivers. The Black Forest, or *Schwarzwald* in German, is a mountainous region that takes its name from the dark coniferous trees that cover its slopes. Its fertile valleys provide good pastureland and produce grapes for wine, and its trees supply the lumber and woodworking industries, as well as toy and cuckoo clock manufacturers. The region's scenic beauty, winter sports facilities, and mineral springs attract many tourists each year.

Q How many national capitals are located on the Danube River?

A Four. The capital cities of Bratislava (Slovakia), Budapest (Hungary), Belgrade (Serbia and Montenegro), and Vienna (Austria) are all found along the banks of the Danube. Five other capitals are located on tributaries of the Danube: Bucharest (Romania), Sofia (Bulgaria), Ljubljana (Slovenia), Zagreb (Croatia), and Sarajevo (Bosnia and Herzegovina).

Old Town of Zagreb, Croatia

Q What is killing the forests of Northern Europe?

A Acid rain. In the atmosphere, airborne pollutants—especially sulfur and nitrogen dioxides from automobile and industrial emissions—adhere to water droplets, and then fall back to Earth as acidified rain, snow, or hail. This precipitation poisons plant and animal life, erodes buildings, and contaminates soil and drinking water. As a result of acid rain, as many as one-half of the trees in Germany's Black Forest and Switzerland's central alpine region are dead or dying. At least 4,000 lakes in Sweden are so acidic that no fish survive in them. To combat acid rain, the countries of the European Union recently agreed to significantly reduce nitrogen oxide and sulfur dioxide emissions.

Q What independent countries were once part of the U.S.S.R.?

A When the Union of Soviet Socialist Republics (U.S.S.R.) broke up in 1991, its 15 republics all became independent countries: Armenia, Azerbaijan, Belarus, Estonia, Georgia, Kazakhstan, Krygyzstan, Latvia, Lithuania, Moldova, Russia, Tajikistan, Turkmenistan, Ukraine, and Uzbekistan.

Q How many times did the name of St. Petersburg, Russia, change in the 20th century?

A Three times. St. Petersburg was founded in 1703 by Peter the Great. In 1914, its name was changed to Petrograd, Russian for "Peter's City," and then in 1924 it was changed again, this time to Leningrad, in honor of Vladimir Lenin, the founder of Russian Communism. In 1991, following the collapse of Communist rule, the city name was changed back to St. Petersburg. Older citizens joke about being born in St. Petersburg, attending school in Petrograd, working in Leningrad, and growing old in St. Petersburg—all while living in the same place.

Q What independent countries were once part of Yugoslavia?

A Prior to 1991, Yugoslavia was comprised of six republics: Bosnia and Herzegovina, Croatia, Macedonia, Montenegro, Serbia, and Slovenia. In 1991-92, four of the six republics—Croatia, Slovenia, Macedonia, and Bosnia and Herzegovina—declared their independence. In 2003, the remaining republics agreed to change the name from Yugoslavia to Serbia and Montenegro.

Q What is the Chunnel?

A "Chunnel" is a nickname for the English Channel Tunnel, which connects England and France via rail under the English Channel. There are actually three separate tunnels: two for trains and a parallel service tunnel. The tunnels run for 31 miles between Coquelles, France, and Folkestone, England, at an average depth of 150 feet (46 m) below the seafloor. Work on the tunnels began in 1987, and the first trains crossed under the Channel in 1994.

Q Where is "Europe's Grand Canyon"?

A Along the Verdon River in the Provence region of southeastern France. The Verdon has carved a deep, narrow gorge, known as the Grand Cañon du Verdon, through the limestone plateau between the town of Castellane and the artificial Lac de Ste-Croix. The gorge stretches for 13 miles (21 km) and reaches a depth of 3,170 feet (965 m). It is considered one of the natural wonders of Europe.

Q What is the only volcano on the European mainland that erupted in the 20th century?

A Mt. Vesuvius (Vesuvio), located in southern Italy nine miles (15 km) east of Naples. It was active through much of the century, with significant eruptions in 1906, 1929, and 1944. Two thousand years ago, most Romans did not recognize Vesuvius as a volcano, and numerous farming communities thrived on the fertile land around its base. Then, in August of A.D. 79, the volcano exploded in a mighty eruption, burying the cities of Pompeii, Herculaneum, and Stabiae under cinders, ash, and mud, and killing more than 3,500 people.

Q How many European countries fall partially within the Arctic Circle?

A Four: Finland, Norway, Russia, and Sweden. Technically, a fifth country could be added to this list: Iceland's mainland ends just short of the Arctic Circle, but one of the country's islands, Grimsey, straddles the line, its northern half sitting within the Circle.

The historic Henningsvaer Port in the Lofoten Islands of Norway, north of the Arctic Circle

Q Where is Waterloo, site of Napoleon's famous defeat?

A Today, Waterloo is a suburb of Brussels, Belgium, although at the time of the battle—June 18, 1815—it lay 12 miles (19 km) away from the city, which was then much smaller. At Waterloo, the troops of French emperor Napoleon I were defeated by British forces under the command of the Duke of Wellington and Prussian forces led by Gebhard Blücher. The French defeat ended the Napoleonic Wars, which had begun in 1803.

Q Is Venice, Italy, really sinking?

A Yes, although at a much slower rate than previously. The city, which dates back to the 4th century A.D., is built on 118 small islands in a lagoon at the top of the Adriatic Sea. Its buildings sit on foundations of wooden pilings driven deep into the underlying sand, silt and clay. Originally the buildings were safely above high tide level, but over the course of 15 centuries, natural compaction of the subsoil caused the city to sink more than 30 inches (76 cm). Earlier this century, groundwater was pumped out of the subsoil to satisfy water needs on the mainland. This proved disastrous for Venice: the city quickly sank another five inches (13 cm) at a time when the sea level was rising by four inches (10 cm). The pumping was stopped, and Venice's sinking has slowed to its earlier "natural" rate. Unfortunately, the foundations of many buildings have been severely damaged by high water.

Gondola and canal, Venice

Q Which independent European countries are smaller than Rhode Island, the smallest U.S. state?

A Seven independent European countries cover a smaller area than Rhode Island's 1,545 square miles (4,002 sq km): Vatican City, Monaco, San Marino, Liechtenstein, Malta, Andorra, and Luxembourg.

Q How many official languages are recognized in Switzerland?

A Four: German, French, Italian, and Romansch. German is the most widely spoken language: 65% of the Swiss speak a dialect known as *Schwyzerdütsch*, or Swiss German. French is spoken by 18% of the population, Italian by 10%, and Romansch by only 1%.

Q Why is Ukraine called "the breadbasket of Europe"?

A Ukraine's topography—flat plains, or "steppes," cover most of the country—and extremely fertile soils combine to make it one of the world's most outstanding agricultural areas. In 1994, the country produced almost 36 million tons (33 metric tons) of grain. Major crops include wheat, rye, barley, corn, potatoes, sunflower seeds, sugar beets, and cotton. Ukraine also has thriving dairy and livestock industries, as well as many food-processing plants.

Q If the Caspian Sea is a *sea*, then how can it be the world's largest *lake*?

A Actually, it is both a sea *and* a lake. The word "sea" is used most often to designate specific regions of the oceans that are more or less surrounded by land; however, it can also apply to inland bodies of water, especially if they are large and/or salty. The Caspian Sea is both large and salty, so it is called a sea. "Lake" is a general term for inland bodies of water of substantial size. The Caspian Sea lies inland and has a surface area of 143,240 square miles (370,990 sq km), so it is also considered to be a lake. Other "sea-lakes" in the world include the Aral Sea, the Dead Sea, the Sea of Galilee, and California's Salton Sea.

Q Where is Transylvania?

A In northwestern Romania. The region is bounded by the Carpathian Mountains in the north and east, the Transylvanian Alps in the south, and by Romania's borders with Hungary and Serbia and Montenegro in the west. A high plateau, averaging 1,000 to 1,600 feet (300 to 500 m) in elevation, covers much of Transylvania. In Bram Stoker's 1897 novel *Dracula*, Transylvania is the home of the blood-sucking Count. Stoker based the story on local vampire legends, many of which persist today: in some parts of eastern Europe, peasants still wear garlic necklaces and hang garlic wreaths from their doors to ward off vampires.

Q What countries contain parts of the Carpathian Mountains?

A Five: the Czech Republic, Slovakia, Poland, Ukraine, and Romania. Curving for more than 900 miles (1,450 km) along the north and east sides of the Danube plain in central and eastern Europe, the Carpathians roughly form a half-circle connecting the Alps and the Balkans. The mountain system consists of two main parts: the Northern Carpathians, which include the Beskid and the Tatra ranges, and the Southern Carpathians, also called the Transylvanian Alps. The Carpathians' highest peak is Gerlachovský štít in Slovakia, which rises to 8,711 feet (2,655 m).

Q Where is Lapland?

A In northern Scandinavia. Lapland is home to the Lapps, a nomadic people who have traditionally engaged in hunting, fishing, and reindeer-herding. When the Finns arrived in the southern part of present-day Finland 2,000 years ago, they found the Lapps already settled there. Over the years, the Lapps have been pushed north, and their territory has expanded to cover parts of northern Norway, Sweden, Finland, and northwestern Russia. Today, there are approximately 42,000 Lapps, most of whom work in a variety of farming, construction, and service fields. The Finnish government has made many efforts to protect the Lapps' language, called Sami, and culture.

Q What European country has a shorter coastline than any other maritime country in the world?

A Monaco, whose Mediterranean coastline is a mere three-and-a-half miles (5.6 km) long. Another European country, Bosnia and Herzegovina, ranks second in this category: its coast on the Adriatic Sea between Croatia and Serbia and Montenegro is only 13 miles (21 km) long. In third place is Slovenia, whose Adriatic coast is 29 miles (47 km) long.

Harbor and coastline, Monaco

Q What European city is the largest city in the world north of the Arctic Circle?

A Murmansk, Russia, a city of 472,900 people located on the Kola Gulf of the Barents Sea. Although Murmansk lies approximately 150 miles north of the Arctic Circle, its harbor remains ice-free throughout the year due to the moderating effect of a warm ocean current called the North Atlantic Drift. While there are thousands of cities and towns north of the Arctic Circle, there are none at all south of the Antarctic Circle at the opposite end of the world.

Questions and Answers

Africa

Q What is the East African Rift System?

A This term refers to a series of rift valleys running through East Africa from Mozambique to the southern end of the Red Sea. These valleys are part of the Great Rift Valley, a 4,000-mile (6,430-km)-long depression that also includes the Red Sea, the Dead Sea, and the rest of the Jordan Valley. The East African Rift System marks the line along which geological forces are splitting East Africa off from the rest of the continent. Eventually, everything east of the Rift System—including all or part of present-day Mozambique, Tanzania, Rwanda, Burundi, Uganda, Kenya, Ethiopia, Djibouti, and Somalia—will be a huge island off of Africa's eastern coast. Madagascar was attached to the African mainland before similar forces split it off into an island 175 million years ago.

Q What is the Serengeti?

A Located in northern Tanzania, east of Lake Victoria and west of Kilimanjaro, the Serengeti is a vast plain of grassland, acacia bushes, forest, and rocky outcrops. Serengeti National Park, established in 1951, covers an area of the plain about the size of Connecticut. The park is home to one of the last great concentrations of African wildlife, including antelope, buffalo, cheetahs, elephants, gazelles, giraffes, hyenas, leopards, lions, black rhinoceroses, wildebeests and zebras. Tourists from all over the world visit the park to observe the wildlife and to witness the large-scale animal migrations that occur in May and June.

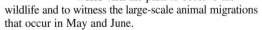
Giraffes on the Serengeti

Q How has the Aswan High Dam affected the Nile Valley ?

A Before the dam was built in 1971, floodwaters inundated the Nile Valley each fall, depositing fresh, fertile silt across the valley floor. This annual replenishment of the soil helped agriculture to thrive in the valley for thousands of years. The dam ended the annual floods, and now much of the Nile's water-borne silt settles to the bottom of Lake Nassar, the enormous artificial lake behind the dam. Water evaporating from the lake's surface has increased the regional humidity, which has accelerated the decay of many of the valley's great tombs and monuments. On the positive side, the dam supplies more than 25% of Egypt's hydro-electric power, and desert irrigation projects using water from Lake Nassar have created 900,000 new acres of arable land.

Q What is remarkable about the delta of the Okavango River?

A It is the largest inland delta in the world. The Okavango originates in the mountains of central Angola and flows 1,000 miles (1,600 km) to the northwest corner of Botswana, where it spills over the Gomare fault and fans out into a swampy delta covering 4,000 square miles (10,350 sq km). Meandering through a myriad of shallow channels, the waters of the Okavango quickly evaporate. The small amount that eventually emerges from the southeastern end of the delta represents less than 5% of the river's pre-delta flow.

Q What African country was previously known as Upper Volta?

A Burkina Faso. The Volta River's three upper branches—the Volta Blanche (White Volta), Volta Rouge (Red Volta), and Volta Noire (Black Volta)—all originate within the country, hence the earlier name. Burkina Faso, the Mossi-dialect name adopted in 1984, translates roughly as "Country of Honest Men."

Q What are the most important crops grown in Africa?

A Africa is the world's leading producer of cocoa beans (55% of the world total) and cassava roots (45% of the world total). It is also a major producer of grain and millet sorghum (27%), coffee (20%), peanuts (20%), palm oil (14%), tea (12%), and olive oil (12%).

Woman in sorghum fields, Bema

Q What object found along the banks of the Orange River in 1867 changed the course of South African history?

A A 21-carat diamond. The discovery of this gem near Hopetown precipitated a huge diamond rush, and thousands of people from all over the continent and the world raced to southern Africa. The town of Kimberley, site of the famous open mine known as the Big Hole, became the diamond capital of the world. Between 1871 and 1914, more than 14 million carats of diamonds were removed from the mine, which eventually reached a depth of 4,000 feet (1,220 m) and a width of one mile (1.6 km).

Q What is Cabinda?

A A coastal province of Angola that lies north of the Congo River and is separated from the rest of the country by a 19-mile (31-km)-wide corridor belonging to the Democratic Republic of the Congo. Most of Cabinda is covered by tropical forest. Offshore lie rich oil fields which produce one million barrels annually.

Q What African country was founded in 1847 by freed American slaves?

A Liberia, whose name comes from the Latin word *liber*, meaning "free." It is the only country in sub-Saharan Africa that has never been ruled by a colonial power. Liberia's capital city, Monrovia, was named for James Monroe, the fifth U.S. president.

Q What two African countries border only a single other country?

A Lesotho and The Gambia. South Africa surrounds Lesotho, and The Gambia is bordered in the north, east, and south by Senegal; to its west lies the Atlantic Ocean.

Q What is the Ngorongoro Crater?

A Located in northern Tanzania, Ngorongoro is the crater of a volcano that has been extinct for several million years. It has a diameter of 9 miles (14.5 km) and its walls rise about 2,000 feet (610 m) above its floor. The crater supports an abundance of wildlife, including wildebeests, elephants, rhinoceroses, hippopotamuses, lions, leopards, and flamingoes. In 1956 Ngorongoro was established as a conservation area, but its ecological balance is threatened by growing numbers of tourists and the large cattle herds of the nomadic Masai people.

Why is it difficult to say how large Lake Chad is?

The lake's size fluctuates dramatically throughout the year. Numerous rivers and streams flow into Lake Chad, but it has no outlet. During the summer rainy season, floodwaters swell the lake to 10,000 square miles (25,900 sq km) and occasionally to twice that size. Even at its maximum size the lake is extremely shallow; its greatest depth is only 25 feet (8 m). By the end of the following spring, evaporation has shrunk the lake by 60%, to about 4,000 square miles (10,360 sq km). In recent decades, Lake Chad's cyclical fluctuations have been greatly affected by recurring droughts, which have reduced the flow of water into the lake and accelerated evaporation. Its volume has dropped by 80% since 1970.

What is significant about the location of Khartoum, Sudan?

Khartoum, the capital of Sudan, is located at the point where the White Nile and Blue Nile rivers meet to form the Nile. Capitalizing on its strategic location, the city has become Sudan's commercial center and transportation hub. It is built on a curving strip of land that resembles the trunk of an elephant: the name "Khartoum" comes from the Arabic *Ras-al-hartum*, which means "end of the elephant's trunk."

What is Africa's newest country?

Eritrea, which officially became independent in 1993. An Italian colony from 1890 to 1941, Eritrea was captured by the British during World War II. In 1952, the United Nations awarded Eritrea to Ethiopia under the condition that it be ruled as a self-governing territory. Ethiopia violated this agreement by annexing Eritrea in 1962, touching off a civil war which lasted more than 30 years. Eritrea formally declared its independence in May 1993, two years after defeating Ethiopia's Marxist regime.

What is the Sahel?

The Sahel (Sudan) is a semiarid region that separates the Sahara Desert from the tropical savanna and rain forests of central Africa. It stretches halfway across the continent, from Mauritania in the west to Chad in the east, in a band averaging more than 1,000 miles (1,600 km) in width. Most of the Sahel is semiarid savanna, with low grasses in the north and tall grasses in the south. Annual precipitation varies from 4 inches to 24 inches (100 to 600 mm). The 8-month dry season makes farming difficult, and the region has experienced several severe droughts in recent decades.

Woman returning from well in the Sahel

In what country would you find Africa's northernmost point?

Tunisia. The northernmost point is Cape Ben Sekka, which lies just north of the continent's northernmost town, Bechater. Parts of five European countries—Greece, Italy, Malta, Portugal, and Spain—lie farther south than Cape Ben Sekka. From the tip of the cape, Africa stretches southward approximately 5,000 miles (8,000 km) to its southernmost point, Cape Agulhas in South Africa.

How has the Sahara Desert changed in the last 5,000 years?

Scientists believe that 5,000 years ago the climate of the Sahara was more temperate and far less arid than it is today. Much of the region was grassland. Around 3000 B.C. global climate patterns began to shift, and the region entered an arid period which continues today. The desert currently covers 3,500,000 square miles (9,100,000 sq km), an area nearly as large as the United States, and its size is increasing. In recent decades, recurring droughts and overgrazing in the Sahel region have contributed to the Sahara's southward expansion.

What is the traditional mode of transportation in the Sahara Desert?

Camel eating leaves

The camel, or more specifically, the one-humped dromedary, which was domesticated at least 3,000 years ago. Dromedaries are extremely well-suited to desert conditions. They have the ability to store water in their hump, and can tolerate water losses equal to one-fourth of their body weight. Their heavy-lidded eyes and closeable nostrils offer protection in sandstorms. Today, as the Saharan road system expands, truck convoys are replacing camel caravans, although trucks require frequent refueling, often overheat in the desert sun, and grind to a halt when sand clogs their engines.

Which African country can boast the greatest known deposits, variety, and output of minerals in the world?

South Africa. It has the world's largest known deposits of chromite, gold, manganese, platinum, and vanadium. The country leads the world in production of gold, chromite, vanadium, and the platinum group metals: platinum, palladium, iridium, rhodium, and ruthenium. It is also one of the leading producers of manganese, antimony, and gem and industrial diamonds.

Where is the Horn of Africa?

This term refers to the horn-shaped area of eastern Africa that juts into the Indian Ocean. Somalia and Ethiopia occupy most of the horn. The cape of Gees Gwardafuy and the city of Caluula sit at the northeastern tip of the horn, marking the entrance to the Gulf of Aden, which connects the Arabian Sea and the Red Sea.

What is the Valley of the Kings?

This narrow valley, across the Nile River from the city of Luxor, contains the tombs of the pharaohs who ruled Egypt during the New Kingdom period, 1550 B.C. to 1200 B.C. The tombs are carved deep into the sandstone walls of the valley; most have five to fifteen rooms. Among the pharaohs buried in the valley are Ramses II, Ramses VI, and Seti I. Upon their death, the pharaohs were mummified and then entombed with all of the material things that they might need in the afterlife, including gold, jeweled ornaments, furniture, clothing, and food. Most of the tombs were soon looted by robbers, who removed all items of value. However, in 1922 the tomb of Tutankhamen—"King Tut"—was discovered with most of its riches untouched.

Questions and Answers

Asia

Q What natural features form the physical boundary between Europe and Asia?

A Europe and Asia share the same huge landmass, which is known as Eurasia. The imaginary line dividing this landmass into two continents runs through the Ural Mountains, the Ural River, the Caspian Sea, the Caucasus mountains, the Black Sea, the Bosporus strait, the Sea of Marmara, and the Dardanelles strait.

Q How many countries lie partially within Europe and partially within Asia?

A Four: Azerbaijan, which is traversed by the Caucasus Mountains; Kazakhstan, whose far western lands lie west of the Ural River; Russia, which is split by the Ural Mountains, and Turkey, which includes a small area on the northwestern side of the Sea of Marmara.

Q Why was the Great Wall of China built?

A To defend China against invasion by the Huns and other enemies. Defensive walls were built in China

The Great Wall winding through a hilly region in northern China

as early as the 6th century B.C. In 214 B.C., under Emperor Shih Huang-ti, the existing walls were connected to form a single continuous wall with watchtowers. This wall was extended during the Han Dynasty (202 B.C. – A.D. 220) and the Sui Dynasty (A.D. 581 – 618). Seven hundred years later the wall had mostly crumbled, and in the late 1400s, under the Ming Emperors, it was completely rebuilt. The portions of the wall that remain today are those that were constructed during this most recent period.

Q How has the Aral Sea changed in recent decades?

A It has shrunk by about 55% since 1960. The sea once covered nearly 25,000 square miles (64,720 sq km) and was the fourth-largest inland body of water in the world. Today it covers only about 11,100 square miles (28,700 sq km), and the former port city of Muynak lies 30 miles (48 km) inland. The sea's shrinkage can be blamed on cotton farming in the surrounding desert. Soviet-era efforts to establish a profitable cotton industry led to the creation of an extensive network of irrigation canals. These huge canals drain large amounts of water from the Syr Darya and Amu Darya, the only two rivers that empty into the sea.

Q What is the Ring of Fire?

A "Ring of Fire" designates the narrow band of active volcanoes encircling the Pacific Ocean basin. Of the approximately 1,500 volcanoes in the world that have been active within the last 10,000 years, more than two-thirds are part of the Ring. Over half of the Ring's active volcanoes are found in its Asian portion, which passes through Russia's Kamchatka Peninsula, the Kuril Islands, Japan, and the Philippines. The Ring of Fire's most recent major volcanic event was the 1991 eruption of Pinatubo on the Philippine island of Luzon, which prompted the evacuation of 250,000 people.

Q What part of Asia is called Indochina?

A "Indochina" refers to the southeastern Asian peninsula situated south of China and east of India. Countries located on the peninsula are Cambodia, Laos, Myanmar (Burma), Thailand, Vietnam, and the western portion of Malaysia. The eastern part of the Indochinese peninsula, including Cambodia, Laos, and Vietnam, was formerly known as French Indochina because of France's strong colonial presence there.

Q The Khyber Pass links which two countries?

A Afghanistan and Pakistan. Approximately 33 miles (53 km) long and reaching a maximum elevation of about 3,500 feet (1,067 m), the pass cuts through the Safed Koh mountains just south of the Kabul River, connecting the high plateau of Afghanistan with the Indus Valley. It has been used for centuries as a caravan route and as an invasion route into India. Today it is also traversed by a paved highway and, in Pakistan, by a railroad. In the 1980s several million refugees fleeing Afghanistan's civil war crossed into Pakistan via the pass.

Q What Persian Gulf country is a federation of seven Arab sheikdoms?

A United Arab Emirates, formed in 1971 through the unification of the sheikdoms of Abu Dhabi, Ajman, Dubai, Fujeirah, Sharjah, and Umm al-Qawain. Ras al-Khaimah joined the federation in 1972. Underdeveloped a few decades ago, the U.A.E. has been transformed by oil wealth into a modern and affluent country.

Q What Asian country contains, or is bordered by, six of the world's ten highest mountains?

A Nepal. Within Nepal or along its borders with China and India are found the following peaks: Mt. Everest (highest in the world), Kanchenjunga (3rd), Makalu (4th), Dhawalāgiri (5th), Annapurna (7th), and Xixabangma Feng (9th). Nanda Devi (10th) lies only 50 miles (80 km) northwest of Nepal's western border.

Q Where is the Empty Quarter?

A This hostile desert is found in the southern third of the Arabian Peninsula. Called *Ar Rub' Al-Khālī*, or "the Empty Quarter" in Arabic, it covers 250,000 square miles (647,000 sq km) and is the world's largest continuous sand body. Few people live in the Empty Quarter, and much of the region has never been explored.

Q What Asian volcanic eruption has been called the loudest natural explosion in recorded history?

A The 1883 eruption of Krakatau (Krakatoa), an island volcano between Sumatra and Java. Krakatau exploded three times on August 26 and 27, 1883, shooting tremendous amounts of gas and ash 50 miles (80 km) into the atmosphere. The explosions were so violent that they were heard nearly 3,000 miles (4,653 km) away on Rodrigues Island in the western Indian Ocean. Krakatau collapsed into itself, and when the explosions were over most of the island was submerged under 900 feet of water. Tsunamis up to 130 feet (40 m) high slammed the coasts of Sumatra and Java, washing away hundreds of villages and killing more than 36,000 people.

Q **At their closest point, how far apart are Asia and North America?**

A At the narrowest point of the Bering Strait, Asia and North America are separated by only 56 miles (90 km). Russia's Big Diomede (Ratmanov) Island and the United States' Little Diomede Island, which lie in the middle of the strait, are only 2.5 miles (4 km) apart.

Q **Where is the Fertile Crescent?**

A This term refers to a crescent-shaped area of fertile land in the Middle East which runs along the eastern coast of the Mediterranean Sea, then turns southeast through Mesopotamia, the land between the Tigris and Euphrates rivers, and ends at the head of the Persian Gulf. The Fertile Crescent was the birthplace of some of the world's oldest civilizations, including the Sumerians, Babylonians, and Assyrians.

Q **What country was Pakistan part of before it became independent?**

A India. Conflicts between Hindus and Muslims in British India led to the creation of Pakistan as a separate Muslim state in 1947. Originally, Pakistan included the two main centers of Muslim population, which lay in northwest and east India. The two areas, West Pakistan and East Pakistan, were separated by 1,000 miles (1,600 km). In 1971, East Pakistan declared its independence and changed its name to Bangladesh. The name "Pakistan" comes from the Urdu words *pakh*, meaning "pure," and *stan*, meaning "land."

Q **What was Sri Lanka called before 1972?**

A Ceylon, which is the name the British had given to the island when they claimed it in 1796. The island became independent in 1948, and in 1972 was renamed Sri Lanka, which in the Sinhala language means "Resplendent Land."

The Taj Mahal

Q **What is India's most famous tomb?**

A The Taj Mahal, located in the city of Agra. Often described as one of the world's most beautiful buildings, it was built by the Mogul emperor Shah Jahan to honor the memory of his wife, Mumtaz-i-Mahal. Construction began in 1631 and was completed in 1648.

Q **What two seas are linked by the Suez Canal?**

A The Red Sea and the Mediterranean Sea. Before the 101-mile (163-km) canal was built in the mid-1800s, ships traveling between Europe and the Far East had to sail all the way around the southern tip of Africa. Depending on the origin and destination of the ship, the canal could shorten its trip dramatically. For example, a ship sailing from London to Bombay would have to travel almost 11,000 miles (17,700 km) around the African continent. Using the Suez Canal, the trip could be shortened to 6,300 miles (10,140 km), a distance reduction of over 40%.

Q **Which independent Asian country has the highest population density?**

A The tiny republic of Singapore, with 17,814 people per square mile (6,879 per sq km). Singapore's 4,375,000 people occupy an island measuring only 26 miles east-to-west and 14 miles north-to-south. Mongolia has the lowest density: 4.4 people per square mile (1.7 per sq km). Mongolia's land area is 2,458 times larger than Singapore's, but it holds only 2,675,000 people.

Q **How long is Japan, from north to south?**

A The islands of Japan stretch approximately 1,900 miles (3,060 km) from Hokkaido in the north to the Sakishima Archipelago in the south. This is approximately equal to the distance between New York City and Denver.

Landscape on Hokkaido, Japan's northernmost island

Q **What region is known as the "Roof of the World"?**

A Tibet, the high plateau region which lies north of the Himalayas. Covering 471,000 square miles (1,220,000 sq km), and with an average elevation of 15,000 feet (4,600 m), the Tibetan Plateau is the largest and highest plateau in the world. Much of Tibet is uninhabited; the region's fewer than two million people are concentrated in the valleys of the Brahmaputra (Yarlung) River and its tributaries.

Q **Which Asian country leads the world in number of earthquake-related deaths since 1900?**

A China, where 48 deadly earthquakes have killed an estimated 967,420 people since 1900. During the same period Iran has lost 147,293 people in 57 earthquakes, and in Japan 32 earthquakes have killed 123,462 people.

Q **What cities mark the endpoints of the Trans-Siberian Railway?**

A The longest railway line in the world, the Trans-Siberian Railway stretches 5,764 miles (9,297 km) between Moscow in the west and the Pacific Coast port city of Nakhodka (near Vladivostok) in the east. The eight-day journey between the two cities includes stops in 92 Russian cities and towns.

Q **How many people live on the Indonesian island of Java?**

A Java is home to approximately 118 million people. It is the world's most populous island, although it is only the 13th-largest in area. By contrast, the island of Cuba is four-fifths the size of Java, but its population is only one-eleventh as large.

Q **What was the name of Ho Chi Minh City, Vietnam, prior to 1975?**

A Saigon. When the city fell to North Vietnamese forces in 1975, it was renamed for Ho Chi Minh, founder of the Indochina Communist Party and president of North Vietnam from 1945 until his death in 1969.

Questions and Answers

Oceania (including Australia and New Zealand)

What is Oceania?

The name "Oceania" refers to the scattered islands of a vast area of the Pacific Ocean, from Palau in the west to Easter Island in the east, and from the Midway Islands in the north to New Zealand in the south. The three main island groups of Oceania are Melanesia, Micronesia, and Polynesia. The continent of Australia and the islands of New Zealand are sometimes considered part of Oceania.

What is the Outback?

This nickname refers to Australia's vast, largely uninhabited interior. Over the years, the Outback's harsh beauty and its remoteness from the rest of Australia have made it popular with adventurous explorers and travelers. Through depictions in literature, art, and film, the region has become an integral part of Australia's identity. However, it is difficult to characterize the Outback, for its boundaries are undefined and its landscape varies from hot deserts to lush wilderness.

Eucalyptus tree in the Outback, Northern Territory

Why is Australia sometimes referred to as "the Land Down Under"?

This nickname originated with the British, who began colonizing Australia in the late 1700s. Because of its extreme southern location in relation to Britain, Australia was considered "Down." The "Under" part of the phrase refers to the continent's position "under" the Eurasian landmass. But while people from the Northern Hemisphere think of Australia as "Down Under," Australians do not.

How much of Australia is arid or semiarid?

More than two-thirds of the continent is considered to be arid or semiarid. The arid areas comprise several large deserts, including the Great Victoria Desert, the Gibson Desert, the Great Sandy Desert, and the Simpson Desert.

What distinction does Wellington, New Zealand have among national capitals of independent countries?

Located at 41°18' south latitude, Wellington is the world's southernmost national capital. In second place is Canberra, Australia, which lies at 35°17' south latitude.

What is unusual about how the island of Nauru was formed?

Nauru, the world's smallest republic, began as a coral atoll. Over the millennia, accumulated bird droppings filled in the central lagoon and created an 8-square-mile (21-sq-km) island whose highest point rises 210 feet (64 m) above sea level. The droppings are a rich source of phosphate, which is used in making fertilizers. Phosphate mining has long been Nauru's economic mainstay, but the resource will soon be exhausted.

What are the principal islands of New Zealand?

Two islands, North Island and South Island, account for more than 98% of New Zealand's total land area. The country also includes Stewart Island, the Chatham Islands, the Antipodes Islands, the Auckland Islands, and hundreds of tiny islets.

What is Ayers Rock?

Ayers Rock, now called by its Aboriginal name, Uluru, is a huge, red, oval-shaped rock outcropping that rises 2,831 feet (863 m) above the plains of central Australia. One of the largest monoliths in the world, Uluru is actually the summit of a massive sandstone hill, most of which is hidden underground. Aborigines consider Uluru sacred and incorporate numerous places around it into their ceremonial life.

What is the ratio of sheep to humans in Australia and New Zealand?

Because both countries are major wool, mutton, and lamb producers, Australia and New Zealand each have a high ratio of sheep to humans. In Australia, there are 132 million sheep, or seven sheep for each human in the country. In New Zealand, the ratio is even greater: the country's 50 million sheep translate into 14 sheep for each human.

How many of Oceania's countries have become independent since 1975?

Eight. Papua New Guinea became independent in 1975, the Solomon Islands and Tuvalu in 1978, Kiribati in 1979, Vanuatu in 1980, the Marshall Islands and the Federated States of Micronesia in 1986, and Palau (Belau) in 1994.

What is the Great Barrier Reef?

This vast coral reef system is the longest in the world, stretching 1,250 miles (2,000 km) along Australia's northeast coast. It is composed of reefs, shoals, and hundreds of islands. Popular with divers, the Great Barrier Reef is home to a myriad of aquatic creatures.

On what island is Robert Louis Stevenson buried?

Stevenson, author of *Dr. Jekyll and Mr. Hyde*, *Kidnapped*, and *Treasure Island*, is buried on the island of Upolu in Western Samoa. Born in Edinburgh, Scotland in 1850, Stevenson sailed to the South Pacific in 1888 and settled permanently in Samoa in 1890. He died there in 1894.

Where does Sydney rank among Australia's most populous cities?

Harbor and skyline of Sydney

Measured by actual city population, Sydney is not even ranked in the top hundred: only 13,501 people live within its tiny city limits. Brisbane is Australia's largest city, with 751,115 people. The Sydney metropolitan area, however, is by far the largest in Australia, with 3,538,749 people.

What is Australia's only island state?

Tasmania, which lies about 150 miles (240 km) south of the Australian mainland. Measuring 26,200 square miles (67,800 sq km) in area, it is the smallest of Australia's six states and accounts for less than 1% of the country's area. Originally part of New South Wales, Tasmania became a separate colony in 1825 and a state in 1901. Hobart, its capital, is home to 45% of the state's population.

Countries and Flags

This 12-page section presents basic information about each of the world's countries, along with an illustration of each country's flag. A total of 198 countries are listed: the world's 191 fully independent countries, and 7 internally independent countries which are under the protection of other countries in matters of defense and foreign affairs. Colonies and other dependent political entities are not listed.

The categories of information provided for each country are as follows.

Flag: In many countries two or more versions of the national flag exist. For example, there is often a "civil" version which the average person flies, and a "state" version which is flown only at government buildings and government functions. A common difference between the two is the inclusion of a coat of arms on the state version.

Country name: The short form of the English translation of the official country name.

Official name: The long form of the English translation of the official country name.

Population: The population figures listed are 2002 estimates based on U.S. census bureau figures and other available information.

Area: Figures provided represent total land area and all inland water. They are based on official data or U.N. data.

Population density: The number of people per square mile and square kilometer, calculated by dividing the country's population figure by its area figure.

Capital: The city that serves as the official seat of government. Population figures follow the capital name. These figures are based upon the latest official data.

AFGHANISTAN
Official Name: Islamic State of Afghanistan
Population: 27,280,000
Area: 251,826 sq mi (652,225 sq km)
Density: 108/sq mi (42/sq km)
Capital: Kābul, 1,424,400

ALGERIA
Official Name: People's Democratic Republic of Algeria
Population: 32,005,000
Area: 919,595 sq mi (2,381,741 sq km)
Density: 35/sq mi (13/sq km)
Capital: Algiers (El Djazaïr),1,507,241

ANGUILLA
Official Name: Anguilla
Population: 12,000
Area: 35 sq mi (91 sq km)
Density: 342/sq mi (132/sq km)
Capital: The Valley, 1,462

ALBANIA
Official Name: Republic of Albania
Population: 3,525,000
Area: 11,100 sq mi (28,748 sq km)
Density: 318/sq mi (123/sq km)
Capital: Tiranë, 243,000

ANDORRA
Official Name: Principality of Andorra
Population: 68,000
Area: 175 sq mi (453 sq km)
Density: 389/sq mi (150/sq km)
Capital: Andorra, 20,437

ANTIGUA AND BARBUDA
Official Name: Antigua and Barbuda
Population: 67,000
Area: 171 sq mi (442 sq km)
Density: 393/sq mi (152/sq km)
Capital: St. John's, 24,359

ANGOLA
Official Name: Republic of Angola
Population: 10,480,000
Area: 481,354 sq mi (1,246,700 sq km)
Density: 22/sq mi (8.4/sq km)
Capital: Luanda, 1,459,900

Countries and Flags *continued*

ARGENTINA
Official Name: Argentine Republic
Population: 37,600,000
Area: 1,073,519 sq mi (2,780,400 sq km)
Pop. Density: 35/sq mi (14/sq km)
Capital: Buenos Aires, 2,960,976

ARMENIA
Official Name: Republic of Armenia
Population: 3,335,000
Area: 11,506 sq mi (29,800 sq km)
Pop. Density: 290/sq mi (112/sq km)
Capital: Yerevan, 1,199,000

AUSTRALIA
Official Name: Commonwealth of Australia
Population: 19,455,000
Area: 2,969,910 sq mi (7,692,030 sq km)
Pop. Density: 6.6/sq mi (2.5/sq km)
Capital: Canberra, 298,847

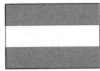

AUSTRIA
Official Name: Republic of Austria
Population: 8,160,000
Area: 32,378 sq mi (83,859 sq km)
Pop. Density: 252/sq mi (97/sq km)
Capital: Vienna (Wien), 1,539,848

AZERBAIJAN
Official Name: Azerbaijani Republic
Population: 7,785,000
Area: 33,437 sq mi (86,600 sq km)
Pop. Density: 233/sq mi (90/sq km)
Capital: Baku (Bakı), 1,080,500

BAHAMAS
Official Name: Commonwealth of The
  Bahamas
Population: 300,000
Area: 5,382 sq mi (13,939 sq km)
Pop. Density: 56/sq mi (22/sq km)
Capital: Nassau, 141,000

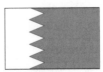

BAHRAIN
Official Name: Kingdom of Bahrain
Population: 650,000
Area: 267 sq mi (691 sq km)
Pop. Density: 2,436/sq mi (941/sq km)
Capital: Al Manāmah, 127,578

BANGLADESH
Official Name: People's Republic of
  Bangladesh
Population: 132,315,000
Area: 55,598 sq mi (143,998 sq km)
Pop. Density: 2,380/sq mi (919/sq km)
Capital: Dhaka (Dacca), 3,637,892

BARBADOS
Official Name: Barbados
Population: 275,000
Area: 166 sq mi (430 sq km)
Pop. Density: 1,657/sq mi (640/sq km)
Capital: Bridgetown, 5,928

BELARUS
Official Name: Republic of Belarus
Population: 10,340,000
Area: 80,155 sq mi (207,600 sq km)
Pop. Density: 129/sq mi (50/sq km)
Capital: Minsk, 1,661,000

BELGIUM
Official Name: Kingdom of Belgium
Population: 10,265,000
Area: 11,787 sq mi (30,528 sq km)
Pop. Density: 871/sq mi (336/sq km)
Capital: Brussels (Bruxelles), 136,424

BELIZE
Official Name: Belize
Population: 260,000
Area: 8,866 sq mi (22,963 sq km)
Pop. Density: 29/sq mi (11/sq km)
Capital: Belmopan, 8,130

BENIN
Official Name: Republic of Benin
Population: 6,690,000
Area: 43,475 sq mi (112,600 sq km)
Pop. Density: 154/sq mi (59/sq km)
Capital: Porto-Novo (designated), 179,138,
  and Cotonou (de facto), 536,827

BHUTAN
Official Name: Kingdom of Bhutan
Population: 2,070,000
Area: 17,954 sq mi (46,500 sq km)
Pop. Density: 115/sq mi (45/sq km)
Capital: Thimphu, 12,000

BOLIVIA
Official Name: Republic of Bolivia
Population: 8,375,000
Area: 424,165 sq mi (1,098,581 sq km)
Pop. Density: 20/sq mi (7.6/sq km)
Capital: La Paz (seat of government),
  792,611, and Sucre (designated), 194,888

BOSNIA AND HERZEGOVINA
Official Name: Republic of Bosnia and
  Herzegovina
Population: 3,950,000
Area: 19,741 sq mi (51,129 sq km)
Pop. Density: 200/sq mi (77/sq km)
Capital: Sarajevo, 367,703

BOTSWANA
Official Name: Republic of Botswana
Population: 1,590,000
Area: 224,712 sq mi (582,000 sq km)
Pop. Density: 7.1/sq mi (2.7/sq km)
Capital: Gaborone, 133,468

BRAZIL
Official Name: Federative Republic of Brazil
Population: 175,260,000
Area: 3,300,172 sq mi (8,547,404 sq km)
Pop. Density: 53/sq mi (21/sq km)
Capital: Brasília, 1,947,133

BRUNEI
Official Name: Negara Brunei Darussalam
Population: 345,000
Area: 2,226 sq mi (5,765 sq km)
Pop. Density: 155/sq mi (60/sq km)
Capital: Bandar Seri Begawan, 45,867

BULGARIA
Official Name: Republic of Bulgaria
Population: 7,665,000
Area: 42,855 sq mi (110,994 sq km)
Pop. Density: 179/sq mi (69/sq km)
Capital: Sofia (Sofiya), 1,190,126

BURKINA FASO
Official Name: Burkina Faso
Population: 12,435,000
Area: 105,869 sq mi (274,200 sq km)
Pop. Density: 117/sq mi (45/sq km)
Capital: Ouagadougou, 441,514

BURUNDI
Official Name: Republic of Burundi
Population: 6,300,000
Area: 10,745 sq mi (27,830 sq km)
Pop. Density: 586/sq mi (226/sq km)
Capital: Bujumbura, 226,628

CAMBODIA
Official Name: Kingdom of Cambodia
Population: 12,630,000
Area: 69,898 sq mi (181,035 sq km)
Pop. Density: 181/sq mi (70/sq km)
Capital: Phnom Penh (Phnum Pénh),
620,000

CAMEROON
Official Name: Republic of Cameroon
Population: 15,995,000
Area: 183,568 sq mi (475,440 sq km)
Pop. Density: 87/sq mi (34/sq km)
Capital: Yaoundé, 620,000

CANADA
Official Name: Canada
Population: 31,750,000
Area: 3,855,103 sq mi (9,984,670 sq km)
Pop. Density: 8.2/sq mi (3.2/sq km)
Capital: Ottawa, 323,340

CAPE VERDE
Official Name: Republic of Cape Verde
Population: 405,000
Area: 1,557 sq mi (4,033 sq km)
Pop. Density: 260/sq mi (100/sq km)
Capital: Praia, 61,644

CENTRAL AFRICAN REPUBLIC
Official Name: Central African Republic
Population: 3,610,000
Area: 240,536 sq mi (622,984 sq km)
Pop. Density: 15/sq mi (5.8/sq km)
Capital: Bangui, 451,690

CHAD
Official Name: Republic of Chad
Population: 8,850,000
Area: 495,755 sq mi (1,284,000 sq km)
Pop. Density: 18/sq mi (6.9/sq km)
Capital: N'Djamena, 546,572

CHILE
Official Name: Republic of Chile
Population: 15,415,000
Area: 292,135 sq mi (756,626 sq km)
Pop. Density: 53/sq mi (20/sq km)
Capital: Santiago, 4,295,593

CHINA
Official Name: People's Republic of China
Population: 1,278,720,000
Area: 3,690,045 sq mi (9,557,172 sq km)
Pop. Density: 347/sq mi (134/sq km)
Capital: Beijing (Peking), 6,690,000

COLOMBIA
Official Name: Republic of Colombia
Population: 40,680,000
Area: 440,831 sq mi (1,141,748 sq km)
Pop. Density: 92/sq mi (36/sq km)
Capital: Bogotá, 4,931,796

COMOROS
Official Name: Union of the Comoros
Population: 605,000
Area: 863 sq mi (2,235 sq km)
Pop. Density: 701/sq mi (271/sq km)
Capital: Moroni, 23,432

CONGO
Official Name: Republic of the Congo
Population: 2,925,000
Area: 132,047 sq mi (342,000 sq km)
Pop. Density: 22/sq mi (8.6/sq km)
Capital: Brazzaville, 693,712

**CONGO, DEMOCRATIC REPUBLIC OF
THE**
Official Name: Democratic Republic
of the Congo
Population: 54,455,000
Area: 905,446 sq mi (2,345,095 sq km)
Pop. Density: 60/sq mi (23/sq km)
Capital: Kinshasa, 3,000,000

COSTA RICA
Official Name: Republic of Costa Rica
Population: 3,805,000
Area: 19,730 sq mi (51,100 sq km)
Pop. Density: 193/sq mi (74/sq km)
Capital: San José, 309,672

Countries and Flags *continued*

COTE D'IVOIRE
Official Name: Republic of Cote d'Ivoire
Population: 16,600,000
Area: 124,518 sq mi (322,500 sq km)
Pop. Density: 133/sq mi (51/sq km)
Capital: Abidjan (de facto), 1,929,079, and
 Yamoussoukro (designated), 106,786

CROATIA
Official Name: Republic of Croatia
Population: 4,365,000
Area: 21,829 sq mi (56,538 sq km)
Pop. Density: 200/sq mi (77/sq km)
Capital: Zagreb, 867,865

CUBA
Official Name: Republic of Cuba
Population: 11,205,000
Area: 42,804 sq mi (110,861 sq km)
Pop. Density: 262/sq mi (101/sq km)
Capital: Havana (La Habana), 2,189,716

CYPRUS
Official Name: Republic of Cyprus
Population: 765,000
Area: 3,572 sq mi (9,251 sq km)
Pop. Density: 214/sq mi (83/sq km)
Capital: Nicosia (Levkosía), 84,436

CZECH REPUBLIC
Official Name: Czech Republic
Population: 10,260,000
Area: 30,450 sq mi (78,866 sq km)
Pop. Density: 337/sq mi (130/sq km)
Capital: Prague (Praha), 1,214,174

DENMARK
Official Name: Kingdom of Denmark
Population: 5,360,000
Area: 16,639 sq mi (43,094 sq km)
Pop. Density: 322 sq mi (124/sq km)
Capital: Copenhagen (København), 487,969

DJIBOUTI
Official Name: Republic of Djibouti
Population: 465,000
Area: 8,958 sq mi (23,200 sq km)
Pop. Density: 52/sq mi (20/sq km)
Capital: Djibouti, 329,337

DOMINICA
Official Name: Commonwealth of Dominica
Population: 70,000
Area: 305 sq mi (790 sq km)
Pop. Density: 230/sq mi (89/sq km)
Capital: Roseau, 9,348

DOMINICAN REPUBLIC
Official Name: Dominican Republic
Population: 8,650,000
Area: 18,704 sq mi (48,442 sq km)
Pop. Density: 462/sq mi (179/sq km)
Capital: Santo Domingo, 1,609,966

EAST TIMOR
Official Name: Democratic Republic of
 Timor-Leste
Population: 795,000
Area: 5,743 sq mi (14,874 sq km)
Pop. Density: 138/sq mi (53/sq km)
Capital: Dili, 50,000

ECUADOR
Official Name: Republic of Ecuador
Population: 13,315,000
Area: 105,037 sq mi (272,045 sq km)
Pop. Density: 127/sq mi (49/sq km)
Capital: Quito, 1,100,847

EGYPT
Official Name: Arab Republic of Egypt
Population: 70,125,000
Area: 386,662 sq mi (1,001,449 sq km)
Pop. Density: 181/sq mi (70/sq km)
Capital: Cairo (Al Qāhirah), 6,801,695

EL SALVADOR
Official Name: Republic of El Salvador
Population: 6,295,000
Area: 8,124 sq mi (21,041 sq km)
Pop. Density: 775/sq mi (299/sq km)
Capital: San Salvador, 415,346

EQUATORIAL GUINEA
Official Name: Republic of Equatorial Guinea
Population: 490,000
Area: 10,831 sq mi (28,051 sq km)
Pop. Density: 45/sq mi (17/sq km)
Capital: Malabo, 31,630

ERITREA
Official Name: State of Eritrea
Population: 4,380,000
Area: 36,170 sq mi (93,679 sq km)
Pop. Density: 121/sq mi (47/sq km)
Capital: Asmera, 358,100

ESTONIA
Official Name: Republic of Estonia
Population: 1,420,000
Area: 17,413 sq mi (45,100 sq km)
Pop. Density: 82/sq mi (31/sq km)
Capital: Tallinn, 403,981

ETHIOPIA
Official Name: Federal Democratic Republic
 of Ethiopia
Population: 66,780,000
Area: 446,953 sq mi (1,157,603 sq km)
Pop. Density: 149/sq mi (58/sq km)
Capital: Addis Ababa (Adis Abeba), 2,084,588

FIJI
Official Name: Republic of the Fiji Islands
Population: 850,000
Area: 7,056 sq mi (18,274 sq km)
Pop. Density: 120/sq mi (47/sq km)
Capital: Suva, 77,366

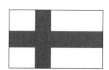

FINLAND
Official Name: Republic of Finland
Population: 5,180,000
Area: 130,559 sq mi (338,145 sq km)
Pop. Density: 40/sq mi (15/sq km)
Capital: Helsinki (Helsingfors), 512,686

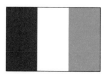

FRANCE
Official Name: French Republic
Population: 59,660,000
Area: 208,482 sq mi (539,965 sq km)
Pop. Density: 286/sq mi (110/sq km)
Capital: Paris, 2,147,857

GABON
Official Name: Gabonese Republic
Population: 1,225,000
Area: 103,347 sq mi (267,667 sq km)
Pop. Density: 12/sq mi (4.6/sq km)
Capital: Libreville, 337,700

THE GAMBIA
Official Name: Republic of The Gambia
Population: 1,435,000
Area: 4,127 sq mi (10,689 sq km)
Pop. Density: 348/sq mi (134/sq km)
Capital: Banjul, 42,407

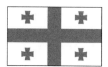

GEORGIA
Official Name: Republic of Georgia
Population: 4,975,000
Area: 26,911 sq mi (69,700 sq km)
Pop. Density: 185/sq mi (71/sq km)
Capital: Tbilisi, 1,279,000

GERMANY
Official Name: Federal Republic of Germany
Population: 83,145,000
Area: 137,822 sq mi (356,955 sq km)
Pop. Density: 603/sq mi (233/sq km)
Capital: Berlin, 3,425,759

GHANA
Official Name: Republic of Ghana
Population: 20,070,000
Area: 92,098 sq mi (238,533 sq km)
Pop. Density: 218/sq mi (84/sq km)
Capital: Accra, 949,113

GREECE
Official Name: Hellenic Republic
Population: 10,635,000
Area: 50,949 sq mi (131,957 sq km)
Pop. Density: 209/sq mi (81/sq km)
Capital: Athens (Athína), 772,072

GREENLAND
Official Name: Greenland
Population: 56,000
Area: 840,004 sq mi (2,175,600 sq km)
Pop. Density: 0.07/sq mi (0.03/sq km)
Capital: Godthåb (Nuuk), 13,445

GRENADA
Official Name: Grenada
Population: 89,000
Area: 133 sq mi (344 sq km)
Pop. Density: 670/sq mi (259/sq km)
Capital: St. George's, 4,439

GUATEMALA
Official Name: Republic of Guatemala
Population: 13,145,000
Area: 42,042 sq mi (108,889 sq km)
Pop. Density: 313/sq mi (121/sq km)
Capital: Guatemala, 823,301

GUINEA
Official Name: Republic of Guinea
Population: 7,690,000
Area: 94,926 sq mi (245,857 sq km)
Pop. Density: 81/sq mi (31/sq km)
Capital: Conakry, 950,000

GUINEA-BISSAU
Official Name: Republic of Guinea-Bissau
Population: 1,330,000
Area: 13,948 sq mi (36,125 sq km)
Pop. Density: 95/sq mi (37/sq km)
Capital: Bissau, 125,000

GUYANA
Official Name: Co-operative Republic of Guyana
Population: 695,000
Area: 83,000 sq mi (214,969 sq km)
Pop. Density: 8.4/sq mi (3.2/sq km)
Capital: Georgetown, 78,500

HAITI
Official Name: Republic of Haiti
Population: 7,015,000
Area: 10,714 sq mi (27,750 sq km)
Pop. Density: 655/sq mi (253/sq km)
Capital: Port-au-Prince, 846,247

HONDURAS
Official Name: Republic of Honduras
Population: 6,485,000
Area: 43,277 sq mi (112,088 sq km)
Pop. Density: 150/sq mi (58/sq km)
Capital: Tegucigalpa, 576,661

HUNGARY
Official Name: Republic of Hungary
Population: 10,090,000
Area: 35,919 sq mi (93,030 sq km)
Pop. Density: 281/sq mi (108/sq km)
Capital: Budapest, 1,906,798

Countries and Flags *continued*

ICELAND
Official Name: Republic of Iceland
Population: 280,000
Area: 39,769 sq mi (103,000 sq km)
Pop. Density: 7.0/sq mi (3.0/sq km)
Capital: Reykjavik, 100,850

INDIA
Official Name: Republic of India
Population: 1,037,955,000
Area: 1,222,559 sq mi (3,166,414 sq km)
Pop. Density: 849/sq mi (328/sq km)
Capital: New Delhi, 294,783

INDONESIA
Official Name: Republic of Indonesia
Population: 230,260,000
Area: 735,310 sq mi (1,904,443 sq km)
Pop. Density: 313/sq mi (121/sq km)
Capital: Jakarta, 8,227,746

IRAN
Official Name: Islamic Republic of Iran
Population: 66,365,000
Area: 630,578 sq mi (1,633,189 sq km)
Pop. Density: 105/sq mi (41/sq km)
Capital: Tehrān, 6,758,845

IRAQ
Official Name: Republic of Iraq
Population: 23,665,000
Area: 169,235 sq mi (438,317 sq km)
Pop. Density: 140/sq mi (54/sq km)
Capital: Baghdād, 3,841,268

IRELAND
Official Name: Ireland
Population: 3,860,000
Area: 27,133 sq mi (70,273 sq km)
Pop. Density: 142/sq mi (55/sq km)
Capital: Dublin (Baile Átha Cliath), 481,854

ISRAEL
Official Name: State of Israel
Population: 5,985,000
Area: 8,019 sq mi (20,770 sq km)
Pop. Density: 746/sq mi (288/sq km)
Capital: Jerusalem (Yerushalayim), 633,700

ITALY
Official Name: Italian Republic
Population: 57,700,000
Area: 116,342 sq mi (301,323 sq km)
Pop. Density: 496/sq mi (191/sq km)
Capital: Rome (Roma), 2,649,765

JAMAICA
Official Name: Jamaica
Population: 2,670,000
Area: 4,244 sq mi (10,991 sq km)
Pop. Density: 629/sq mi (243/sq km)
Capital: Kingston, 516,500

JAPAN
Official Name: Japan
Population: 126,880,000
Area: 145,850 sq mi (377,750 sq km)
Pop. Density: 870/sq mi (336/sq km)
Capital: Tōkyō, 7,967,614

JORDAN
Official Name: Hashemite Kingdom of
Jordan
Population: 5,230,000
Area: 35,135 sq mi (91,000 sq km)
Pop. Density: 149/sq mi (57/sq km)
Capital: 'Ammān, 963,490

KAZAKHSTAN
Official Name: Republic of Kazakhstan
Population: 16,735,000
Area: 1,049,156 sq mi (2,717,300 sq km)
Pop. Density: 16/sq mi (6.2/sq km)
Capital: Astana, 286,000

KENYA
Official Name: Republic of Kenya
Population: 30,960,000
Area: 224,961 sq mi (582,646 sq km)
Pop. Density: 138/sq mi (53/sq km)
Capital: Nairobi, 2,143,254

KIRIBATI
Official Name: Republic of Kiribati
Population: 95,000
Area: 313 sq mi (811 sq km)
Pop. Density: 303/sq mi (117/sq km)
Capital: Bairiki, 2,226

KOREA, NORTH
Official Name: Democratic People's Republic
of Korea
Population: 22,100,000
Area: 46,540 sq mi (120,538 sq km)
Pop. Density: 475/sq mi (183/sq km)
Capital: P'yŏngyang, 2,355,000

KOREA, SOUTH
Official Name: Republic of Korea
Population: 48,120,000
Area: 38,230 sq mi (99,016 sq km)
Pop. Density: 1,259/sq mi (486/sq km)
Capital: Seoul (Sŏul), 10,627,790

KUWAIT
Official Name: State of Kuwait
Population: 2,075,000
Area: 6,880 sq mi (17,818 sq km)
Pop. Density: 302/sq mi (116/sq km)
Capital: Kuwait (Al Kuwayt), 28,859

KYRGYZSTAN
Official Name: Kyrgyz Republic
Population: 4,785,000
Area: 76,641 sq mi (198,500 sq km)
Pop. Density: 62/sq mi (24/sq km)
Capital: Bishkek, 631,300

LAOS
Official Name: Lao People's Democratic
  Republic
Population: 5,705,000
Area: 91,429 sq mi (236,800 sq km)
Pop. Density: 62/sq mi (24/sq km)
Capital: Viangchan (Vientiane), 464,000

LATVIA
Official Name: Republic of Latvia
Population: 2,375,000
Area: 24,595 sq mi (63,700 sq km)
Pop. Density: 97/sq mi (37/sq km)
Capital: Rīga, 874,200

LEBANON
Official Name: Republic of Lebanon
Population: 3,655,000
Area: 4,016 sq mi (10,400 sq km)
Pop. Density: 910/sq mi (351/sq km)
Capital: Beirut (Bayrūt), 509,000

LESOTHO
Official Name: Kingdom of Lesotho
Population: 2,195,000
Area: 11,720 sq mi (30,355 sq km)
Pop. Density: 187/sq mi (72/sq km)
Capital: Maseru, 137,837

LIBERIA
Official Name: Republic of Liberia
Population: 3,255,000
Area: 38,250 sq mi (99,067 sq km)
Pop. Density: 85/sq mi (33/sq km)
Capital: Monrovia, 465,000

LIBYA
Official Name: Great Socialist People's
  Libyan Arab Jamahiriya
Population: 5,305,000
Area: 679,362 sq mi (1,759,540 sq km)
Pop. Density: 7.8/sq mi (3.0/sq km)
Capital: Tripoli (Tarābulus), 591,062

LIECHTENSTEIN
Official Name: Principality of Liechtenstein
Population: 33,000
Area: 62 sq mi (160 sq km)
Pop. Density: 534/sq mi (206/sq km)
Capital: Vaduz, 5,106

LITHUANIA
Official Name: Republic of Lithuania
Population: 3,605,000
Area: 25,213 sq mi (65,300 sq km)
Pop. Density: 143/sq mi (55/sq km)
Capital: Vilnius, 578,639

LUXEMBOURG
Official Name: Grand Duchy of Luxembourg
Population: 445,000
Area: 999 sq mi (2,586 sq km)
Pop. Density: 446/sq mi (172/sq km)
Capital: Luxembourg, 81,800

MACEDONIA
Official Name: Republic of Macedonia
Population: 2,050,000
Area: 9,928 sq mi (25,713 sq km)
Pop. Density: 206/sq mi (80/sq km)
Capital: Skopje, 440,577

MADAGASCAR
Official Name: Republic of Madagascar
Population: 16,225,000
Area: 226,658 sq mi (587,041 sq km)
Pop. Density: 72/sq mi (28/sq km)
Capital: Antananarivo, 1,250,000

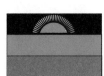

MALAWI
Official Name: Republic of Malawi
Population: 10,625,000
Area: 45,747 sq mi (118,484 sq km)
Pop. Density: 232/sq mi (90/sq km)
Capital: Lilongwe, 435,964

MALAYSIA
Official Name: Malaysia
Population: 22,445,000
Area: 127,320 sq mi (329,758 sq km)
Pop. Density: 176/sq mi (68/sq km)
Capital: Kuala Lumpur (de facto), 1,297,526 and
  Putrajaya (future)

MALDIVES
Official Name: Republic of Maldives
Population: 315,000
Area: 115 sq mi (298 sq km)
Pop. Density: 2,737/sq mi (1,057/sq km)
Capital: Male', 55,130

MALI
Official Name: Republic of Mali
Population: 11,170,000
Area: 482,077 sq mi (1,248,574 sq km)
Pop. Density: 23/sq mi (8.9/sq km)
Capital: Bamako, 658,275

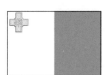

MALTA
Official Name: Republic of Malta
Population: 395,000
Area: 122 sq mi (316 sq km)
Pop. Density: 3,238/sq mi (1,250/sq km)
Capital: Valletta, 7,262

MARSHALL ISLANDS
Official Name: Republic of the Marshall Islands
Population: 72,000
Area: 70 sq mi (181 sq km)
Pop. Density: 1,029/sq mi (397/sq km)
Capital: Majuro (island)

MAURITANIA
Official Name: Islamic Republic of Mauritania
Population: 2,790,000
Area: 397,956 sq mi (1,030,700 sq km)
Pop. Density: 7.0/sq mi (2.7/sq km)
Capital: Nouakchott, 393,325

Countries and Flags *continued*

MAURITIUS
Official Name: Republic of Mauritius
Population: 1,195,000
Area: 788 sq mi (2,040 sq km)
Pop. Density: 1,517/sq mi (586/sq km)
Capital: Port Louis, 132,460

MEXICO
Official Name: United Mexican States
Population: 102,640,000
Area: 758,452 sq mi (1,964,382 sq km)
Pop. Density: 135/sq mi (52/sq km)
Capital: Mexico City (Ciudad de México),
 8,489,007

MICRONESIA, FEDERATED STATES OF
Official Name: Federated States of
 Micronesia
Population: 135,000
Area: 271 sq mi (702 sq km)
Pop. Density: 498/sq mi (192/sq km)
Capital: Palikir, 5,047

MOLDOVA
Official Name: Republic of Moldova
Population: 4,435,000
Area: 13,012 sq mi (33,700 sq km)
Pop. Density: 341/sq mi (132/sq km)
Capital: Chişinău (Kishinev), 676,700

MONACO
Official Name: Principality of Monaco
Population: 32,000
Area: 0.8 sq mi (2.0 sq km)
Pop. Density: 40,000/sq mi (16,000/sq km)
Capital: Monaco, 32,000

MONGOLIA
Official Name: Mongolia
Population: 2,675,000
Area: 604,829 sq mi (1,566,500 sq km)
Pop. Density: 4.4/sq mi (1.7/sq km)
Capital: Ulan Bator (Ulaanbaatar), 616,900

MOROCCO
Official Name: Kingdom of Morocco
Population: 30,905,000
Area: 172,414 sq mi (446,550 sq km)
Pop. Density: 179/sq mi (69/sq km)
Capital: Rabat, 717,000

MOZAMBIQUE
Official Name: Republic of Mozambique
Population: 19,495,000
Area: 308,642 sq mi (799,380 sq km)
Pop. Density: 63/sq mi (24/sq km)
Capital: Maputo, 966,837

MYANMAR
Official Name: Union of Myanmar
Population: 42,120,000
Area: 261,228 sq mi (676,577 sq km)
Pop. Density: 161/sq mi (62/sq km)
Capital: Rangoon (Yangon), 2,705,053

NAMIBIA
Official Name: Republic of Namibia
Population: 1,810,000
Area: 317,818 sq mi (823,144 sq km)
Pop. Density: 5.7/sq mi (2.2/sq km)
Capital: Windhoek, 147,056

NAURU
Official Name: Republic of Nauru
Population: 12,000
Area: 8.0 sq mi (21 sq km)
Pop. Density: 1,481/sq mi (571/sq km)
Capital: Yaren District

NEPAL
Official Name: Kingdom of Nepal
Population: 25,580,000
Area: 56,827 sq mi (147,181 sq km)
Pop. Density: 450/sq mi (174/sq km)
Capital: Kathmandu, 421,258

NETHERLANDS
Official Name: Kingdom of the Netherlands
Population: 16,025,000
Area: 16,164 sq mi (41,864 sq km)
Pop. Density: 991/sq mi (383/sq km)
Capital: Amsterdam (designated), 727,053,
 and The Hague ('s-Gravenhage) (seat of
 government), 440,743

NEW ZEALAND
Official Name: New Zealand
Population: 3,885,000
Area: 104,454 sq mi (270,534 sq km)
Pop. Density: 37/sq mi (14/sq km)
Capital: Wellington, 150,301

NICARAGUA
Official Name: Republic of Nicaragua
Population: 4,970,000
Area: 50,054 sq mi (129,640 sq km)
Pop. Density: 99/sq mi (38/sq km)
Capital: Managua, 864,201

NIGER
Official Name: Republic of Niger
Population: 10,495,000
Area: 489,192 sq mi (1,267,000 sq km)
Pop. Density: 21/sq mi (8.3/sq km)
Capital: Niamey, 392,165

NIGERIA
Official Name: Federal Republic of Nigeria
Population: 128,285,000
Area: 356,669 sq mi (923,768 sq km)
Pop. Density: 360/sq mi (139/sq km)
Capital: Abuja, 250,000

NIUE
Official Name: Niue
Population: 2,000
Area: 100 sq mi (259 sq km)
Pop. Density: 20/sq mi (7.7/sq km)
Capital: Alofi, 682

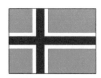

NORTHERN MARIANA ISLANDS
Official Name: Commonwealth of the Northern
  Mariana Islands
Population: 76,000
Area: 184 sq mi (477 sq km)
Pop. Density: 413/sq mi (159/sq km)
Capital: Saipan (island)

NORWAY
Official Name: Kingdom of Norway
Population: 4,515,000
Area: 149,405 sq mi (386,958 sq km)
Pop. Density: 30/sq mi (12/sq km)
Capital: Oslo, 504,040

OMAN
Official Name: Sultanate of Oman
Population: 2,665,000
Area: 82,030 sq mi (212,457 sq km)
Pop. Density: 32/sq mi (13/sq km)
Capital: Muscat (Masqat), 34,683

PAKISTAN
Official Name: Islamic Republic of Pakistan
Population: 146,145,000
Area: 339,732 sq mi (879,902 sq km)
Pop. Density: 430/sq mi (166/sq km)
Capital: Islāmābād, 204,364

PALAU
Official Name: Republic of Palau
Population: 19,000
Area: 196 sq mi (508 sq km)
Pop. Density: 97/sq mi (37/sq km)
Capital: Koror (de facto), 9,018, and
  Melekeok (future), 42

PANAMA
Official Name: Republic of Panama
Population: 2,865,000
Area: 29,157 sq mi (75,517 sq km)
Pop. Density: 98/sq mi (38/sq km)
Capital: Panamá, 415,964

PAPUA NEW GUINEA
Official Name: Independent State of Papua
  New Guinea
Population: 5,110,000
Area: 178,704 sq mi (462,840 sq km)
Pop. Density: 29/sq mi (11/sq km)
Capital: Port Moresby, 246,664

PARAGUAY
Official Name: Republic of Paraguay
Population: 5,810,000
Area: 157,048 sq mi (406,752 sq km)
Pop. Density: 37/sq mi (14/sq km)
Capital: Asunción, 502,426

PERU
Official Name: Republic of Peru
Population: 27,720,000
Area: 496,225 sq mi (1,285,216 sq km)
Pop. Density: 56/sq mi (22/sq km)
Capital: Lima, 371,122

PHILIPPINES
Official Name: Republic of the Philippines
Population: 83,685,000
Area: 115,831 sq mi (300,000 sq km)
Pop. Density: 722/sq mi (279/sq km)
Capital: Manila, 1,654,761

POLAND
Official Name: Republic of Poland
Population: 38,630,000
Area: 120,728 sq mi (312,685 sq km)
Pop. Density: 320/sq mi (124/sq km)
Capital: Warsaw (Warszawa), 1,615,369

PORTUGAL
Official Name: Portuguese Republic
Population: 10,075,000
Area: 35,516 sq mi (91,985 sq km)
Pop. Density: 284/sq mi (110/sq km)
Capital: Lisbon (Lisboa), 663,394

PUERTO RICO
Official Name: Commonwealth of Puerto Rico
Population: 3,950,000
Area: 3,515 sq mi (9,104 sq km)
Pop. Density: 1,124/sq mi (434/sq km)
Capital: San Juan, 421,958

QATAR
Official Name: State of Qatar
Population: 780,000
Area: 4,412 sq mi (11,427 sq km)
Pop. Density: 177/sq mi (68/sq km)
Capital: Ad Dawḩah (Doha), 361,540

ROMANIA
Official Name: Romania
Population: 22,340,000
Area: 91,699 sq mi (237,500 sq km)
Pop. Density: 244/sq mi (94/sq km)
Capital: Bucharest (Bucureşti), 2,067,545

RUSSIA
Official Name: Russian Federation
Population: 145,215,000
Area: 6,592,849 sq mi (17,075,400 sq km)
Pop. Density: 22/sq mi (8.5/sq km)
Capital: Moscow (Moskva), 8,368,449

RWANDA
Official Name: Republic of Rwanda
Population: 7,355,000
Area: 10,169 sq mi (26,338 sq km)
Pop. Density: 723/sq mi (279/sq km)
Capital: Kigali, 232,733

ST. KITTS AND NEVIS
Official Name: Federation of St. Kitts and Nevis
Population: 39,000
Area: 104 sq mi (269 sq km)
Pop. Density: 375/sq mi (145/sq km)
Capital: Basseterre, 11,295

Countries and Flags *continued*

ST. LUCIA
Official Name: St. Lucia
Population: 160,000
Area: 238 sq mi (616 sq km)
Pop. Density: 672/sq mi (260/sq km)
Capital: Castries, 11,147

ST. VINCENT AND THE GRENADINES
Official Name: St. Vincent and the
  Grenadines
Population: 115,000
Area: 150 sq mi (388 sq km)
Pop. Density: 767/sq mi (296/sq km)
Capital: Kingstown, 15,466

SAMOA
Official Name: Independent State of Samoa
Population: 180,000
Area: 1,093 sq mi (2,831 sq km)
Pop. Density: 165/sq mi (64/sq km)
Capital: Apia, 34,126

SAN MARINO
Official Name: Republic of San Marino
Population: 28,000
Area: 24 sq mi (61 sq km)
Pop. Density: 1,186/sq mi (459/sq km)
Capital: San Marino, 2,794

SAO TOME AND PRINCIPE
Official Name: Democratic Republic of Sao
  Tome and Principe
Population: 170,000
Area: 372 sq mi (964 sq km)
Pop. Density: 457/sq mi (176/sq km)
Capital: São Tomé, 5,245

SAUDI ARABIA
Official Name: Kingdom of Saudi Arabia
Population: 23,130,000
Area: 830,000 sq mi (2,149,690 sq km)
Pop. Density: 28/sq mi (11/sq km)
Capital: Riyadh (Ar Riyāḍ), 1,250,000

SENEGAL
Official Name: Republic of Senegal
Population: 10,435,000
Area: 75,951 sq mi (196,712 sq km)
Pop. Density: 137/sq mi (53/sq km)
Capital: Dakar, 1,490,450

SERBIA AND MONTENEGRO
Official Name: Serbia and Montenegro
Population: 10,665,000
Area: 39,449 sq mi (102,173 sq km)
Pop. Density: 270/sq mi (104/sq km)
Capital: Belgrade (Beograd), 1,136,786

SEYCHELLES
Official Name: Republic of Seychelles
Population: 80,000
Area: 176 sq mi (455 sq km)
Pop. Density: 455/sq mi (176/sq km)
Capital: Victoria, 24,907

SIERRA LEONE
Official Name: Republic of Sierra Leone
Population: 5,525,000
Area: 27,925 sq mi (72,325 sq km)
Pop. Density: 198/sq mi (76/sq km)
Capital: Freetown, 469,776

SINGAPORE
Official Name: Republic of Singapore
Population: 4,375,000
Area: 246 sq mi (636 sq km)
Pop. Density: 17,814/sq mi (6,879/sq km)
Capital: Singapore, 4,017,700

SLOVAKIA
Official Name: Slovak Republic
Population: 5,420,000
Area: 18,933 sq mi (49,035 sq km)
Pop. Density: 286/sq mi (111/sq km)
Capital: Bratislava, 441,453

SLOVENIA
Official Name: Republic of Slovenia
Population: 1,930,000
Area: 7,821 sq mi (20,256 sq km)
Pop. Density: 247/sq mi (95/sq km)
Capital: Ljubljana, 292,589

SOLOMON ISLANDS
Official Name: Solomon Islands
Population: 490,000
Area: 10,954 sq mi (28,370 sq km)
Pop. Density: 45/sq mi (17/sq km)
Capital: Honiara, 30,413

SOMALIA
Official Name: Somalia
Population: 7,620,000
Area: 246,201 sq mi (637,657 sq km)
Pop. Density: 31/sq mi (12/sq km)
Capital: Mogadishu (Muqdisho), 600,000

SOUTH AFRICA
Official Name: Republic of South Africa
Population: 43,645,000
Area: 470,693 sq mi (1,219,090 sq km)
Pop. Density: 93/sq mi (36/sq km)
Capital: Pretoria (administrative), 525,583,
  Cape Town (legislative), 854,616, and
  Bloemfontein (judicial), 126,867

SPAIN
Official Name: Kingdom of Spain
Population: 40,060,000
Area: 194,885 sq mi (504,750 sq km)
Pop. Density: 206/sq mi (79/sq km)
Capital: Madrid, 2,882,860

SRI LANKA
Official Name: Democratic Socialist
Republic of Sri Lanka
Population: 19,495,000
Area: 24,962 sq mi (64,652 sq km)
Pop. Density: 781/sq mi (302/sq km)
Capital: Colombo (designated), 612,000,
and Sri Jayewardenepura Kotte (seat of
government), 108,000

SUDAN
Official Name: Republic of the Sudan
Population: 36,585,000
Area: 967,500 sq mi (2,505,813 sq km)
Pop. Density: 38/sq mi (15/sq km)
Capital: Khartoum (Al Kharṭūm), 473,597

SURINAME
Official Name: Republic of Suriname
Population: 435,000
Area: 63,251 sq mi (163,820 sq km)
Pop. Density: 6.9/sq mi (2.7/sq km)
Capital: Paramaribo, 241,000

SWAZILAND
Official Name: Kingdom of Swaziland
Population: 1,115,000
Area: 6,704 sq mi (17,364 sq km)
Pop. Density: 166/sq mi (64/sq km)
Capital: Mbabane (administrative), 38,290,
and Lobamba (legislative)

SWEDEN
Official Name: Kingdom of Sweden
Population: 8,875,000
Area: 173,732 sq mi (449,964 sq km)
Pop. Density: 51/sq mi (20/sq km)
Capital: Stockholm, 674,452

SWITZERLAND
Official Name: Swiss Confederation
Population: 7,295,000
Area: 15,943 sq mi (41,293 sq km)
Pop. Density: 458/sq mi (177/sq km)
Capital: Bern (Berne), 136,338

SYRIA
Official Name: Syrian Arab Republic
Population: 16,940,000
Area: 71,498 sq mi (185,180 sq km)
Pop. Density: 237/sq mi (91/sq km)
Capital: Damascus (Dimashq), 1,549,932

TAIWAN
Official Name: Republic of China
Population: 22,460,000
Area: 13,901 sq mi (36,002 sq km)
Pop. Density: 1,616/sq mi (624/sq km)
Capital: T'aipei, 2,706,453

TAJIKISTAN
Official Name: Republic of Tajikistan
Population: 6,650,000
Area: 55,251 sq mi (143,100 sq km)
Pop. Density: 120/sq mi (46/sq km)
Capital: Dushanbe, 582,400

TANZANIA
Official Name: United Republic of Tanzania
Population: 36,705,000
Area: 364,900 sq mi (945,087 sq km)
Pop. Density: 101/sq mi (39/sq km)
Capital: Dar es Salaam (de facto), 1,096,000,
and Dodoma (legislative), 85,000

THAILAND
Official Name: Kingdom of Thailand
Population: 62,080,000
Area: 198,115 sq mi (513,115 sq km)
Pop. Density: 313/sq mi (121/sq km)
Capital: Bangkok (Krung Thep), 5,620,591

TOGO
Official Name: Republic of Togo
Population: 5,220,000
Area: 21,925 sq mi (56,785 sq km)
Pop. Density: 238/sq mi (92/sq km)
Capital: Lomé, 500,000

TONGA
Official Name: Kingdom of Tonga
Population: 105,000
Area: 288 sq mi (747 sq km)
Pop. Density: 364/sq mi (141/sq km)
Capital: Nuku'alofa, 22,400

TRINIDAD AND TOBAGO
Official Name: Republic of Trinidad and
Tobago
Population: 1,165,000
Area: 1,980 sq mi (5,128 sq km)
Pop. Density: 588/sq mi (227/sq km)
Capital: Port of Spain, 50,878

TUNISIA
Official Name: Republic of Tunisia
Population: 9,760,000
Area: 63,170 sq mi (163,610 sq km)
Pop. Density: 155/sq mi (60/sq km)
Capital: Tunis, 674,142

TURKEY
Official Name: Republic of Turkey
Population: 66,905,000
Area: 302,541 sq mi (783,577 sq km)
Pop. Density: 221/sq mi (85/sq km)
Capital: Ankara, 2,559,471

TURKMENISTAN
Official Name: Turkmenistan
Population: 4,645,000
Area: 188,457 sq mi (488,100 sq km)
Pop. Density: 25/sq mi (10/sq km)
Capital: Ashgabat, 412,200

TUVALU
Official Name: Tuvalu
Population: 11,000
Area: 10 sq mi (26 sq km)
Pop. Density: 1,100/sq mi (423/sq km)
Capital: Funafuti, 2,191

Countries and Flags *continued*

UGANDA
Official Name: Republic of Uganda
Population: 24,335,000
Area: 93,104 sq mi (241,139 sq km)
Pop. Density: 261/sq mi (101/sq km)
Capital: Kampala, 773,463

UKRAINE
Official Name: Ukraine
Population: 48,570,000
Area: 233,090 sq mi (603,700 sq km)
Pop. Density: 208/sq mi (80/sq km)
Capital: Kiev (Kyyiv), 2,630,000

UNITED ARAB EMIRATES
Official Name: United Arab Emirates
Population: 2,425,000
Area: 32,278 sq mi (83,600 sq km)
Pop. Density: 75/sq mi (29/sq km)
Capital: Abū Ẓaby (Abu Dhabi), 242,975

UNITED KINGDOM
Official Name: United Kingdom of Great
  Britain and Northern Ireland
Population: 59,715,000
Area: 94,249 sq mi (244,101 sq km)
Pop. Density: 634/sq mi (245/sq km)
Capital: London, 7,650,944

UNITED STATES
Official Name: United States of America
Population: 279,310,000
Area: 3,717,796 sq mi (9,629,091 sq km)
Pop. Density: 75/sq mi (29/sq km)
Capital: Washington, D.C., 572,059

URUGUAY
Official Name: Oriental Republic of Uruguay
Population: 3,375,000
Area: 68,500 sq mi (177,414 sq km)
Pop. Density: 49/sq mi (19/sq km)
Capital: Montevideo, 1,303,182

UZBEKISTAN
Official Name: Republic of Uzbekistan
Population: 25,355,000
Area: 172,742 sq mi (447,400 sq km)
Pop. Density: 147/sq mi (57/sq km)
Capital: Tashkent, 2,113,300

VANUATU
Official Name: Republic of Vanuatu
Population: 195,000
Area: 4,707 sq mi (12,190 sq km)
Pop. Density: 41/sq mi (16/sq km)
Capital: Port Vila, 19,311

VATICAN CITY
Official Name: State of the Vatican City
Population: 1,000
Area: 0.2 sq mi (0.4 sq km)
Pop. Density: 5,000/sq mi (2,500/sq km)
Capital: Vatican City, 1,000

VENEZUELA
Official Name: Bolivarian Republic of
  Venezuela
Population: 24,105,000
Area: 352,145 sq mi (912,050 sq km)
Pop. Density: 68/sq mi (26/sq km)
Capital: Caracas, 1,822,465

VIETNAM
Official Name: Socialist Republic of Vietnam
Population: 80,520,000
Area: 127,428 sq mi (330,036 sq km)
Pop. Density: 632/sq mi (244/sq km)
Capital: Hanoi, 905,939

YEMEN
Official Name: Republic of Yemen
Population: 18,385,000
Area: 203,850 sq mi (527,968 sq km)
Pop. Density: 90/sq mi (35/sq km)
Capital: Şan'ā', 427,150

ZAMBIA
Official Name: Republic of Zambia
Population: 9,865,000
Area: 290,586 sq mi (752,614 sq km)
Pop. Density: 34/sq mi (13/sq km)
Capital: Lusaka, 982,362

ZIMBABWE
Official Name: Republic of Zimbabwe
Population: 11,375,000
Area: 150,873 sq mi (390,759 sq km)
Pop. Density: 75/sq mi (29/sq km)
Capital: Harare (Salisbury), 1,189,103

Introduction to the Maps and Legend

Continental and regional coverage of the world's land areas is provided by the following section of thematic maps and physical-political reference maps. The reference map section falls into a continental arrangement: North America, South America, Europe, Africa, Asia, and Oceania. Introducing each regional reference map section are several basic thematic maps.

To aid the reader in understanding the relative sizes of continents and of some of the countries and regions, uniform scales for comparable areas were used as far as possible. Most of the world is covered by a series of regional maps at scales of 1:16,000,000 and 1:12,000,000. Maps at 1:10,000,000 provide even greater detail for parts of Europe. The United States and parts of South America are mapped at 1:4,000,000.

Many of the symbols used are self-explanatory. A complete legend below provides a key to the symbols on the reference maps in the atlas.

The color tints on the maps depict the varying elevations and depths of land areas and bodies of water. The Relief legend that accompanies each map shows the specific elevation or depth that each color tint represents.

The surface configuration is represented by hill-shading, which gives the three-dimensional impression of landforms. This terrain representation is superimposed on the layer tints to convey a realistic and readily visualized impression of the surface. The combination of altitudinal tints and hill-shading best shows elevation, relief, steepness of slope, and ruggedness of terrain.

If the world used one alphabet and language, no particular difficulty would arise in understanding place-names. However, some of the people of the world, the Chinese and the Japanese, for example, use non-alphabetic languages. Their symbols are transliterated into the Roman alphabet. In this atlas, a "local-name" policy generally was used for naming cities, towns, and all local topographic and water features. However, for a few major cities the Anglicized name was preferred and the local name given in parentheses: for instance, Moscow (Moskva), Vienna (Wien), Bangkok (Krung Thep). In countries where more than one official language is used, a name appears in the dominant local language. The generic parts of local names for topographic and water features are self-explanatory in many cases because of the associated map symbols or type styles. A complete list of foreign generic names is given in the Glossary.

Physical-Political Reference Map Legend

Cultural Features

Political Boundaries

- International (Demarcated, Undemarcated, and Administrative) / (over water)
- Disputed de facto
- Claim Boundary
- Indefinite or Undefined
- Secondary, State, Provincial, etc. / (over water)
- Parks, Indian Reservations
- City Limits — Urbanized Areas
- Neighborhoods, Sections of City

Populated Places

- ◉ 1,000,000 and over
- ◎ 250,000 to 1,000,000
- ☉ 100,000 to 250,000
- • 25,000 to 100,000
- ○ 0 to 25,000
- TŌKYŌ National Capitals
- Boise Secondary Capitals

Note: On maps at 1:20,000,000 and smaller the town symbols do not follow the specific population classification shown above. On all maps, type size indicates the relative importance of the city.

Transportation

- Railroads
- Railroads On 1:1,000,000 scale maps
- Railroad Ferries
- Roads On 1:1,000,000 scale maps — Major / Other
- On 1:4,000,000 scale maps — Major / Other
- On other scale maps
- Caravan Routes
- ✈ Airports

Other Cultural Features

- Dams
- Pipelines
- ▲ Points of Interest
- Ruins

Land Features

- △ Peaks, Spot Heights
- = Passes
- Sand
- Contours

Water Features

Lakes and Reservoirs

- Fresh Water
- Fresh Water: Intermittent
- Salt Water
- Salt Water: Intermittent

Other Water Features

- Salt Basins, Flats
- Swamps
- Ice Caps and Glaciers
- Rivers
- Intermittent Rivers
- Aqueducts and Canals
- Ship Channels
- Falls
- Rapids
- Springs
- △ Water Depths
- Fishing Banks
- Sand Bars
- Reefs

Note: Country populations used throughout the atlas are 2002 estimates based on 2001 U.S. Census Bureau figures and other available information. City populations in the continent "At a Glance" sections reflect the latest available official data.

ARCTIC OCEAN

Barents Sea

ZEML'A FRANCA-IOSIFA

NOVOSIBIRSKIJE OSTROVA

More Laptevych

NOVAJA ZEML'A

Karskoje More

Arctic Circle

SWEDEN
FINLAND
Helsinki
Archangel'sk
Stockholm
SANKT-PETERBURG
MOSKVA
Noril'sk
Jenisej
Ob'
Lena
Jakutsk

R U S S I A

Anadyr'

75°

60°

POLAND
GERMANY
CZ. REP.
UKRAINE
Kyiv
MOLD.
Nižnij Novgorod
Jakaterinburg
URAL'SKJE
GORY
Novosibirsk
Ozero Bajkal

Sea of Okhotsk

Bering Sea

ALEUTIAN IS. (U.S.)

OSTROV SACHALIN

Petropavlovsk-Kamcatskij

ROM.
AUS.
HUNG.
SLO.
BOS.
SERB.
BUL.

K A Z A K H S T A N

Aral Sea

A S I A

A L T A I

MONGOLIA

GOBI

Harbin

Sea of Japan

45°

ITALY
Roma
GREECE
ALB.
Black Sea
Gora El'brus
5633
GEOR.
ARM.
AZER.
UZBEK.
Taškent
TADŽ.
KYRG.

BEIJING PEKING

KOREA
SEOUL

JAPAN

ŌSAKA
TŌKYŌ

International Date Line

MALTA
Mediterranean Sea
TURKEY
Istanbul
SYRIA
IRAQ
Tehrān
TURKMENISTAN
AFGHANISTAN

C H I N A

Xi'an

Wuhan

Yellow Sea

SHANGHAI

30°

LIBYA
EGYPT
ISRAEL
JORDAN
KUWAIT
AL-QĀHIRAH
CAIRO
SAUDI ARABIA
QATAR
UNITED ARAB EMIRATES
OMAN
PAKISTAN
Karachi
DELHI
HIMALAYA
NEPAL
Mount Everest 8848
Tropic of Cancer
BANGL.
Chongqing

Guangzhou

Xianggang (Hong Kong)

TAIWAN

PACIFIC

WAKE ISLAND (U.S.)

NIGER
CHAD
SUDAN
Al-Kharṭūm
Nile
Red Sea
ERITREA
YEMEN
Adan
MUMBAI
INDIA
Arabian Sea
Chennai
Bay of Bengal
KOLKATA
MYANMAR BURMA
THAILAND
Krung Thep Bangkok
VIETNAM
CAMB.
South China Sea
MANILA
GUAM (U.S.)

Philippine Sea

OCEAN

15°

NIGERIA
CAMEROON
CEN. AFR. REP.
ETHIOPIA
SOMALIA
DJIBOUTI
Colombo
SRI LANKA
MALDIVES
BRUNEI
MALAYSIA
Singapore
BORNEO
PHILIPPINES

M I C R O N E S I A

EQUATORIAL GUINEA
GABON
CONGO
DEM. REP. OF THE CONGO
ZAIRE
UGANDA
RWANDA
BURUNDI
KENYA
Nairobi
Lake Victoria
TANZANIA
Kilimanjaro 5895
Kinshasa

SEYCHELLES

CHAGOS ARCHIPELAGO (B.I.O.T.)

Equator

SUMATERA
JAKARTA
INDONESIA
JAWA
SULAWESI

IRIAN JAYA
NEW GUINEA
PAPUA NEW GUINEA
Port Moresby

Equator

SOLOMON ISLANDS

SOLOMON ISLANDS

KIRIBATI

TUVALU

0°

ANGOLA
ZAMBIA
ZIMBABWE
MOZAMBIQUE
Mozambique Channel
MADAGASCAR
Luanda

I N D I A N

O C E A N

CHRISTMAS ISLAND (Austl.)

EAST TIMOR
TIMOR

M E L A N E S I A

VANUATU

Cairns

Coral Sea

NEW CALEDONIA (Fr.)

FIJI

15°

NAMIBIA
BOTSWANA
SWAZILAND
Johannesburg
LESOTHO
SOUTH AFRICA
Durban
Cape Town
CAPE OF GOOD HOPE

REUNION (Fr.)

MAURITIUS

Tropic of Capricorn

A U S T R A L I A

Perth

Brisbane

Sydney

Melbourne
Mount Kosciuszko 2230

Tasman Sea

NEW ZEALAND

30°

ÎLES KERGUELEN (F.S.A.T.)

TASMANIA

Wellington

45°

SOUTHERN   OCEAN

Antarctic Circle

ENDERBY LAND

WILKES LAND

60°

75°

Kilometers | 0 1000 2000 3000 Km.
Miles | 0 1000 2000 3000 Mi.

Robinson Projection

A N T A R C T I C A

World Physical

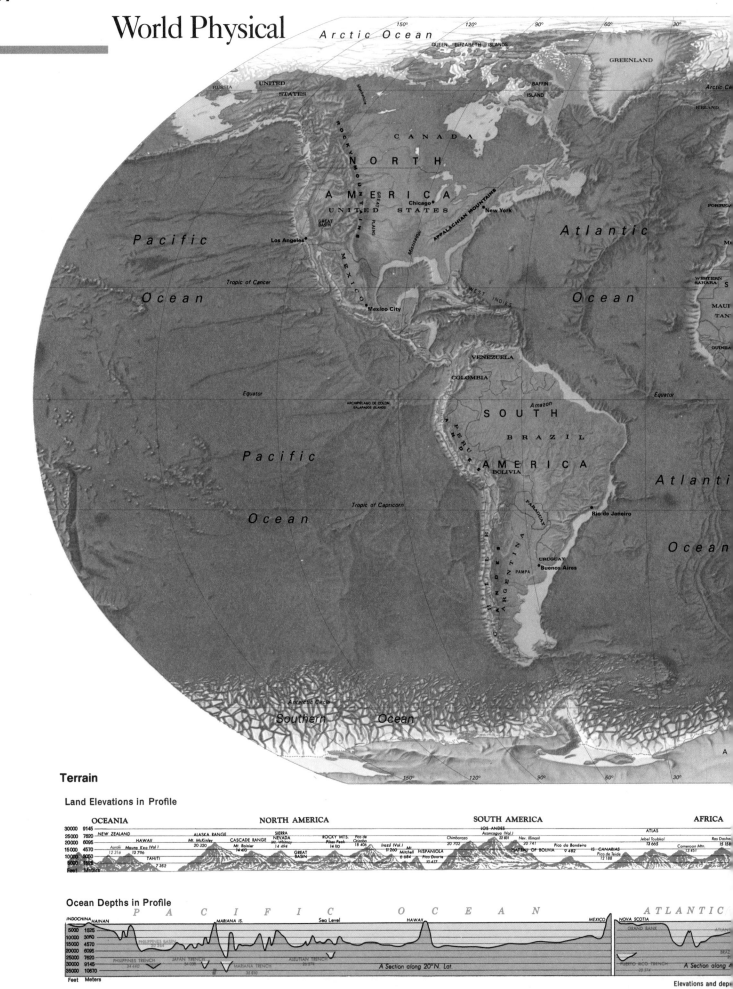

Arctic Ocean

QUEEN ELIZABETH ISLANDS

GREENLAND

RUSSIA

UNITED STATES

BAFFIN ISLAND

ICELAND

Arctic C

CANADA

NORTH

AMERICA

UNITED STATES

PORTUGA

Chicago

New York

Atlantic

Pacific

Los Angeles

GREAT BASIN

ROCKY MOUNTAINS

GREAT PLAINS

MEXICO

APPALACHIAN MOUNTAINS

Mississippi

WESTERN SAHARA

Tropic of Cancer

Ocean

M

Ocean

MAUR

TAN

Mexico City

WEST INDIES

GUINEA

VENEZUELA

COLOMBIA

Equator

ARCHIPELAGO DE COLON SALAPAGOS ISLANDS

Amazon

SOUTH

BRAZIL

Equator

Pacific

PERU

AMERICA

Atlanti

BOLIVIA

Ocean

Tropic of Capricorn

PARAGUAY

Rio de Janeiro

Ocean

ANDES

CHILE

ARGENTINA

URUGUAY

Buenos Aires

PAMPA

Antarctic Circle

Southern   Ocean

A

Terrain

Land Elevations in Profile

| | OCEANIA | NORTH AMERICA | SOUTH AMERICA | AFRICA |

LOS ANDES

ATLAS

30000	9145												
25000	7620	NEW ZEALAND	ALASKA RANGE	SIERRA		Aconcagua (Vol.)				
20000	6095	HAWAII	Mt. McKinley	NEVADA	ROCKY MTS. Pico de Orizaba	Chimborazo 22 831	Nev. Illimani		Jebel Toubkal	Ras Dashe
			20 320	Mt. Whitney	Pikes Peak 18 406	20 702	20 741	Pico da Bandeira	13 665	15 158
15000	4570	Aoraki Mauna Kea (Vol.)		Mt. Rainier 14 494	14 110			IS. CANARIAS	Cameroon Mtn.
		12 316 13 796		CASCADE RANGE		Irazú (Vol.) Mt. HISPANIOLA	PLATEAU OF BOLIVIA 9 482	12 188 Pico de Teide	13 451
10000	3050	TAHITI		GREAT	11 200 Mitchell Pico Duarte			
5000	1525	7 352		BASIN	6 684 10 417			
Feet	Meters							

Ocean Depths in Profile

P A C I F I C   O C E A N   A T L A N T I C

INDOCHINA HAINAN

MARIANA IS.

Sea Level

HAWAII

MEXICO

NOVA SCOTIA

GRAND BANK

ATLAS

5000	1525							
10000	3050	PHILIPPINES BASIN						BRAZ
15000	4570							
20000	6095		MARIANA IS.					
25000	7620	PHILIPPINES TRENCH	JAPAN TRENCH	ALEUTIAN TRENCH			PUERTO RICO TRENCH
30000	9145	34 440	34 626	23 376	A Section along 20°N. Lat.		28 374	A Section alor
35000	10670		MARIANA TRENCH 35 810				
Feet	Meters							

Elevations and dep

Arctic   Ocean

30°   60°   90°   120°   150°

Arctic Circle

NORWAY
SWEDEN
FINLAND

RUSSIA

Ob'

Moscow
Volga

Berlin   BELARUS
POLAND
GERMANY
UKRAINE

EUROPE

ITALY
ALPS
Rome

ROMANIA

Black Sea

Caspian Sea

TURKEY

SYRIA
ISRAEL
Tehran
IRAQ
IRAN

Mediterranean Sea

Cairo
LIBYA
EGYPT
SAUDI
ARABIA

Red Sea

Nile

NIGER
CHAD
SUDAN

NIGERIA

CENTRAL
AFRICAN
REPUBLIC
ETHIOPIA

SOMALIA

GABON
Congo
DEM. REP.
OF THE
CONGO
ZAIRE

Lake
Victoria
TANZANIA

ANGOLA
ZAMBIA

ZIMBABWE
MOZAMBIQUE

MADAGASCAR

NAMIBIA
KALAHARI
DESERT
BOTSWANA

SOUTH
AFRICA
Cape Town

A S I A

KAZAKHSTAN

TURKMENISTAN

MONGOLIA

GOBI

CHINA

Beijing

Shanghai

JAPAN
Tokyo

Pacific

Ocean

PAKISTAN
HIMALAYAS
Ganges

INDIA
BNGL.
Kolkata

MYANMAR
THAILAND

Tropic of Cancer

VIETNAM
CAMB.

PHILIPPINES

Mumbai

MALAYSIA

Equator

Jakarta   INDONESIA

PAPUA
NEW GUINEA

EAST TIMOR
TIMOR

GREAT
SANDY
DESERT

AUSTRALIA

Indian

Tropic of Capricorn

GREAT
VICTORIA
DESERT

GREAT DIVIDING RANGE

Kinabalu

Sydney

Ocean

NEW
ZEALAND

Southern   Ocean

Antarctic Circle

A R C T I C A

30°   60°   90°   120°   150°

A-510000-792

© Rand McNally & Co.

0   1000   2000 Mi.

0   1000   2000 Km.

Scale

EUROPE   ASIA   OCEANIA

9145 30000

ALPS   CAUCASUS   ELBURZ   K2   Everest Kanchenjunga   Gongga Shan   NEW GUINEA 7620 25000
PYRENEES   Mt. Blanc   KJÖLEN   Qolleh-ye   Damavand   28 250   29 028   24 790   SUMATRA   BORNEO
Pico de Aneto   15 771   Glittertinden   18 510   18 386   PAMIRS   6095 20000
11 168   Etna (Vol.)   8110   10 902   Dj. ash-Sheikh   PLATEAU OF TIBET   Klyuchevskaya   JAVA   Kinabalu   Mt. Apo   Puncak Jaya 4570 15000
MADAGASCAR   (Hermon)   H I M A L A Y A S   15 584   12 455   9692   16 503
Maromokotro   Hekla (Vol.)   Narodnaya   9 232   Padam Adigalla   SRI LANKA   Semeru   G. Kerinci   3050 10000
9 436   4 892   5 217   GOBI DESERT   12 060   12 467   1525 5000
                                                                                                                                                Meters Feet

MEDITERRANEAN   SEA   I N D I A N   O C E A N   ARCTIC OCEAN   PACIFIC OCEAN

FRANCE   GIBRALTAR   MALTA   ISRAEL   Sea Level   SOEMBA   NORTH POLE   65°N. 65°S.   LITTLE AMERICA   SOUTH POLE

1525 5000
3050 10000
4570 15000
6095 20000
7620 25000
9145 30000
10670 35000

A Section along 10°S. Lat.

Meters Feet

in feet

World Climate

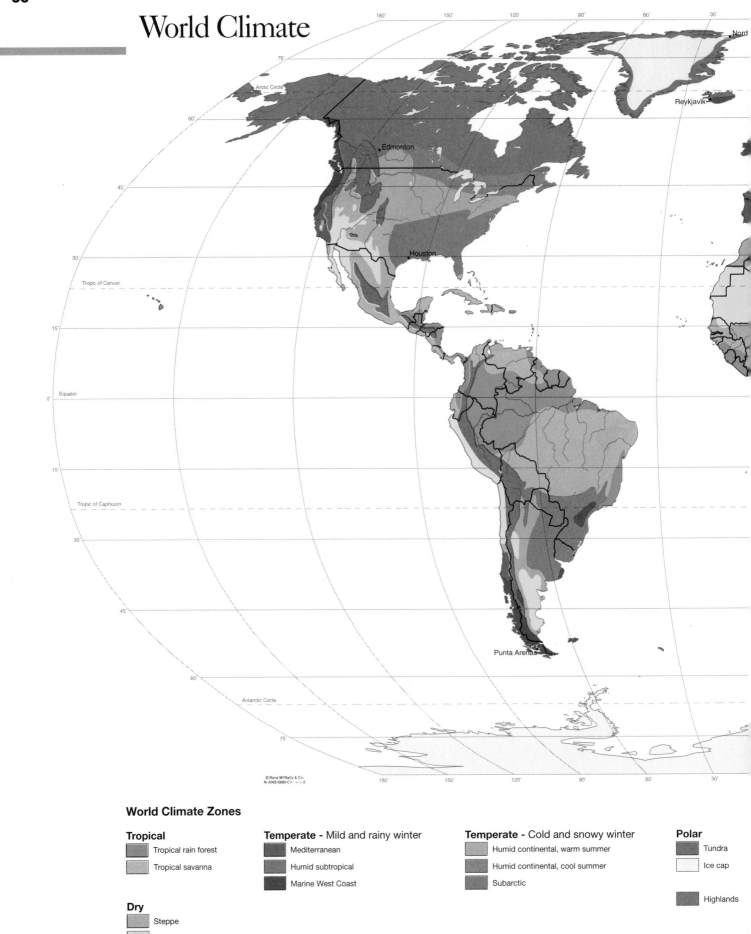

World Climate Zones

Tropical
- Tropical rain forest
- Tropical savanna

Dry
- Steppe
- Desert

Temperate - Mild and rainy winter
- Mediterranean
- Humid subtropical
- Marine West Coast

Temperate - Cold and snowy winter
- Humid continental, warm summer
- Humid continental, cool summer
- Subarctic

Polar
- Tundra
- Ice cap
- Highlands

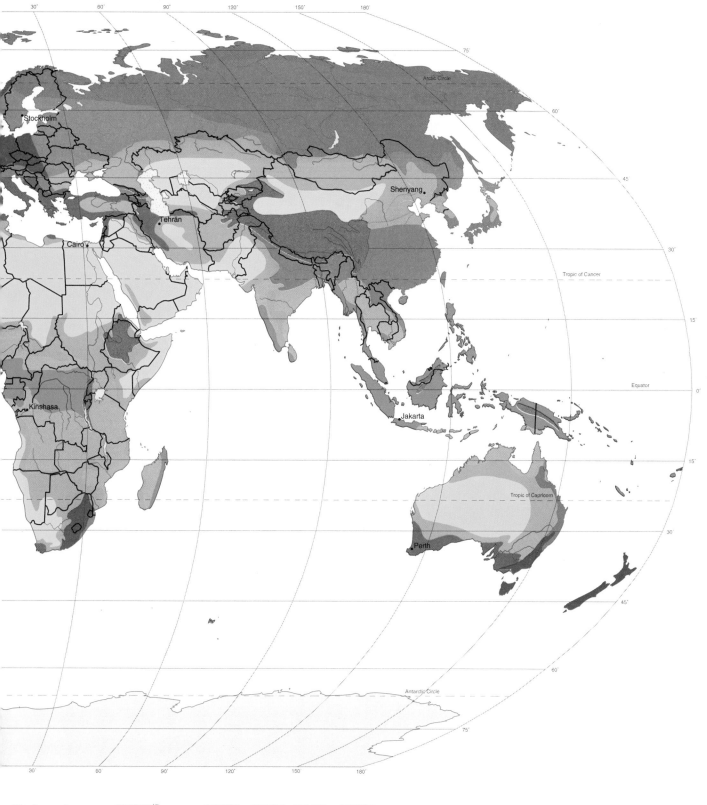

Tinted areas show temperature in degrees Fahrenheit. Vertical bars show precipitation in inches.

Jakarta
Hot and rainy

Kinshasa
Hot with rainy and dry seasons

Tehrān
Semiarid

Cairo
Very dry

Perth
Hot, dry summer / mild, rainy winter

Houston
Warm, humid summer / mild winter

Punta Arenas
Mild and rainy

Shenyang
Warm, humid summer / cold, snowy winter

Stockholm
Cool, humid summer / cold, snowy winter

Edmonton
Short, cool, humid summer / very cold, snowy winter

Reykjavík
Cold and dry

Nord
Very cold, perpetual frost

Extensive uplands
Climate varies with elevation and latitude

World Vegetation

180° 150° 120° 90° 60° 30°

75°

Arctic Circle

60°

45°

ROCKY MOUNTAINS

Great Plains

APPALACHIAN MTS.

New York

30°

Tropic of Cancer

Mexico City

15°

0° Equator

Amazon Basin

15°

ANDES MOUNTAINS

Tropic of Capricorn

Rio de Janeiro

30°

Buenos Aires

Patagonia

45°

© Rand McNally & Co.
N-ANS10000-E1- -:-:-3

60°

Antarctic Circle

75°

180° 150° 120° 90° 60° 30°

Vegetation Regions

■ Tropical and sub-tropical forests	■ Savanna	■ Desert	■ Mediterranean	■ Temperate grassland

Siberia

URALS

Moscow

Balkan
Peninsula

LPS

Cairo

Arabian
Peninsula

Beijing

Tōkyō

HIMALAYAS

Congo
Basin

MADAGASCAR

Great Sandy
Desert

Johannesburg

Sydney

Melbourne

Arctic Circle

Tropic of Cancer

Equator

Tropic of Capricorn

Antarctic Circle

Temperate forest

Taiga (northern forests)

Tundra (lichen and moss)

Mountain

Polar and high mountain

World Population

Population Density
Inhabitants per sq. km. (mi.)

	Uninhabited
	<1 (2)
	1-10 (2-25)
	10-25 (25-60)
	25-50 (60-125)
	50-100 (125-250)
	>100 (250)

© Rand McNally & Co.
N-ANS10000-T1- -<:-)-6

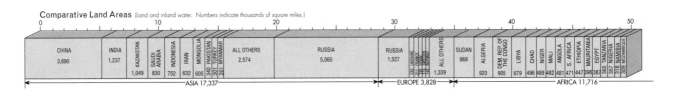

Comparative Land Areas (Land and inland water. Numbers indicate thousands of square miles.)

CHINA 3,690	INDIA 1,237	KAZAKHSTAN 1,049	SAUDI ARABIA 830	INDONESIA 752	IRAN 632	MONGOLIA 605	PAKISTAN 340	TURKEY 301	MYANMAR 261	ALL OTHERS 2,574	RUSSIA 5,065	RUSSIA 1,527	UKRAINE 233	FRANCE 213	SPAIN 195	SWEDEN 174	GERMANY 138	ALL OTHERS 1,339	SUDAN 968	ALGERIA 920	DEM. REP. OF THE CONGO 905	LIBYA 679	CHAD 496	NIGER 489	MALI 482	ANGOLA 481	S. AFRICA 471	ETHIOPIA 447	MAURITANIA 396	EGYPT 387	TANZANIA 365	NIGERIA 357	NAMIBIA 318	MOZAMBIQUE 309

ASIA 17,337 | EUROPE 3,828 | AFRICA 11,716

St. Petersburg

Moscow

sen

İstanbul

Tehrān

Cairo

Karāchi

Delhi

Dhaka

Kolkata

Mumbai

Hyderābād

Chennai

Bangkok

Beijing

Tianjin

Seoul

Tōkyō

Osaka Nagoya

Shanghai

T'aipei

Hong Kong

Manila

Jakarta

Arctic Circle

75°

60°

45°

30°

Tropic of Cancer

15°

Equator

0°

15°

Tropic of Capricorn

30°

45°

60°

Antarctic Circle

75°

WORLD TOTAL 57,900,000 square miles

| ZAMBIA 291 | ALL OTHERS 2,956 | CANADA 3,850 | UNITED STATES 3,787 | GREENLAND 840 | MEXICO 760 | OTHER 292 | BRAZIL 3,286 | ARGENTINA 1,074 | PERU 496 | COLOMBIA 441 | BOLIVIA 424 | VENEZUELA 352 | CHILE 292 | OTHER 518 | AUSTRALIA 2,966 | OTHER 318 | ANTARCTICA 5,400 |

← NORTH AMERICA 9,529 → ← SOUTH AMERICA 6,884 → ← OCEANIA 3,284 → ← ANTARCTICA 5,400 →

World Environments

© Rand McNally & Co.
N-ANS10000-M1- -!-!-3

Environments

Urban	Cropland	Cropland, woodland	Cropland, grazing land	Grassland, grazing land

Forest, woodland   Swamp, marsh   Tundra   Shrub, sparse grass, wasteland   Barren land

Time Zones

Standard time zone of even-numbered hours from Greenwich time	
Standard time zone of odd-numbered hours from Greenwich time	
Time varies from the standard time zone by half an hour	
Time varies from the standard time zone by other than half an hour	

h m   hours, minutes

The standard time zone system, fixed by international agreement and by law in each country, is based on a theoretical division of the globe into 24 zones of 15° longitude each. The mid-meridian of each zone fixes the hour for the entire zone. The zero time zone extends 7½° east and 7½° west of the Greenwich meridian, 0° longitude. Since the earth rotates toward the east, time zones to the west of Greenwich are earlier, to the east, later.

Plus and minus hours at the top of the map are added to or subtracted from local time to find Greenwich time. Local standard time can be determined for any area in the world by adding one hour for each time zone counted in an easterly direction from one's own, or by subtracting one hour for each zone counted in a westerly direction. To separate one day from the next, the 180th meridian has been designated as the international date line. On both sides of the line the time of day is the same, but west of the line it is one day later than it is to the east. Countries that adhere to the international zone system adopt the zone applicable to their location. Some countries, however, establish time zones based on political boundaries, or adopt the time zone of a neighboring unit. For all or part of the year some countries also advance their time by one hour, thereby utilizing more daylight hours each day.

North America

North America is the world's third-largest continent, covering an area of 9.5 million square miles (24.7 million sq km). It lies primarily between the Arctic Circle and the Tropic of Cancer, and comes within 500 miles (800 km) of both the North Pole and the Equator. The continent's western flank is dominated by the spectacular Rocky Mountains. Covering vast stretches of the central United States and Canada are the fertile Great Plains, a large part of which is drained by the Mississippi River and its tributaries.

In the north, Hudson Bay is frozen for much of the year. Mexico, located in the continent's southern third, is mostly mountainous and dry, but farther south, the climate is wet. Many of the small Central American countries have volcanoes along the Pacific Coast.

North America at a glance

Land area: 9,500,000 square miles (24,700,000 sq km)

Estimated population: 488,780,000

Population density: 51/square mile (20/sq km)

Mean elevation: 2,000 feet (610 m)

Highest point: Mt. McKinley, Alaska, U.S. 20,230 feet (6,194 m)

Lowest point: Death Valley, California, U.S., 282 feet (86 m) below sea level

Longest river: Mississippi-Missouri, 3,740 mi (6,019 km)

Number of countries (incl. dependencies): 38

Largest independent country: Canada, 3,855,103 square miles (9,984,670 sq km)

Smallest independent country: St. Kitts and Nevis, 104 square miles (269 sq km)

Most populous independent country: United States, 279,310,000

Least populous independent country: St. Kitts and Nevis, 39,000

Largest city: Mexico City, pop. 8,489,007

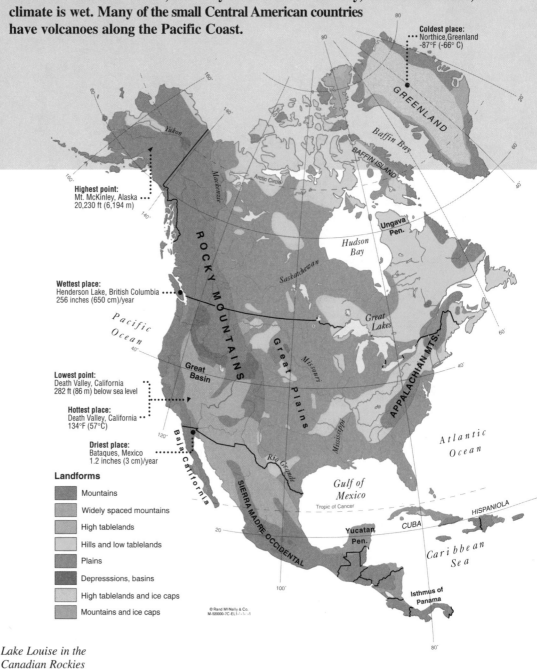

Landforms
- Mountains
- Widely spaced mountains
- High tablelands
- Hills and low tablelands
- Plains
- Depresssions, basins
- High tablelands and ice caps
- Mountains and ice caps

Lake Louise in the Canadian Rockies

Climate

North America contains almost every type of climate that can be found in the world. Ice and tundra cover northern Canada and Greenland. Much of the central and eastern parts of the U.S. and Canada are temperate, with great seasonal changes marked by warm summers and cold winters. The Pacific Ocean moderates weather changes along the west coast, where it is cool and wet in the north and warm and dry in the south. Desert and semi-desert cover much of the southwestern U.S. and Mexico. The tropical southern region of the continent and the islands of the Caribbean Sea are hot and rainy.

Tinted areas show temperature in degrees Fahrenheit. Vertical bars show precipitation in inches.

Belize City — Hot and rainy

Havana — Hot with rainy and dry seasons

Monterrey — Semiarid

Las Vegas — Very dry

Los Angeles — Hot, dry summer / mild, rainy winter

Houston — Warm, humid summer / mild winter

Seattle — Mild and rainy

Chicago — Warm, humid summer / cold, snowy winter

Toronto — Cool, humid summer / cold, snowy winter

Edmonton — Short, cool, humid summer / very cold, snowy winter

Barrow — Cold and dry

Nord — Very cold, perpetual frost

Extensive uplands — Climate varies with elevation and latitude

© Rand McNally & Co.
M-520000-6A-EL1-ᴸ·ᴸ·-1

Population

About 60% of all North Americans live in the United States, the world's third most-populous country. Canada is the continent's largest country, but one of the world's least densely populated; most Canadians live within 100 miles (160 km) of the country's southern border. Mexico, with approximately 20% of North America's inhabitants, has one of the world's largest and fastest growing metropolitan areas, Mexico City, which is home to more than 20 million people.

Canada is populated mostly by descendants of French and British settlers, as well as native Americans, such as the Inuit (Eskimos) of the far north. The United States' populace reflects the country's diverse history of immigration, with European ancestry being the most common. The people of Mexico and Central America trace their origins to Spaniards and native Americans. The population of the Caribbean islands includes many descendants of African slaves and European settlers.

Fastest-Growing Countries

Montserrat, 13.39% (annual rate of natural increase)

Turks and Caicos Islands, 3.41%

Belize, 2.7%

Slowest-Growing Countries

Dominica, -0.98%

Trinidad and Tobago, -0.51%

Saint Kitts and Nevis, -0.11%

Inhabitants per sq. km. (mi.)
- Uninhabited
- <1 (2)
- 1-10 (2-25)
- 10-25 (25-60)
- 25-50 (60-125)
- 50-100 (125-250)
- >100 (250)

© Rand McNally
M-520000-1P-EL1-ᴸ·ᴸ·-1

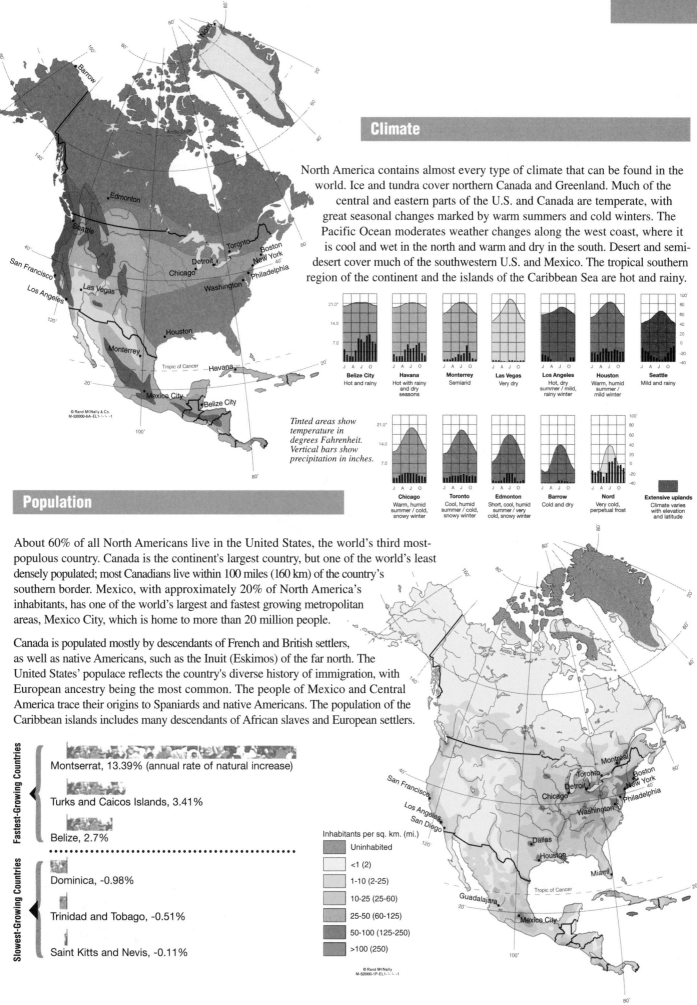

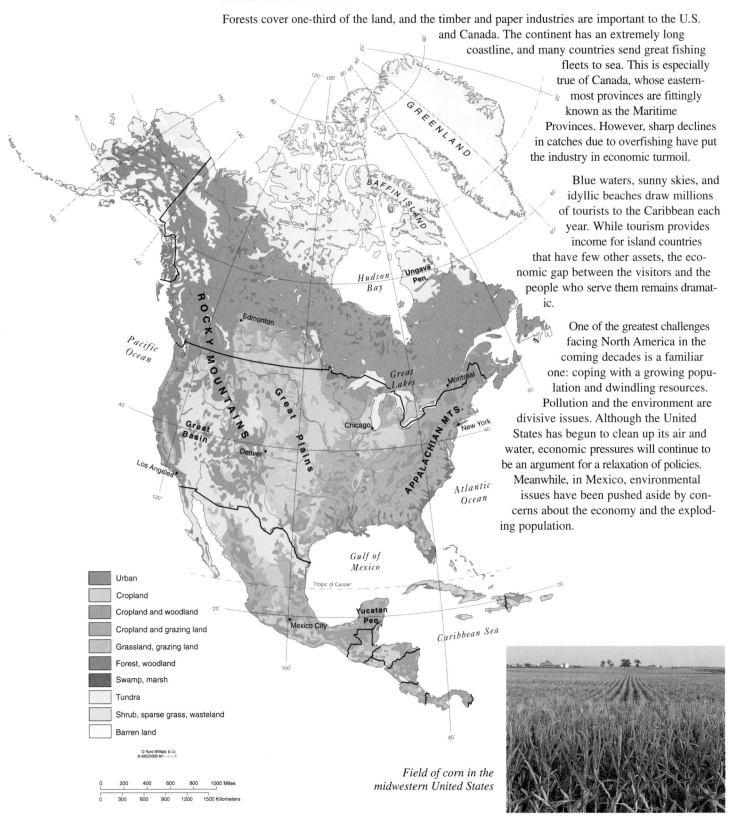

Environments and Land Use

Although only 12% of the continent is suitable for agriculture, North America is the world's leading food producer. Unlike other parts of the world, famine is virtually unknown. Large quantities of food, such as grains from the central U.S. and Canada, are exported worldwide. Sixteen percent of the continent is used for grazing, and the livestock raised on these lands are also an important source of food at home and abroad.

Forests cover one-third of the land, and the timber and paper industries are important to the U.S. and Canada. The continent has an extremely long coastline, and many countries send great fishing fleets to sea. This is especially true of Canada, whose easternmost provinces are fittingly known as the Maritime Provinces. However, sharp declines in catches due to overfishing have put the industry in economic turmoil.

Blue waters, sunny skies, and idyllic beaches draw millions of tourists to the Caribbean each year. While tourism provides income for island countries that have few other assets, the economic gap between the visitors and the people who serve them remains dramatic.

One of the greatest challenges facing North America in the coming decades is a familiar one: coping with a growing population and dwindling resources. Pollution and the environment are divisive issues. Although the United States has begun to clean up its air and water, economic pressures will continue to be an argument for a relaxation of policies. Meanwhile, in Mexico, environmental issues have been pushed aside by concerns about the economy and the exploding population.

Urban
Cropland
Cropland and woodland
Cropland and grazing land
Grassland, grazing land
Forest, woodland
Swamp, marsh
Tundra
Shrub, sparse grass, wasteland
Barren land

© Rand McNally & Co.
N-ANS20000-M1- ⊟ ⊟ -1

| 0 | 200 | 400 | 600 | 800 | 1000 Miles |

| 0 | 300 | 600 | 900 | 1200 | 1500 Kilometers |

Field of corn in the midwestern United States

Urbanization in North America

Seen from the air, large portions of North America still bear the checkerboard imprint left by the people who settled the continent: a vast array of small farms that could be worked by one man and a horse. As industrialization swept through the United States in the second half of the 19th century, many farmers left their farms. Great numbers moved to fast-growing cities such as Chicago and St. Louis. Many small towns saw their populations dwindle.

In the cities, change was continuous. The former farm families were joined by waves of European immigrants. Over the next 100 years, urban populations continued to grow, and cities that had once been separate became part of vast urban megalopolises. An example can be seen in the eastern United States, where a band of urban centers stretches almost continuously from Boston south through New York City to Washington D.C. (see map at right).

After World War II, as the U. S. middle class expanded, large numbers of families moved out of the city centers into suburban communities of mass-produced, affordable homes. Many of those who remained were economically disadvantaged. A shrinking tax base meant that cities could not support their infrastructures, and conditions in the inner cities worsened. In the suburbs the opposite was true: vast sums were spent building new roads, houses, and shopping centers.

The same process that transformed the U.S. is now occurring in Mexico. In 1945, 25% of the population was considered urban, but today the figure surpasses 70% (see graph above). Not content to lead lives as subsistence farmers, scores of Mexicans arrive in the cities each day in search of jobs that will enable them to provide a better life for their families.

Sadly, these dreams are often elusive. Most of the people end up in low-paying jobs, with their meager wages going to pay for the food that they once grew themselves. City officials are hard-pressed to provide clean water to their ever-growing populations, let alone electricity, transportation and education.

As elsewhere in the world, coping with the pressures of growing populations is one of the greatest challenges facing North Americans today.

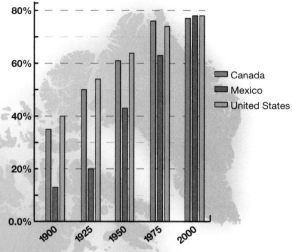

Rising Urban Population
Urban population as a percentage of total population, 1900-2000

Legend: Canada, Mexico, United States

(The definition of "urban" varies from country to country. In Canada, all towns with more than 1,000 people are considered urban, while in the U.S. and Mexico only towns with more than 2,500 people are defined as urban.)

Urban Centers

- 50,000-99,999 people
- 100,000-500,000 people
- Over 500,000 people

© Rand McNally
M-520000-9E-EL1- -1

Mexico City, whose metropolitan area population exceeds 20 million, sprawls toward the distant mountains.

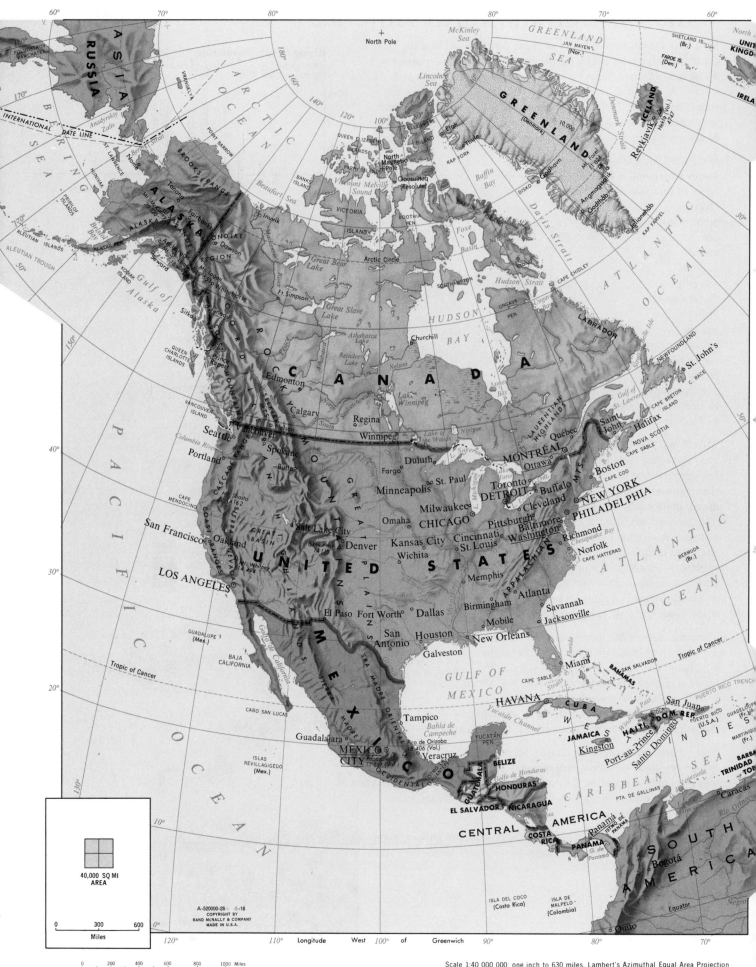

40,000 SQ MI
AREA

0   300   600
Miles

A-520000-26   -5-18
COPYRIGHT BY
RAND McNALLY & COMPANY
MADE IN U.S.A.

0   200   400   600   800   1000 Miles
0   400   800   1200   1600 Kilometers

120° Longitude   West   100°   of   Greenwich   90°

Scale 1:40 000 000; one inch to 630 miles. Lambert's Azimuthal Equal Area Projection
Elevations and depressions are given in feet

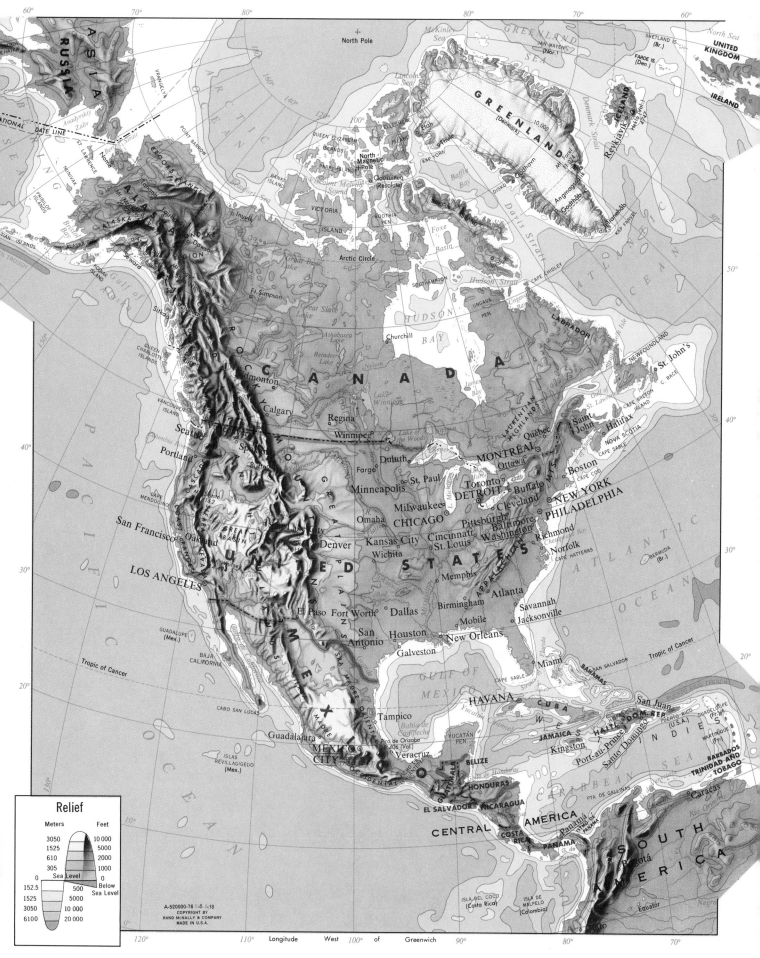

Relief

Meters		Feet
3050		10 000
1525		5000
610		2000
305		1000
0	Sea Level	0
		Below
152.5		500 Sea Level
1525		5000
3050		10 000
6100		20 000

A-520000-76 2-5-5-18
COPYRIGHT BY
RAND McNALLY & COMPANY
MADE IN U.S.A.

Longitude West of Greenwich

0   200   400   600   800   1000 Miles
0   400   800   1200   1600 Kilometers

Scale 1:40 000 000; one inch to 630 miles. Lambert's Azimuthal Equal Area Projection
Elevations and depressions are given in feet

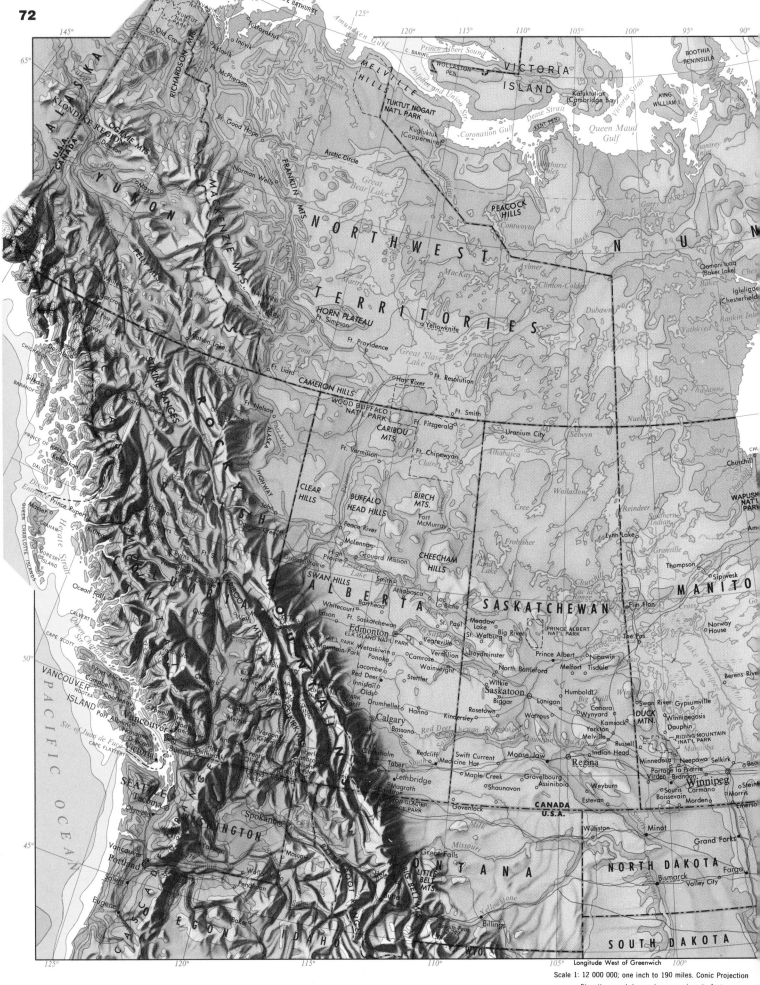

Scale 1: 12 000 000; one inch to 190 miles. Conic Projection
Elevations and depressions are given in feet

a

Scale 1:12 000 000; one inch to 190 miles. Polyconic Projection
Elevations and depressions are given in feet

GULF OF MEXICO

ATLANTIC OCEAN

Cities and Towns

0 to 50,000 ○
50,000 to 500,000 ⊙
500,000 to 1,000,000 ◉
1,000,000 and over

40,000 SQ MI AREA

0   100   200

Miles

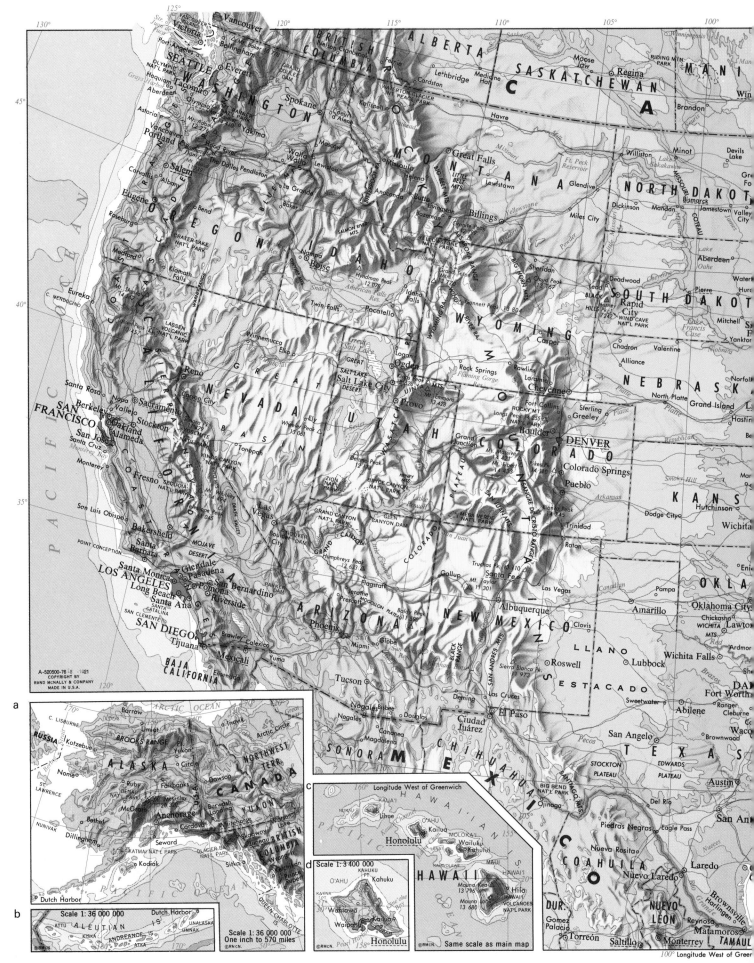

Scale 1:12 000 000; one inch to 190 miles. Polyconic Proje

Elevations and depressions are given in feet

Relief

Meters		Feet
3050		10 000
1525		5000
610		2000
305		1000
152.5		500
Sea Level	0	Sea Level
152.5		500 Below
1525		5 000
3050		10 000
6100		20 000

Cities and Towns

0 to 50,000   ○   500,000 to 1,000,000   ◎

50,000 to 500,000   ⊙   1,000,000 and over

25 50 75 100	200	300	400	500 Miles
100	200	400	600	800 Kilometers

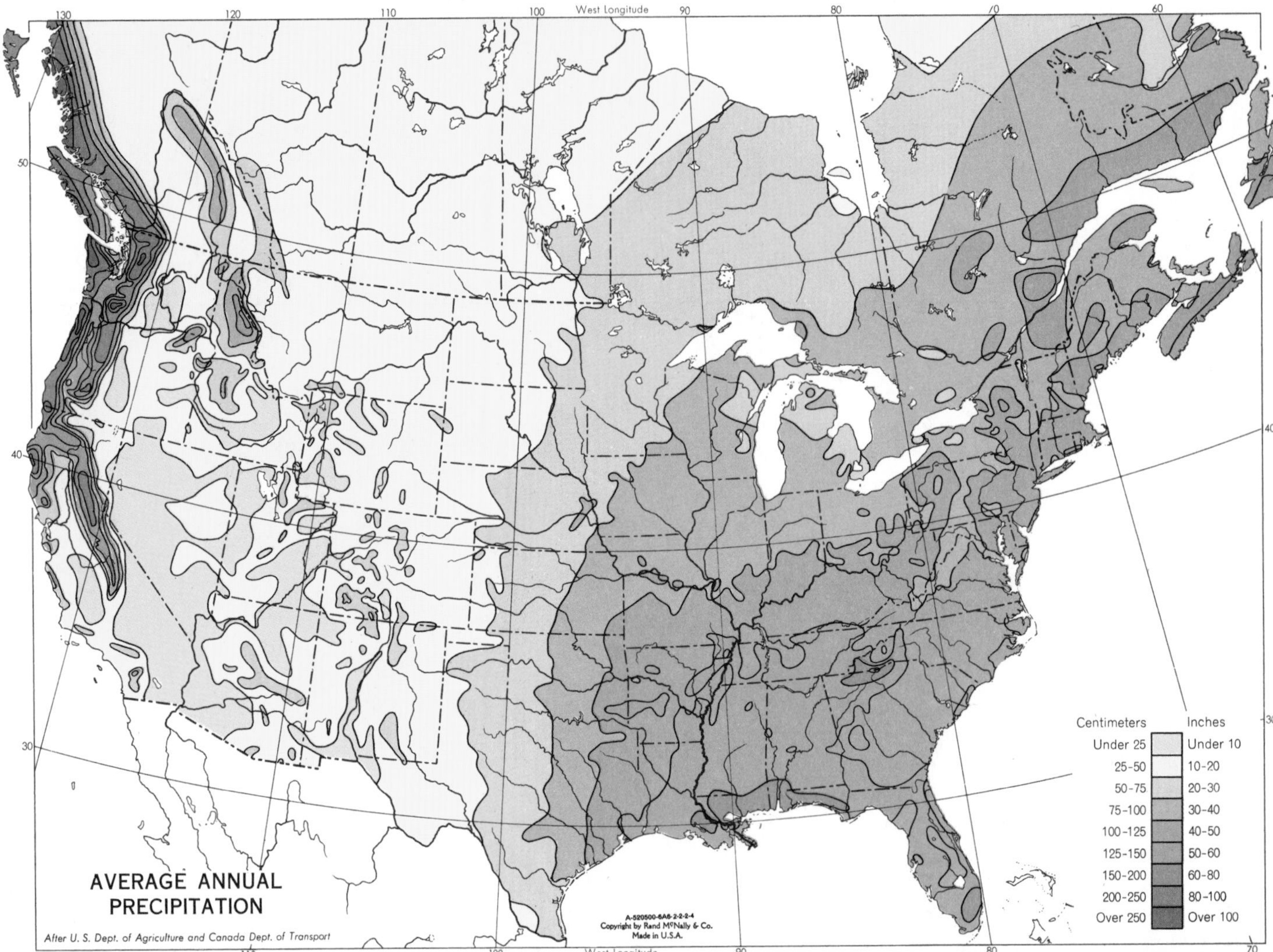

AVERAGE ANNUAL PRECIPITATION
After U. S. Dept. of Agriculture and Canada Dept. of Transport
West Longitude
Centimeters | Inches
Under 25 | Under 10
25-50 | 10-20
50-75 | 20-30
75-100 | 30-40
100-125 | 40-50
125-150 | 50-60
150-200 | 60-80
200-250 | 80-100
Over 250 | Over 100
A-520500-6A6-2-2-2-4
Copyright by Rand McNally & Co.
Made in U.S.A.

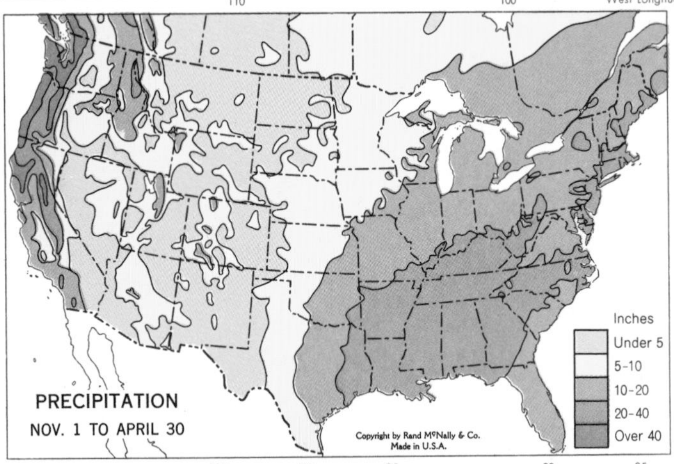

PRECIPITATION
NOV. 1 TO APRIL 30
Inches
Under 5
5-10
10-20
20-40
Over 40
Copyright by Rand McNally & Co.
Made in U.S.A.

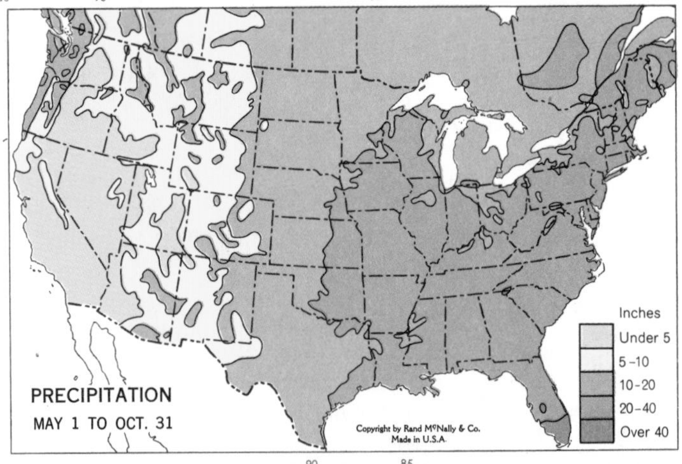

PRECIPITATION
MAY 1 TO OCT. 31
Inches
Under 5
5-10
10-20
20-40
Over 40
Copyright by Rand McNally & Co.
Made in U.S.A.

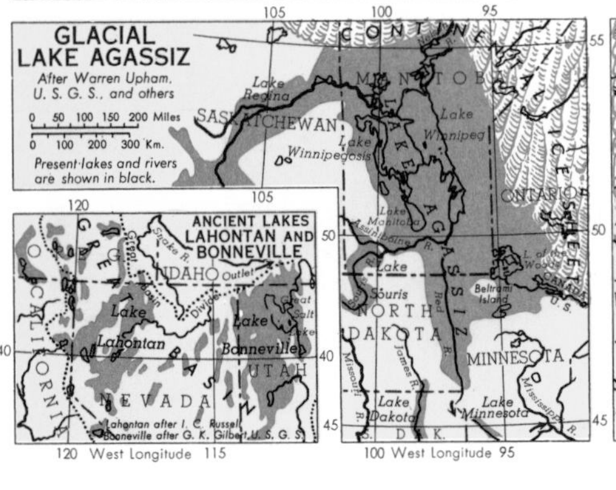

GLACIAL LAKE AGASSIZ
After Warren Upham, U. S. G. S., and others
0 50 100 150 200 Miles
0 100 200 300 Km.
Present lakes and rivers are shown in black.
SASKATCHEWAN
MANITOBA
ONTARIO
Lake Regina
Lake Winnipegosis
Lake Winnipeg
Lake Manitoba
NORTH DAKOTA
MINNESOTA
Lake Dakota
Lake Minnesota
Beltrami Island
L. of the Woods
Souris
100 West Longitude 95
ANCIENT LAKES LAHONTAN AND BONNEVILLE
IDAHO
UTAH
NEVADA
Lake Lahontan
Lake Bonneville
Lahontan after I. C. Russell
Bonneville after G. K. Gilbert, U. S. G. S.
120 West Longitude 115

GLACIAL LAURENTIAN LAKES
EARLY STAGE
After Taylor and Leverett
CONTINENTAL ICE SHEET
Lake Chicago
Lake Maumee
Huron-Erie Lobe
Mississippi R.
Marginal moraines in red
90 85 West Longitude 80 75

GLACIAL LAURENTIAN LAKES
LATER STAGE
After Taylor and Leverett
CONTINENTAL ICE SHEET
LAKE ALGONQUIN
Trent Outlet
Lake Iroquois
Lake Erie
Chicago Outlet
Mohawk Outlet
Mississippi R.
Marginal moraines in red
90 85 West Longitude 80 75

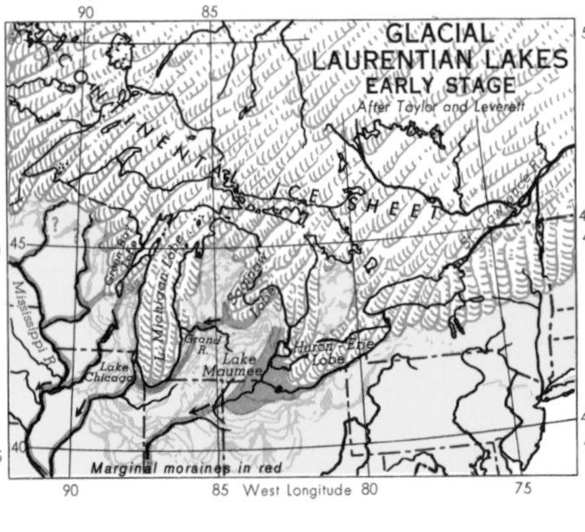

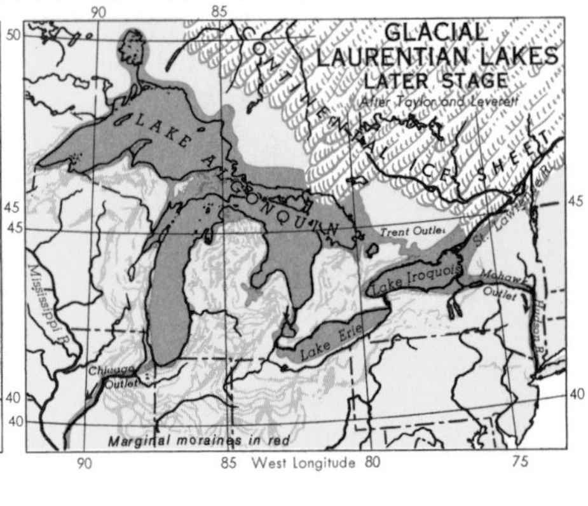

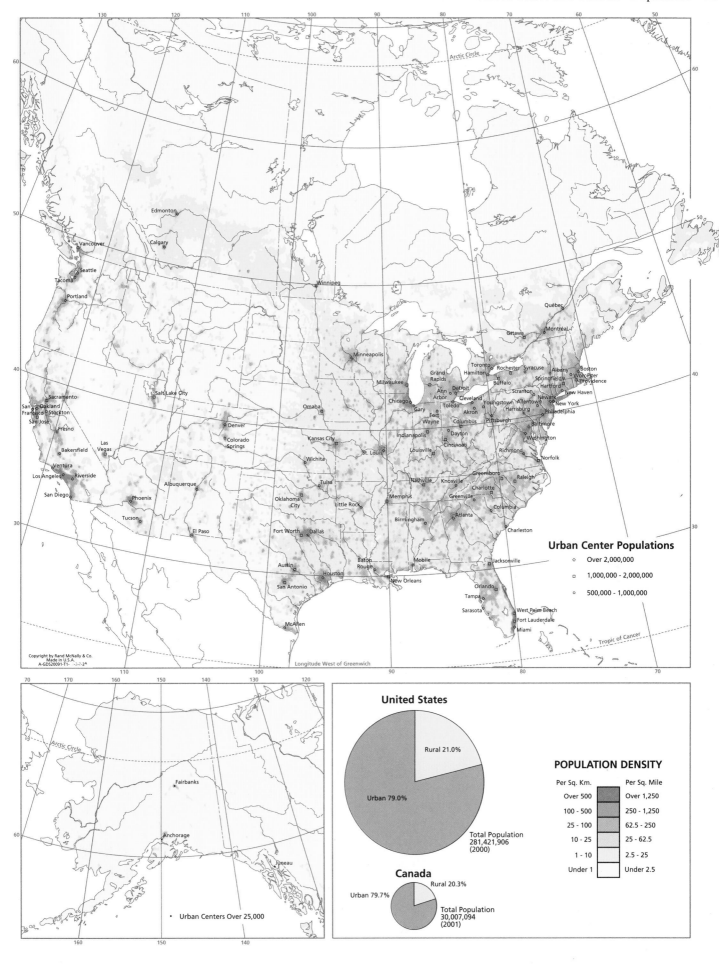

Urban Center Populations

◇ Over 2,000,000

□ 1,000,000 - 2,000,000

○ 500,000 - 1,000,000

Copyright by Rand McNally & Co.
Made in U.S.A.
A-GDS20091-T1-

Longitude West of Greenwich

• Urban Centers Over 25,000

United States

Rural 21.0%

Urban 79.0%

Total Population
281,421,906
(2000)

Canada

Rural 20.3%

Urban 79.7%

Total Population
30,007,094
(2001)

POPULATION DENSITY

Per Sq. Km.	Per Sq. Mile
Over 500	Over 1,250
100 - 500	250 - 1,250
25 - 100	62.5 - 250
10 - 25	25 - 62.5
1 - 10	2.5 - 25
Under 1	Under 2.5

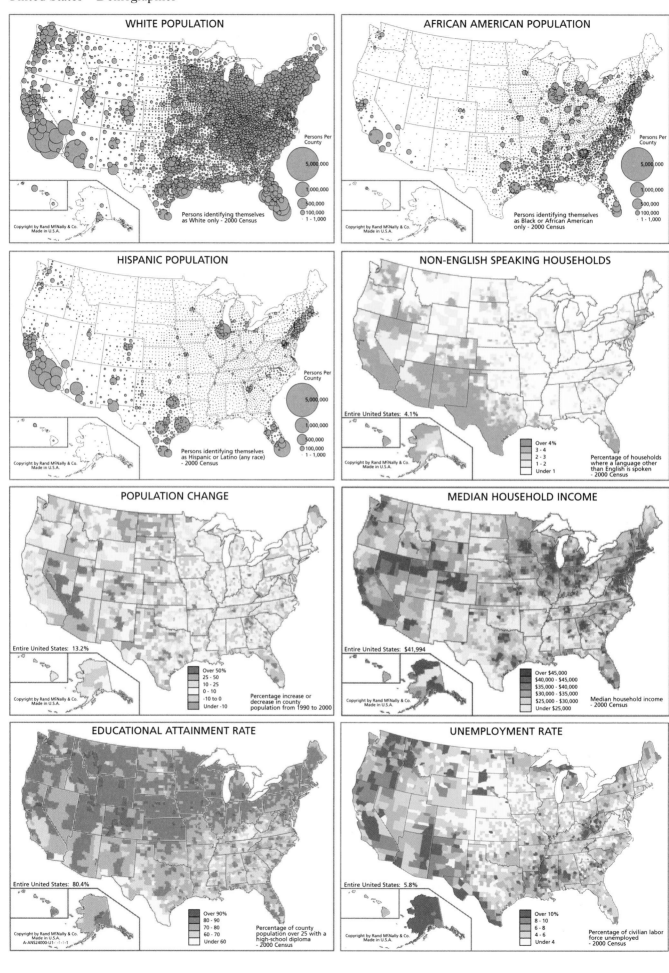

WHITE POPULATION

Persons Per County
5,000,000
1,000,000
500,000
100,000
1 - 1,000

Persons identifying themselves as White only - 2000 Census

Copyright by Rand McNally & Co.
Made in U.S.A.

AFRICAN AMERICAN POPULATION

Persons Per County
5,000,000
1,000,000
500,000
100,000
1 - 1,000

Persons identifying themselves as Black or African American only - 2000 Census

Copyright by Rand McNally & Co.
Made in U.S.A.

HISPANIC POPULATION

Persons Per County
5,000,000
1,000,000
500,000
100,000
1 - 1,000

Persons identifying themselves as Hispanic or Latino (any race) - 2000 Census

Copyright by Rand McNally & Co.
Made in U.S.A.

NON-ENGLISH SPEAKING HOUSEHOLDS

Entire United States: 4.1%

Over 4%
3 - 4
2 - 3
1 - 2
Under 1

Percentage of households where a language other than English is spoken - 2000 Census

Copyright by Rand McNally & Co.
Made in U.S.A.

POPULATION CHANGE

Entire United States: 13.2%

Over 50%
25 - 50
10 - 25
0 - 10
-10 to 0
Under -10

Percentage increase or decrease in county population from 1990 to 2000

Copyright by Rand McNally & Co.
Made in U.S.A.

MEDIAN HOUSEHOLD INCOME

Entire United States: $41,994

Over $45,000
$40,000 - $45,000
$35,000 - $40,000
$30,000 - $35,000
$25,000 - $30,000
Under $25,000

Median household income - 2000 Census

Copyright by Rand McNally & Co.
Made in U.S.A.

EDUCATIONAL ATTAINMENT RATE

Entire United States: 80.4%

Over 90%
80 - 90
70 - 80
60 - 70
Under 60

Percentage of county population over 25 with a high-school diploma - 2000 Census

Copyright by Rand McNally & Co.
Made in U.S.A.
A-ANS24000-U1- -1 -1 -1

UNEMPLOYMENT RATE

Entire United States: 5.8%

Over 10%
8 - 10
6 - 8
4 - 6
Under 4

Percentage of civilian labor force unemployed - 2000 Census

Copyright by Rand McNally & Co.
Made in U.S.A.

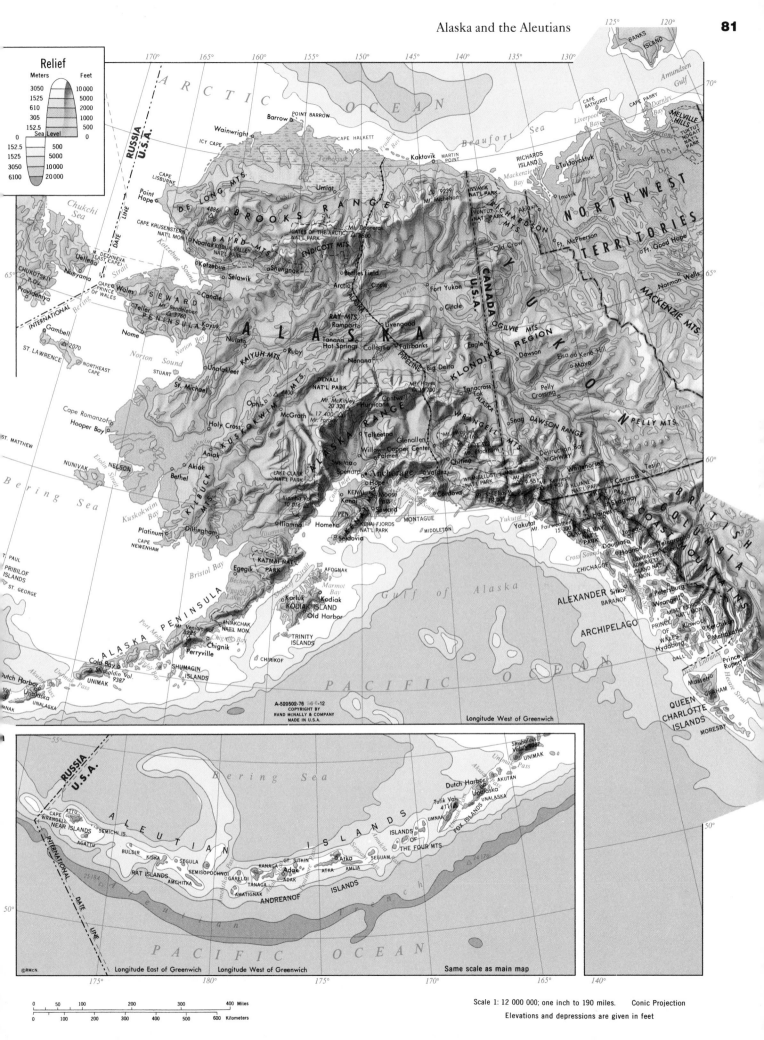

Relief

Meters	Feet
3050	10 000
1525	5000
610	2000
305	1000
152.5	500
0 Sea Level	
152.5	500
1525	5000
3050	10 000
6100	20 000

A-520502-76 9-6-6-12
COPYRIGHT BY
RAND McNALLY & COMPANY
MADE IN U.S.A.

Longitude West of Greenwich

Longitude East of Greenwich   Longitude West of Greenwich   Same scale as main map

Scale 1: 12 000 000; one inch to 190 miles.   Conic Projection

Elevations and depressions are given in feet

0 50 100 200 300 400 Miles
0 100 200 300 400 500 600 Kilometers

124° 120° 118° 116°

BRITISH COLUMBIA

CANADA
U.S.A.

N. Vancouver
Vancouver
New Westminster
Nanaimo
Ladysmith
Steveston
Blaine
Lynden
Chilliwack
Grand Forks
Rossland
Trail
Duncan
VANCOUVER ISLAND
SAN JUAN ISLANDS
Bellingham
Sedro Woolley
Mt. Baker 10,778
Concrete
Newhalem
Ross Lake
Oroville
Northport
Porthill
Bonners Ferry
CAPE FLATTERY
MAKAH IND. RES.
Esquimalt
Victoria
Port Angeles
Port Townsend
Anacortes
Mount Vernon
Arlington
NORTH CASCADES NAT'L PARK
Glacier Peak 10,541
Lake Chelan
Okanogan
COLVILLE IND. RES.
Colville
Chewelah
KALISPEL IND. RES.
Sandpoint
Troy
Libby
Lake Koocanusa
CABINET MTS.
Noxon Res.

48°

OLYMPIC MTS.
OLYMPIC NATIONAL PARK
Mt. Olympus 7965
Everett
Snohomish
Monroe
TULALIP IND. RES.
Leavenworth
Cashmere
WENATCHEE
Chelan
Entiat
WELLS DAM
GRAND COULEE DAM
Franklin D. Roosevelt Lake
SPOKANE IND. RES.
Deer Park
Spirit Lake
Lake Pend Oreille
Newport

QUINAULT IND. RES.
Moclips
SEATTLE
Bremerton
Kirkland
Bellevue
Renton
Cascade Tunnel
Mansfield
Davenport
Spokane
Medical Lake
Cheney
Opportunity
Coeur d'Alene
Kellogg
Wallace
Mullan
Thompson Falls
BITTER

Shelton
Tacoma
Lakewood Center
Auburn
Enumclaw
Cle Elum
Roslyn
ROCK ISLAND DAM
Ephrata
Odessa
COEUR D'ALENE IND. RES.
St. Maries
WASHINGTON

Hoquiam
Aberdeen
Montesano
Elma
Olympia
Puyallup
Carbonado
Ellensburg
Moses Lake
Ritzville
Crab Cr.
Rock
Tekoa
Moscow
Elk River
Dworshak Res.

Grays Harbor
Cosmopolis
Raymond
South Bend
Centralia
Chehalis
Mt. Rainier 14,410
MOUNT RAINIER NATIONAL PARK
Yakima
Toppenish
Potholes Res.
Sunnyside
LOWER MONUMENTAL DAM
Colfax
Pullman
Palouse
LOWER GRANITE DAM

Willapa Bay
Ilwaco
Castle Rock
Kelso
Mt. Saint Helens 8364
Mt. Adams 12,276
YAKIMA INDIAN RESERVATION
PRIEST RAPIDS DAM
Richland
Pasco
Waitsburg
LITTLE GOOSE DAM
Pomeroy
Clarkston
Lewiston
Winchester
NEZ PERCE IND. RES.
Asotin
Nez Perce

46°

Columbia R.
Warrenton
Astoria
Longview
Rainier
Kalama
Saint Helens
Goldendale
JOHN DAY DAM
Prosser
Kennewick
ICE HARBOR DAM
Walla Walla
Dayton
Milton-Freewater
CLEARWA...
MOUNTAI...

Tillamook Bay
Seaside
Vancouver
Camas
Hood River
BONNEVILLE DAM
The Dalles
THE DALLES DAM
Wasco
McNARY DAM
Pendleton
UMATILLA IND. RES.
Elgin
Wallowa
Enterprise
Grangeville

Tillamook
Hillsboro
Forest Grove
Milwaukie
Gresham
Oregon City
W. Linn
Mt. Hood 11,239
Heppner
Condon
Blue Mountains
La Grande
Union
WALLOWA MTS.
HELLS CANYON
New Meadows

McMinnville
Newberg
Lake Oswego
PORTLAND
Woodburn
WARM SPRINGS IND. RES.
John Day
Baker
Brownlee Res.
Oxbow Res.

Sheridan
Dallas
Silverton
SALEM
Detroit Res.
Mt. Jefferson 10,497
Lake Simtustus
Lake Billy Chinook
Burnt R.
Weiser

Newport
Independence
Albany
Lebanon
Corvallis
Green Peter Lake
Prineville
Payette
Ontario
PACIFIC OCEAN

44°

Toledo
Eugene
Springfield
McKenzie R.
Bend
Crooked R.
Prineville Res.
Vale
Beulah Res.
Malheur R.

Reedsport
Cottage Grove
Lookout Pt. Lake
Hills Creek Lake
Cougar Res.
Crane Prairie Res.
GREAT SANDY DESERT
Emmett
Caldwell
Boise

North Bend
Coos Bay
Coquille
Diamond Peak 8744
Burns
Warm Sprs. Res.
Lake Owyhee
Nampa
Lucky Peak Lake
OWYHEE MTS.

Cook Bay
Bandon
Myrtle Point
Roseburg
HARNEY BASIN
Harney Lake
Malheur Lake
Mountain Home

CAPE BLANCO
CRATER LAKE NATIONAL PARK
Mt. Scott 8926
Crater Lake
Lake Sumner
Lake Abert
Donner and Blitzen R.
Jordan Cr.
Glenns Ferry
C.J. Strike Res.

OREGON
Grants Pass
Medford
Mt. McLoughlin 9495
Klamath Falls
Swan Lake
STEENS MTN.
Trout Cr.
Rattlesnake Cr.

42°

Brookings
KLAMATH MTS.
Ashland
OREGON CAVES NAT'L MON.
CASCADE-SISKIYOU NAT'L MON.
Lakeview
WARNER MTS.
FORT McDERMITT IND. RES.
DUCK VALLEY IND. RES.

Crescent City
Happy Camp
Yreka
Lower Klamath Lake
Clear Lake Res.
Goose Lake
Upper Lake
SUMMIT LAKE IND. RES.
PINE FOREST RA.
Paradise Valley
Independence Mts.

REDWOOD N.P.
HOOPA VALLEY IND. RES.
Weed
Mt. Shasta 14,162
LAVA BEDS NAT'L MON.
Alturas
Lower Lake
Eagle Peak 9892
SANTA ROSA RA.
Midas
Tuscarora

Arcata
Fieldbrook
Dunsmuir
CALIFORNIA
NEVADA
BLACK ROCK DESERT
Humboldt R.

Eureka
Fortuna
Redding
Anderson
Weaverville
LASSEN VOLCANIC NATIONAL PARK
Lassen Peak (Vol.) 10,457
Eagle Lake
SMOKE CREEK DESERT
Winnemucca
Battle Mountain

Ferndale
Scotia
MENDOCINO
Rye Patch Res.
Elko
A-520597-76
COPYRIGHT BY
RAND McNALLY & CO.
MADE IN U.S.A.

Longitude West of Greenwich
124° 122° 120° 118° 116°

Scale 1: 4,000 000; one inch to 64 miles. Conic Projecti...
Elevations and depressions are given in feet

SASKATCHEWAN

ALBERTA

CANADA
U.S.A.

MONTANA

WYOMING

UTAH

COLO.

N. DAK.

WATERTON GLACIER
INTERNATIONAL
PEACE PARK

BLACKFEET
IND. RES.

FORT PECK
IND. RES.

FT. BELKNAP
IND. RES.

ROCKY BOYS
IND. RES.

Fort Peck
Lake

CROW IND. RES.

NORTHERN CHEYENNE
IND. RES.

LITTLE
BIGHORN
BATTLEFIELD
NAT'L.
MON.

YELLOWSTONE

NATIONAL

PARK

Yellowstone Lake
7733 ft above
sea level

GRAND TETON
NAT'L PARK

BIG HOLE NAT'L.
BATTLEFIELD

CRATERS OF
THE MOON
NAT'L. MON.

DINOSAUR
NAT'L. MON.

DEVILS TOWER
NAT'L. MON.

WIND RIVER
IND. RES.

FORT HALL
IND. RES.

UINTAH AND OURAY
IND. RES.

GREAT
SALT LAKE
DESERT

Great
Salt
Lake

GREAT DIVIDE
BASIN

ROCKY

SWAN RANGE

MISSION RANGE

BITTERROOT RANGE

PIONEER
MTS.

BEAVERHEAD
MTS.

LEMHI RANGE

LOST RIVER RA.

SNAKE RIVER PLAIN

BIG BELT MTS.

LITTLE BELT MTS.

CRAZY
MTS.

ABSAROKA RANGE

BIGHORN MOUNTAINS

WIND RIVER RANGE

WIND RIVER RANGE

WYOMING RANGE

SALT RIVER RA.

BEAR RIVER RANGE

WASATCH RANGE

UINTA MTS.

PARK RANGE

MOUNTAINS

Homer Youngs Peak
10 621

Electric Peak
10 992

Mt. Washburn
10 243

Grand Teton
13 770

Gannett Peak
13 804

Fremont
Peak 13 745

Cloud Peak
13 167

Borah Pk.
12 662

Hyndman Peak
12 009

Kings Peak
13 528

Mt. Emmons
13 440

Cities and towns:
Browning, Cut Bank, Shelby, Valier, Conrad, Choteau, Sunburst, Great Falls, Belt, Fort Benton, Havre, Chinook, Harlem, Malta, Hogeland, Morgan, Opheim, Scobey, Plentywood, Grenora, Williston, Sidney, Glasgow, Wolf Point, Poplar, Ft. Peck, Brockway, Glendive, Beach, Terry, Miles City, Baker, Marmarth, Winifred, Lewistown, Winnett, Roundup, Forsyth, Colstrip, Lame Deer, Sheridan, Buffalo, Gillette, Moorcroft, Sundance

Kalispell, Whitefish, Columbia Falls, Polson, Ronan, Missoula, Lolo, Stevensville, Hamilton, Philipsburg, Anaconda, Butte, Helena, East Helena, Townsend, White Sulphur Spgs., Neihart, Harlowton, Big Timber, Bozeman, Livingston, Columbus, Laurel, Billings, Hardin, Crow Agency, Huntley

Salmon, Mackay, Arco, Idaho Falls, Shelley, Blackfoot, Pocatello, American Falls, Rupert, Burley, Oakley, Wendover, Rexburg, Rigby, St. Anthony, Ashton, Gardiner, Cody, Powell, Lovell, Greybull, Basin, Worland, Ten Sleep, Thermopolis, Shoshoni, Riverton, Lander, Kaycee, Midwest, Powder River, Casper, Glenrock, Douglas, Orin

Deer Lodge, Walkerville, Three Forks, Twin Bridges, Dillon, Lima, Gebo

Soda Springs, Lava Hot Spgs., Montpelier, Afton, Kemmerer, Granger, Green River, Rock Springs, Superior, Rawlins, Wheatland, Hanna, Steamboat Spgs., Craig, Oak Creek

Malad City, Preston, Lewiston, Richmond, Smithfield, Logan, Providence, Wellsville, Brigham, Huntsville, Garland, Ogden, Farmington, Bountiful, Salt Lake City, Murray, Midvale, Park City, Heber City, Tooele, Evanston, Vernal

Rivers and lakes:
Missouri, Milk, Marias, Teton, Sun, Musselshell, Yellowstone, Bighorn, Little Bighorn, Tongue, Powder, Snake, Green, Sweetwater, North Platte, Bear, Clark Fork, Blackfoot, Bitterroot, Flathead, Hungry Horse Res., Lake Elwell, Fresno Res., Fort Peck Lake, Hebgen Lake, Ennis Lake, Canyon Ferry Lake, Shoshone Lake, Jackson Lake, Boysen Res., Bighorn Lake, Medicine Lake, American Falls Res., Blackfoot Reservoir, Palisades Res., Flaming Gorge Res., Fontenelle Res., Pathfinder Res., Seminoe Res., Alcova Res., Bear Lake, Great Salt Lake, Lake Walcott

Relief		
Meters		Feet
3050		10000
1525		5000
610		2000
305		1000
152.5		500
0	Sea Level	0
1525		500

20 40 60 80 100 120 Miles
20 40 60 80 100 120 140 160 180 200 Kilometers

Scale 1:4 000 000; one inch to 64 miles. Conic Projection
Elevations and depressions are given in feet

Relief

Meters		Feet
3050		10000
1525		5000
610		2000
305		1000
152.5		500
0	Sea Level	0
152.5		500 Below
1525		5000 Sea Level
3050		10000

UTAH

Great Salt Lake
GREAT SALT LAKE DESERT
Salt Lake City
Murray
West Jordan
Tooele
Park City
Midvale
Heber City
American Fork
Lehi
Orem
Provo
Springville
Spanish Fork
Payson
Eureka
Delta
Nephi
Fairview
Helper
Price
Sunnyside
Mount Pleasant
Moroni
Hiawatha
Ephraim
Manti
Castle Dale
Gunnison
Salina
Green River
Fillmore
Richfield
Monroe
Milford
Beaver
Delano Pk. 12 169
Parowan
Panguitch
Escalante
Cedar City
CEDAR BREAKS NATL. MON.
BRYCE CANYON NATL. PARK
GRAND STAIRCASE-ESCALANTE NATL. MON.
ZION NATL. PARK
Hurricane
Saint George
Kanab
GOSHUTE IND. RES.
GREAT BASIN NATL. PARK
Sevier Lake
Little Salt Lake

WASATCH PLATEAU
WEST TAVAPUTS PLATEAU
EAST TAVAPUTS PLATEAU
UINTAH AND OURAY IND. RES.
Duchesne
Roosevelt
Vernal
Oak Creek
Meeker
Rifle
Glenwood Springs
UINTA A PLATEAU

CAPITOL REEF NATL. PARK
Mt. Ellen 11 522
ARCHES NATL. PARK
Moab
Mt. Peale 12 721
CANYONLANDS NATL. PARK
La Sal
Monticello
Abajo Pk. 11 360
Blanding
NATURAL BRIDGES NAT'L. MON.
GLEN CANYON NATL. RECR. AREA
Lake Powell
RAINBOW BRIDGE NATL. MON.
Mexican Hat
GLEN CANYON DAM
Page
INSCRIPTION HOUSE RUIN
KEET SEEL RUIN
BETATAKIN RUIN
NAVAJO NATL. MON.
HOVENWEEP NAT'L MON.
CANYONS OF THE ANCIENTS NATL. MON.
Cortez
MESA VERDE NAT'L PARK
Durango
Pagosa Springs

COLORADO
Grand Junction
Fruita
COLORADO NATL. MON.
Delta
Montrose
UNCOMPAHGRE PLATEAU
Gunnison
BLACK CANYON OF THE GUNNISON NATL. PARK
Blue Mesa Res.
Crested Butte
Castle Pk. 14 265
Aspen
Mt. Massive 14 421
Mt. Elbert 14 433
Leadville
Buena Vista
Mt. Harvard 14 420
Cripple Creek
Salida
Canon City
SANGRE DE CRISTO MTS.
GREAT SAND DUNES N.M.
Monte Vista
Alamosa
Del Norte
Blanca Pk. 14 345
Antonito
Mt. Sneffels 14 150
Ouray
Telluride
Uncompahgre Pk. 14 309
Silverton
SAN JUAN MTS.
Summit Peak 13 300
ROCKY
Bond
Glenwood Springs

NAVAJO INDIAN RESERVATION
PAINTED DESERT
Moenkopi
BLACK MESA
NAVAJO HOPI JOINT USE AREA
CANYON DE CHELLY NATL. MON.
CHUSKA MTS.
Farmington
Aztec
AZTEC RUINS NATL. MON.
JICARILLA APACHE INDIAN RESERVATION
Navajo Res.
SOUTHERN UTE INDIAN RES.
UTE MTN. IND. RES.
El Vado Res.
Abiquiu Res.
SANTA CLARA IND. RES.
Truchas Pk. 13 101
Los Alamos
BANDELIER NATL. MON.
Santa Fe
Santo Pecos
SANTO DOMINGO IND. RES.
SAN FELIPE IND. RES.
Galisteo
Bernalillo
SANDIA IND. RES.
Albuquerque
Wheeler Pk. 13 161
Taos

ARIZONA
Chloride
Lake Havasu City
Parker Dam
Bill Williams
COLORADO RIVER IND. RES.
Quartzsite
Bouse
Ajo
ORGAN PIPE CACTUS N.M.
TOHONO O'ODHAM INDIAN RESERVATION
GILA RIVER IND. RES.
Painted Rock Res.
Gila Bend
Casa Grande
CASA GRANDE RUINS NATL. MON.
IRONWOOD FOREST NAT'L MON.
San Manuel
SAN XAVIER IND. RES.
Tucson
SAGUARO NATL. PARK
Benson
TUMACACORI NATL. MON.
Nogales
Fort Huachuca
Tombstone
Bisbee
Lowell
Pirtleville
Douglas
Willcox
Willcox Playa Lake
CHIRICAHUA NATL. MON.
Columbus
Playas Lake
FLORIDA MTS.
Deming
Las Cruces
Mesilla
Ysleta
El Paso
Ciudad Juárez
Franklin Mtn. 7192

KAIBAB PLATEAU
KANAB PLATEAU
GRAND CANYON NATIONAL PARK
GRAND CANYON PARASHANT NATL. MON.
SHIVWITS PLATEAU
HUALAPAI IND. RES.
Mt. Bangs 8012
PIPE SPRING NATL. MON.
KAIBAB IND. RES.
UINKARET PLATEAU
GRAND CANYON
MARBLE CANYON
LITTLE COLORADO
COCONINO PLATEAU
Williams
Ash Fork
Flagstaff
Humphreys Pk. 12 633
SUNSET CRATER N.M.
WUPATKI NATL. MON.
WALNUT CANYON NATL. MON.
Winslow
Holbrook
PETRIFIED FOREST NATL. PARK
Sanders
Gallup
ZUNI IND. RES.
EL MORRO NATL. MON.
Mt. Taylor 11 301
ACOMA IND. RES.
LAGUNA IND. RES.
ISLETA IND. RES.
Belen
Socorro
Magdalena
ALAMO IND. RES.
SALINAS NATL. MON.
San Marcial
Truth or Consequences
Caballo Res.
Elephant Butte
Sierra Blanca Peak 11 973
WHITE SANDS NATL. MON.
Alamogordo
Tularosa
MESCALERO APACHE IND. RES.
Carrizozo
Bayard
Silver City
Bard
Lordsburg
PELONCILLO MTS.
BLACK RANGE
GILA CLIFF DWELLINGS NATL. MON.
Glenwood
Morenci
Clifton
Safford
Hayden
Miami
Globe
SAN CARLOS INDIAN RESERVATION
San Carlos Lake
Superior
Florence
Casa Grande
Phoenix
Glendale
Mesa
Tempe
SALT RIVER IND. RES.
THEODORE ROOSEVELT DAM
Theodore Roosevelt Lake
TONTO NATL. MON.
Maverick
FORT APACHE INDIAN RESERVATION
Mt. Ord 11 357
Baldy Peak 11 403
McNary
Springerville
Saint Johns
MOGOLLON RIM
Jerome
Clarkdale
TUZIGOOT NATL. MON.
MONTEZUMA CASTLE NATL. MON.
Prescott
AGUA FRIA NATL. MON.
Wickenburg
HUALAPAI MTS.

NEW MEXICO

MEXICO
USA
SONORA
CHIHUAHUA

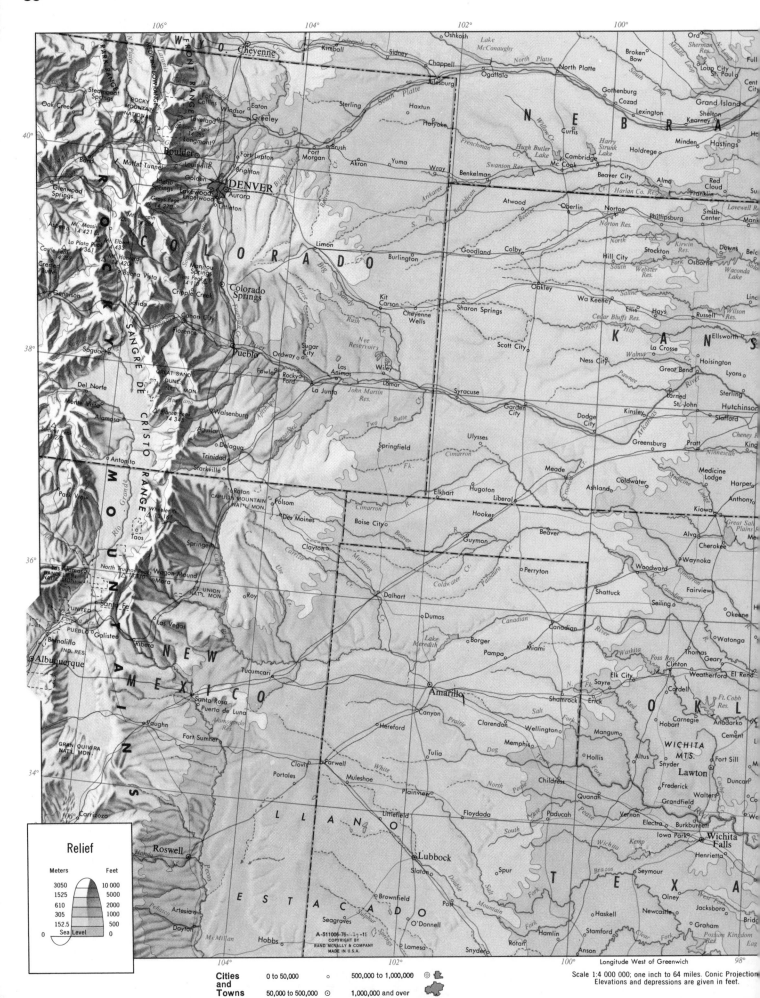

Relief

Meters	Feet
3050	10 000
1525	5000
610	2000
305	1000
152.5	500
0	Sea Level

Cities and Towns

0 to 50,000 ○
50,000 to 500,000 ⊙
500,000 to 1,000,000 ◎
1,000,000 and over

A-511006-76-11
COPYRIGHT BY
RAND McNALLY & COMPANY
MADE IN U.S.A.

Scale 1:4 000 000; one inch to 64 miles. Conic Projection
Elevations and depressions are given in feet.

Longitude West of Greenwich

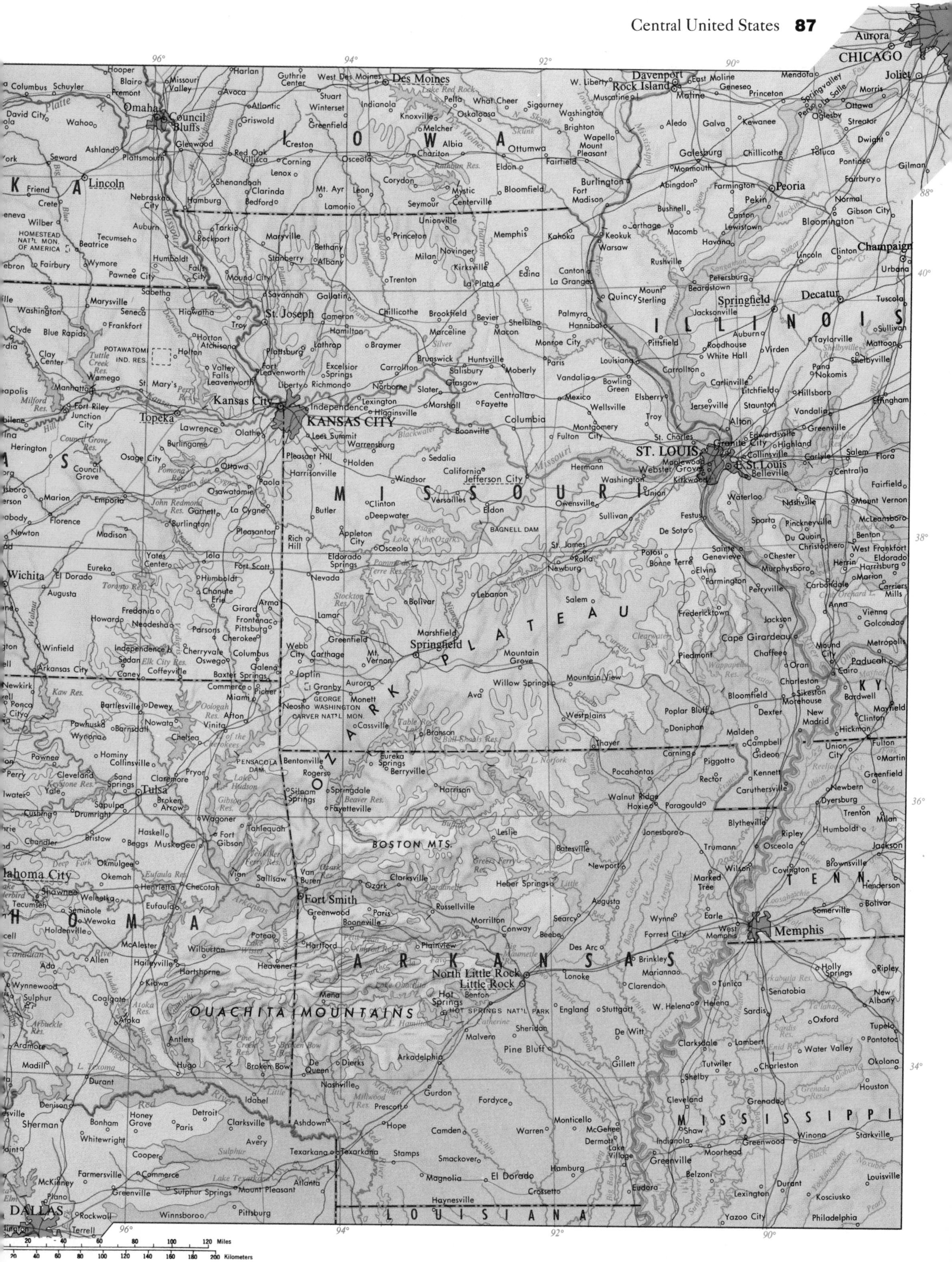

CHICAGO
Aurora
Joliet

I O W A
I L L I N O I S
K A N S A S
M I S S O U R I
O K L A H O M A
A R K A N S A S
O U A C H I T A   M O U N T A I N S
O Z A R K   P L A T E A U
BOSTON MTS.
LOUISIANA
MISSISSIPPI
TENN.
KY.

Des Moines
Davenport
Rock Island
Omaha
Council Bluffs
Lincoln
Topeka
Kansas City
KANSAS CITY
St. Joseph
ST. LOUIS
E. St. Louis
Springfield
Decatur
Champaign
Peoria
Jefferson City
Wichita
Tulsa
Oklahoma City
Fort Smith
Little Rock
North Little Rock
Hot Springs
HOT SPRINGS NAT'L PARK
Memphis
DALLAS

Lake of the Ozarks
BAGNELL DAM
PENSACOLA DAM
GEORGE WASHINGTON CARVER NAT'L MON.
HOMESTEAD NAT'L MON. OF AMERICA
POTAWATOMI IND. RES.

96°   94°   92°   90°

20 40 60 80 100 120 Miles
20 40 60 80 100 120 140 160 180 200 Kilometers

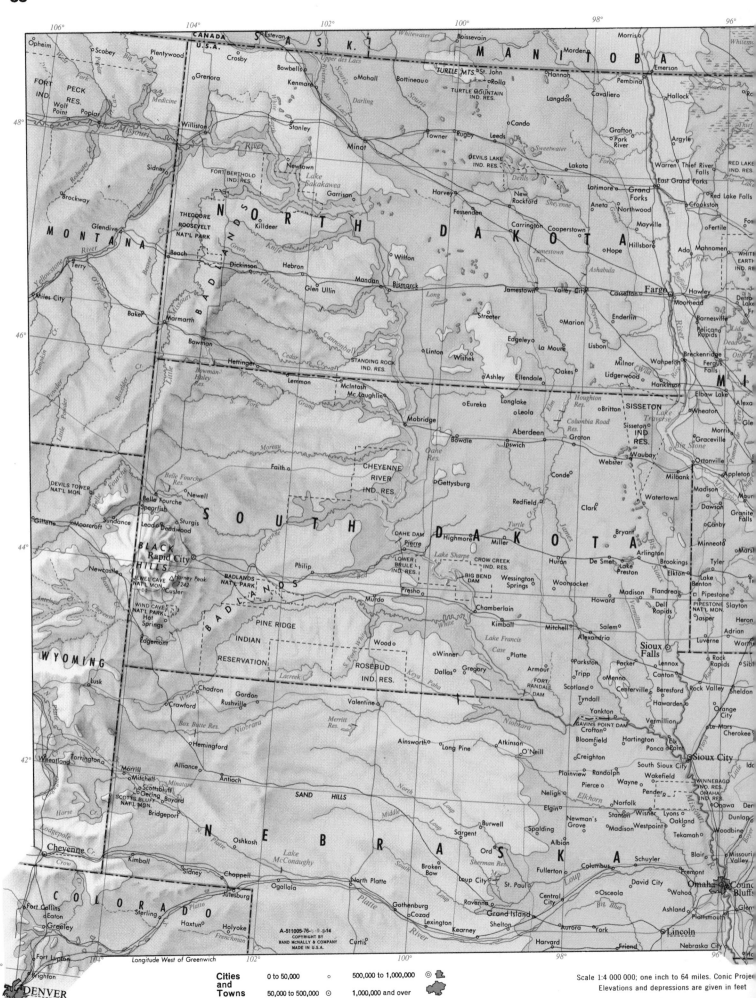

Cities and Towns

0 to 50,000 •

50,000 to 500,000 ⊙

500,000 to 1,000,000 ◉

1,000,000 and over

Scale 1:4 000 000; one inch to 64 miles. Conic Projec
Elevations and depressions are given in feet

A-511005-76- -9-8-14
COPYRIGHT BY
RAND McNALLY & COMPANY
MADE IN U.S.A.

Longitude West of Greenwich

Cities and Towns

0 to 50,000	o
50,000 to 500,000	⊙

500,000 to 1,000,000	◎
1,000,000 and over	

Longitude West of Greenwich

Scale 1:4 000 000; one inch to 64 miles. Conic Projection
Elevations and depressions are given in feet

Scale 1:4 000 000; one inch to 64 miles. Conic Projecti
Elevations and depressions are given in feet

Longitude West of Greenwich

GULF OF MEXICO

A-520598-76   -7-7-14
COPYRIGHT BY
RAND McNALLY & COMPANY
MADE IN U.S.A.

Relief

Meters	Feet
1525	5000
610	2000
305	1000
152.5	500
0 Sea Level	0
152.5	500
1525	5000

Same scale as main map

a

ATLANTIC OCEAN

GULF OF MEXICO

20 40 60 80 100 120 Miles
20 40 60 80 100 120 140 160 180 200 Kilometers

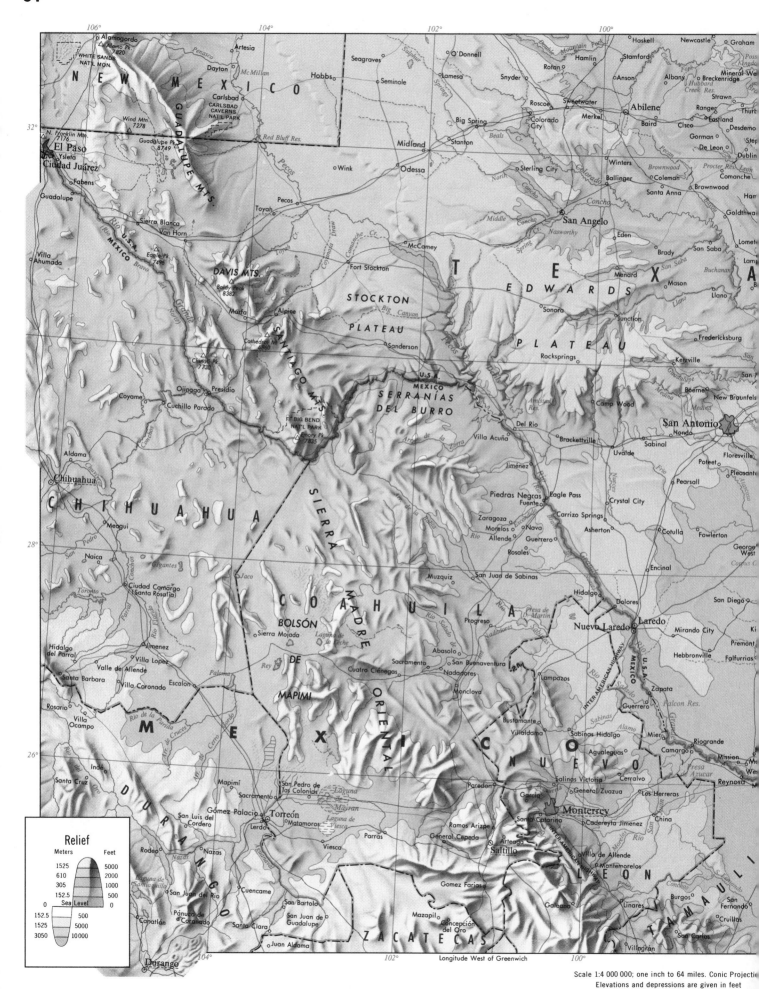

NEW MEXICO

Alamogordo
WHITE SANDS NAT'L MON.
Alamo Pk. 7820
Artesia
Dayton
McMillan
Penasco
Hobbs
O'Donnell
Seagraves
Haskell
Newcastle
Graham
Mineral Wells

Carlsbad
CARLSBAD CAVERNS NAT'L PARK
Wind Mtn. 7278
Hamlin
Stamford
Albany
Breckenridge
Hubbard Creek Res.
Strawn

32°
N. Franklin Mtn. 7176
El Paso
Ysleta
Ciudad Juárez
Fabens
Guadalupe
Guadalupe Pk. 8749
GUADALUPE MTS.
Red Bluff Res.
Wink
Pecos
Odessa
Midland
Stanton
Big Spring
Roscoe
Colorado City
Sweetwater
Merkel
Abilene
Baird
Cisco
Ranger
Eastland
Desdemo
Gorman
De Leon
Dublin

Villa Ahumada
Sierra Blanca
Van Horn
Toyah
Pecos
Eagle Pk. 7496
DAVIS MTS.
Baldy Peak 8382
Marfa
Alpine
Toyah Cr.
Coyanosa Draw
Comanche Cr.
McCamey
Fort Stockton
STOCKTON PLATEAU
Big Canyon
Sanderson
Rio U.S.A. MEXICO Bravo
Rio Grande del Norte
Chinati Pk. 7730
Cathedral Mtn. 6860
SANTIAGO MTS.
Ojinaga
Presidio
Coyame
Cuchillo Parado

Chihuahua
BIG BEND NAT'L PARK
Emory Pk. 7835
Aldama
Conchos
U.S.A. MEXICO
SERRANÍAS DEL BURRO
Arroyo de la Zorra
Del Rio
Villa Acuña
Jiménez
Piedras Negras
Fuente
Eagle Pass
Zaragoza
Morelos
Nava
Allende
Guerrero
Rosales

CHIHUAHUA
Meoqui
San Pedro
Naica
Toronto
Gigantes
Jaco
SIERRA
Muzquiz
San Juan de Sabinas
Hidalgo
Dolores
San Diego

28°
Ciudad Camargo
Santa Rosalía
Parral
Conchos
COAHUILA
BOLSÓN
Sierra Mojada
Laguna de la Leche
Rey
Cuatro Ciénegas
Sacramento
San Buenaventura
Nadadores
Abasolo
Progreso
Presa de D. Martín
Nadadores
Hidalgo
Nuevo Laredo
Laredo
Mirando City
Premont

Hidalgo del Parral
Jiménez
Villa López
Valle de Allende
Santa Barbara
Villa Coronado
Escalón
Palama
MADRE
DE
Lampazos
Monclova
Bustamante
Villaldama
Sabinas Hidalgo
Zapata
Falcon Res.
Guerrero
Mier
Riogrande

26°
Rosario
Villa Ocampo
Rio de la Parida
MEXICO
MAPIMI
ORIENTAL
Aguaaguas
Camargo
Mission

Inde
Santa Cruz
Mapimí
San Pedro de las Colonias
Laguna de Mayran
Paredón
Salinas Victoria
Garcia
General Zuazua
Cerralvo
Los Herreras
Reynosa
Presa Azucar

DURANGO
Rodeo
Nazas
San Luis del Cordero
Gómez Palacio
Torreón
Lerdo
Matamoros
Laguna de Viesca
Ramos Arizpe
Santa Catarina
Monterrey
Cadereyta Jiménez
China

Cuencame
San Juan del Rio
Sacramento
Viesca
Parras
General Cepeda
Arteaga
Saltillo
Villa de Allende
Montemorelos
LEON

Durango
Canatlán
Pánuco de Coronado
Santa Clara
San Bartolo
San Juan de Guadalupe
Gomez Farias
Mazapil
Concepción del Oro
Galeana
Linares
Burgos
San Fernando

ZACATECAS
Juan Aldama
Villagran
Cruillas
San Carlos
TAMAULIPAS

TEXAS
EDWARDS PLATEAU
San Angelo
Eden
Brady
San Saba
Menard
Mason
Llano
Sonora
Rocksprings
Junction
Fredericksburg
Kerrville
Camp Wood
Boerne
New Braunfels
San Antonio
Hondo
Uvalde
Sabinal
Floresville
Poteet
Pearsall
Crystal City
Asherton
Cotulla
Fowlerton
Carrizo Springs
Brackettville
Encinal
George West
Corpus C
San Diego

Relief
Meters / Feet
1525 / 5000
610 / 2000
305 / 1000
152.5 / 500
0 Sea Level 0
152.5 / 500
1525 / 5000
3050 / 10 000

Longitude West of Greenwich
Scale 1:4 000 000; one inch to 64 miles. Conic Projection
Elevations and depressions are given in feet

Scale 1:1 000 000

Cities	0 to 50,000	500,000 to 1,000,000
and		
Towns	50,000 to 500,000	1,000,000 and over

a

Caribbean Sea

Colón
Coco Solito
Rainbow City
Margarita
GATUN LOCKS
Gatun
Lago
Gatun

Salud Mt
1182
Nuevo
San Juan
Isaaca Mt
1847

East Mt
608

Chilibre

West Mt
537

North
Gamboa

Balboa Mt
1149

Oro Hill
662

GAILLARD

PEDRO MIGUEL LOCKS
MIRAFLORES LOCKS
Paraiso
Pedro
Miguel

Río
Abajo

Cocoli
Diablo Hts
Balboa
Balboa Heights
Cerro Galera
1205

Ancón
Panamá

PANAMA

La Chorrera

Bahía de Panamá

TABOGA
TABOGUILLA

©RMCN.

Scale 1:1 000 000

10 Miles

16 Kilometers

A-530000-76-9 9-26 EL
COPYRIGHT BY
RAND McNALLY & COMPANY
MADE IN U.S.A.

Scale 1:16 000 000; one inch to 250 miles. Polyconic Project
Elevations and depressions are given in feet

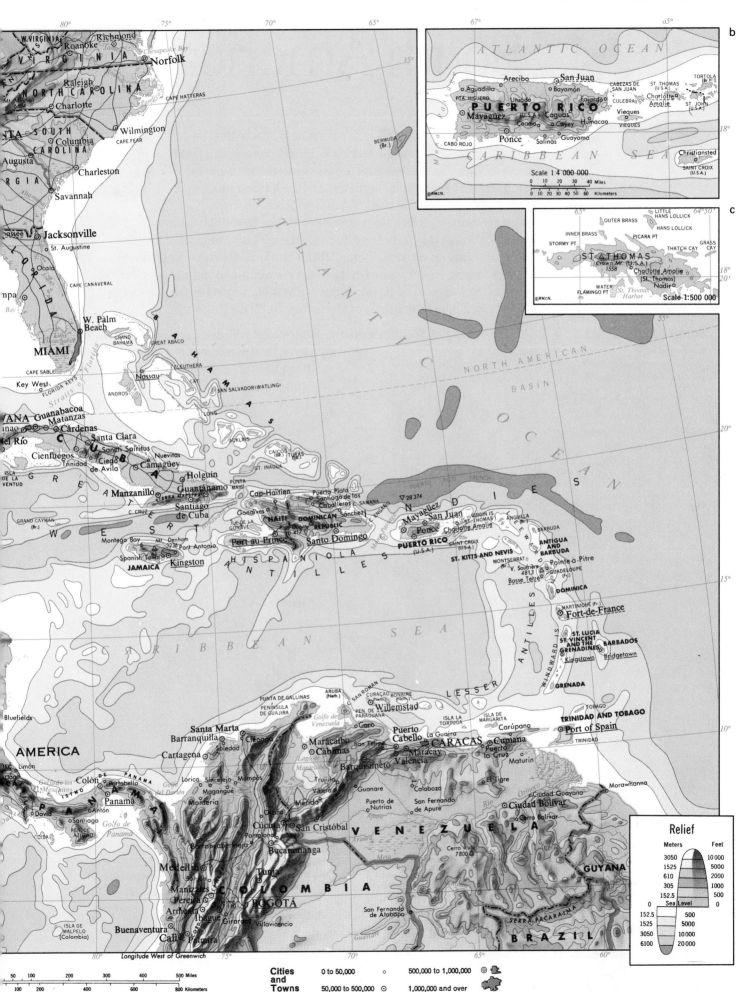

South America

Floodplain of the Amazon River, Brazil

With an area of 6.9 million square miles (17.8 million sq km), triangular-shaped South America is fourth among the continents in size. The Andes, which pass through seven of the continent's 13 mainland countries, are the longest mountain chain in the world. The mighty Amazon River carries a greater volume of water than any other river: 46 million gallons per second flow into the Atlantic Ocean. The Amazon basin contains an estimated one-fifth of the world's fresh water and is home to the world's largest rain forest with its countless plant and animal species. Angel Falls, in a remote Venezuelan forest, is the world's highest waterfall, dropping 3,212 feet (979 m), or almost the height of three Empire State Buildings.

One of South America's other great wonders is manmade. High in the Peruvian Andes lie the ruins of the sacred city of Machu Picchu, built centuries ago by the Incas. The city has an exquisite design and was built with remarkable skill. The Inca population, like most of South America's other native peoples, declined rapidly after the arrival of Europeans in the early 16th century.

South America at a glance

Land area: 6,900,000 square miles (17,800,000 sq km)

Estimated population: 352,960,000

Population density: 51/square mile (20/sq km)

Mean elevation: 1,800 feet (550 m)

Highest point: Aconcagua, Argentina, 22,831 feet (6,959 m)

Lowest point: Salinas Chicas, Argentina, 138 feet (42 m) below sea level

Longest river: Amazon-Ucayali, 4,000 mi (6,400 km)

Number of countries (incl. dependencies): 15

Largest independent country: Brazil, 3,300,172 square miles (8,547,404 sq km)

Smallest independent country: Suriname, 63,251 square miles (163,820 sq km)

Most populous independent country: Brazil, 175,260,000

Least populous independent country: Suriname, 435,000

Largest city: São Paulo, pop. 9,713,692

Wettest place: Quibdó, Colombia 354 inches (899 cm)/year

Driest place: Arica, Chile .03 inches (.08 cm)/year

Hottest place: Rivadavia, Argentina 120°F (49°C)

Highest point: Cerro Aconcagua, Argentina 22,831 ft (6,959 m)

Lowest point: Salinas Chicas, Argentina 138 ft (42 m) below sea level

Coldest place: Sarmiento, Argentina -27°F (-33°C)

Landforms
- Mountains
- Widely spaced mountains
- High tablelands
- Hills and low tablelands
- Plains
- Depresssions, basins
- High tablelands and ice caps
- Mountains and ice caps

© Rand McNally & Co.

The Andes, at the western edge of Argentina's Patagonia region.

Climate

South America's most predominant climate zones are the vast tropical rain forests and tropical savannas which cover most of the northern half of the continent. In the rain forests, rain falls throughout the year, averaging 60 to 80 inches (152 to 203 cm) annually. Daytime temperatures usually exceed 80° F (27° C). The tropical savanna regions experience the same high temperatures but less rainfall, with a dry season in winter. A temperate climate, with milder temperatures and moderate rainfall, prevails throughout much of southern South America, east of the Andes. Arid to semiarid conditions are found in the far south and at Brazil's eastern tip.

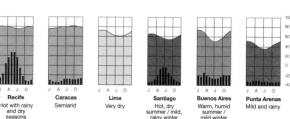

Tinted areas show temperature in degrees Fahrenheit. Vertical bars show precipitation in inches.

Manaus Hot and rainy	**Recife** Hot with rainy and dry seasons	**Caracas** Semiarid
Lima Very dry	**Santiago** Hot, dry summer / mild, rainy winter	**Buenos Aires** Warm, humid summer / mild winter
Punta Arenas Mild and rainy	**Extensive uplands** Climate varies with elevation and latitude	

© Rand McNally & Co.
M-540000-6A-EL1-!-!-!-1'

Population

South America shares the rank of fourth most-densely populated continent with North America, with 51 people per square mile (20 per sq km). Despite this relatively low figure, the continent is intensely urban because the Andes and the Amazon rain forest render most of it either inaccessible or unsuitable for farming. More than 90% of South America's 353 million people live within 150 miles (240 km) of the coast. São Paulo, Brazil, with a metropolitan population of more than 17 million, is the world's sixth-largest metropolitan area. Most South Americans are *mestizo*—of mixed European and Indian descent. Spanish is the predominant language, followed by Portuguese. More than 90% of the people are Roman Catholics.

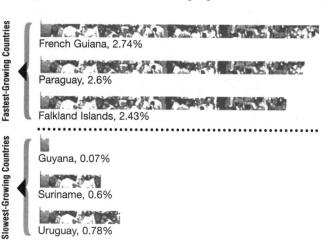

Fastest-Growing Countries

French Guiana, 2.74%

Paraguay, 2.6%

Falkland Islands, 2.43%

Slowest-Growing Countries

Guyana, 0.07%

Suriname, 0.6%

Uruguay, 0.78%

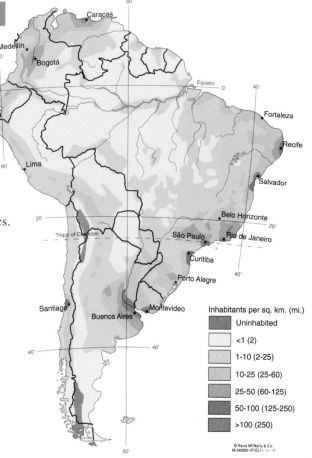

Inhabitants per sq. km. (mi.)

	Uninhabited
	<1 (2)
	1-10 (2-25)
	10-25 (25-60)
	25-50 (60-125)
	50-100 (125-250)
	>100 (250)

© Rand McNally & Co.
M-540000-1P-EL1-!-!-!-1'

Environments and Land Use

Land suitable for farming is very limited in South America, covering only about 6% of the continent. Small, family-run subsistence farms are common, and typical crops are maize, wheat, and potatoes. Despite the scarcity of arable land, commercial agriculture for export is a major part of the economies of several countries. Ecuador is the world's leading exporter of bananas, while Brazil and Colombia grow almost 40% of the world's coffee beans. Brazil is also a major exporter of sugar. Chile has developed a large trade in produce—such as tomatoes and grapes—that is exported to North America during its winter months (South America's summer months). Production of coca, the basis for illicit drugs, has become a part of the rural economies of Colombia, Bolivia, and Peru.

Cattle ranching is centered on the vast, grassy Pampas region, which extends through northern Argentina, Uruguay, and southern Brazil. Sheep, raised both for meat and wool, are important throughout the Andes and southern Argentina. About 25% of the continent is suitable for grazing.

As South America's population grows, pressure builds to clear more land for farming. Much expansion has taken place in the Amazon basin at the cost of millions of acres of rain forest, which are cleared of trees and drained. Balancing the demands of the population with the need to preserve the rain forest is one of the continent's most pressing issues.

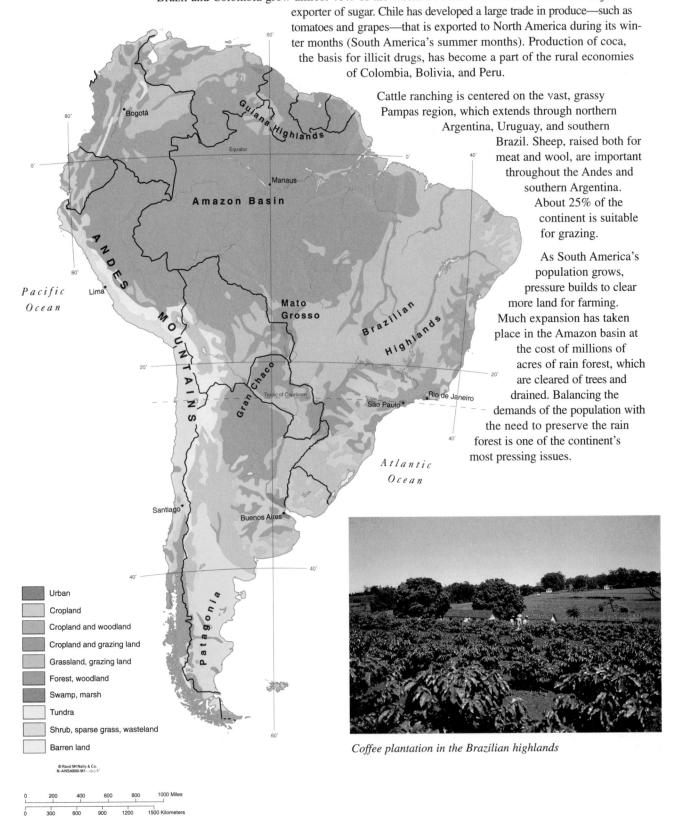

Legend:
- Urban
- Cropland
- Cropland and woodland
- Cropland and grazing land
- Grassland, grazing land
- Forest, woodland
- Swamp, marsh
- Tundra
- Shrub, sparse grass, wasteland
- Barren land

© Rand McNally & Co.
N-ANS40000-M1- -:-:-1'

| 0 | 200 | 400 | 600 | 800 | 1000 Miles |
| 0 | 300 | 600 | 900 | 1200 | 1500 Kilometers |

Coffee plantation in the Brazilian highlands

Destruction of the Rain Forest

The Amazonian rain forest contains an abundance and diversity of life that is matched by few places in the world. In fact, it has been estimated that the plant and animal species of Amazonia account for nearly one-half of those found on Earth. New plants and animals are constantly being discovered, and scientists have found in Amazonian plants a treasure trove of new substances, some of which are now being used to produce life-saving medicines. It is thought that cures for many more diseases could be found in the plants yet to be studied.

In recent decades, nearly 10% of the rain forest's original 1.58 million square miles (4.09 million sq km) has been cleared (see map below) for farming, cattle ranching, mining, and commercial logging. The most effective way to clear the land is the "slash-and-burn" method, which has been practiced by indigenous peoples on an insignificant scale for centuries. Today, widespread usage of this method is destroying vast areas of the rain forest, and smoke from the fires is polluting the atmosphere and possibly contributing to global warming. The destruction also imperils the Indians living within the forest; their numbers have shrunk by more than half in this century alone.

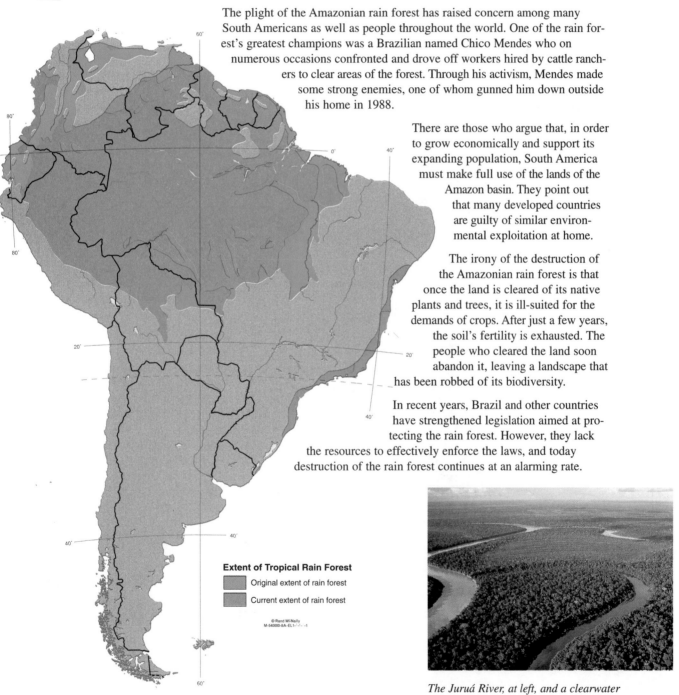

The plight of the Amazonian rain forest has raised concern among many South Americans as well as people throughout the world. One of the rain forest's greatest champions was a Brazilian named Chico Mendes who on numerous occasions confronted and drove off workers hired by cattle ranchers to clear areas of the forest. Through his activism, Mendes made some strong enemies, one of whom gunned him down outside his home in 1988.

There are those who argue that, in order to grow economically and support its expanding population, South America must make full use of the lands of the Amazon basin. They point out that many developed countries are guilty of similar environmental exploitation at home.

The irony of the destruction of the Amazonian rain forest is that once the land is cleared of its native plants and trees, it is ill-suited for the demands of crops. After just a few years, the soil's fertility is exhausted. The people who cleared the land soon abandon it, leaving a landscape that has been robbed of its biodiversity.

In recent years, Brazil and other countries have strengthened legislation aimed at protecting the rain forest. However, they lack the resources to effectively enforce the laws, and today destruction of the rain forest continues at an alarming rate.

Extent of Tropical Rain Forest
Original extent of rain forest
Current extent of rain forest

© Rand McNally
M-540000-8A-EL1-........-1

The Juruá River, at left, and a clearwater slough wind through the dense Amazon rain forest near Eirunepé, Brazil.

Scale 1:40 000 000; one inch to 630 miles. Lambert's Azimuthal, Equal Area Projection
Elevations and depressions are given in feet

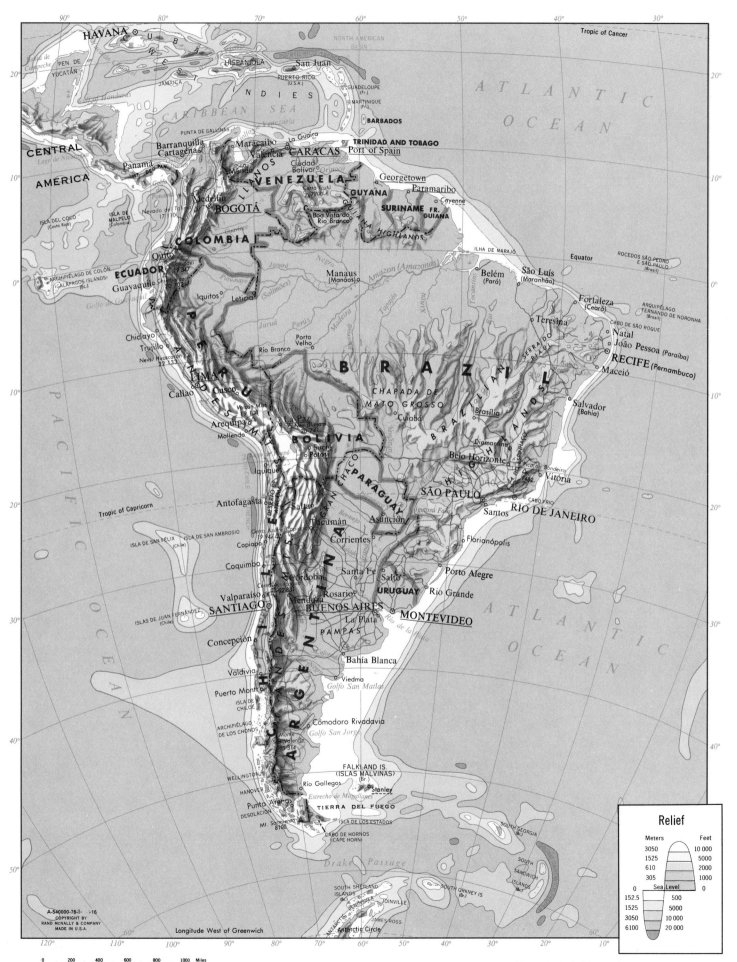

Longitude West of Greenwich

Scale 1:40 000 000; one inch to 630 miles. Lambert's Azimuthal, Equal Area Projection
Elevations and depressions are given in feet

Relief

Meters	Feet
3050	10 000
1525	5000
610	2000
305	1000
0 Sea Level	0
152.5	500
1525	5000
3050	10 000
6100	20 000

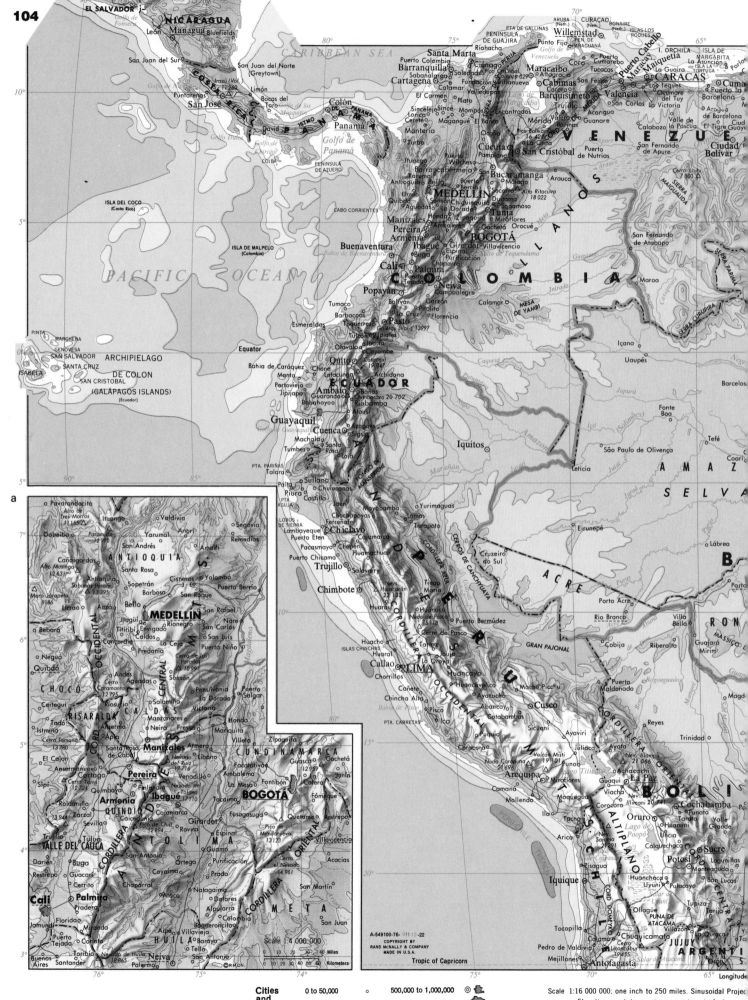

**Cities
and
Towns**

0 to 50,000　　　○

50,000 to 500,000　　⊙

500,000 to 1,000,000　　◉

1,000,000 and over

Scale 1:16 000 000; one inch to 250 miles. Sinusoidal Proje

Elevations and depressions are given in feet

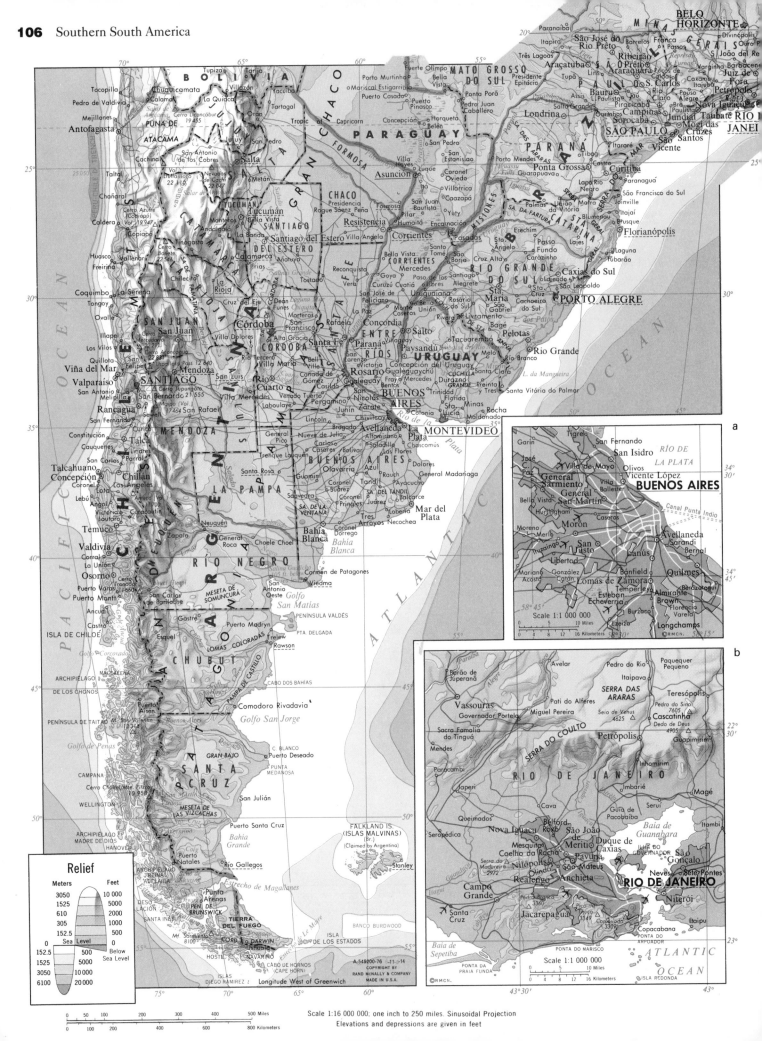

Relief

Meters	Feet
3050	10 000
1525	5000
610	2000
305	1000
152.5	500
Sea Level	0
152.5	500
1525	5000
3050	10 000
6100	20 000

Below Sea Level

a
BUENOS AIRES
Scale 1:1 000 000

b
RIO DE JANEIRO
Scale 1:1 000 000

Scale 1:16 000 000; one inch to 250 miles. Sinusoidal Projection
Elevations and depressions are given in feet

A-549200-76 -11- -14
COPYRIGHT BY
RAND McNALLY & COMPANY
MADE IN U.S.A.

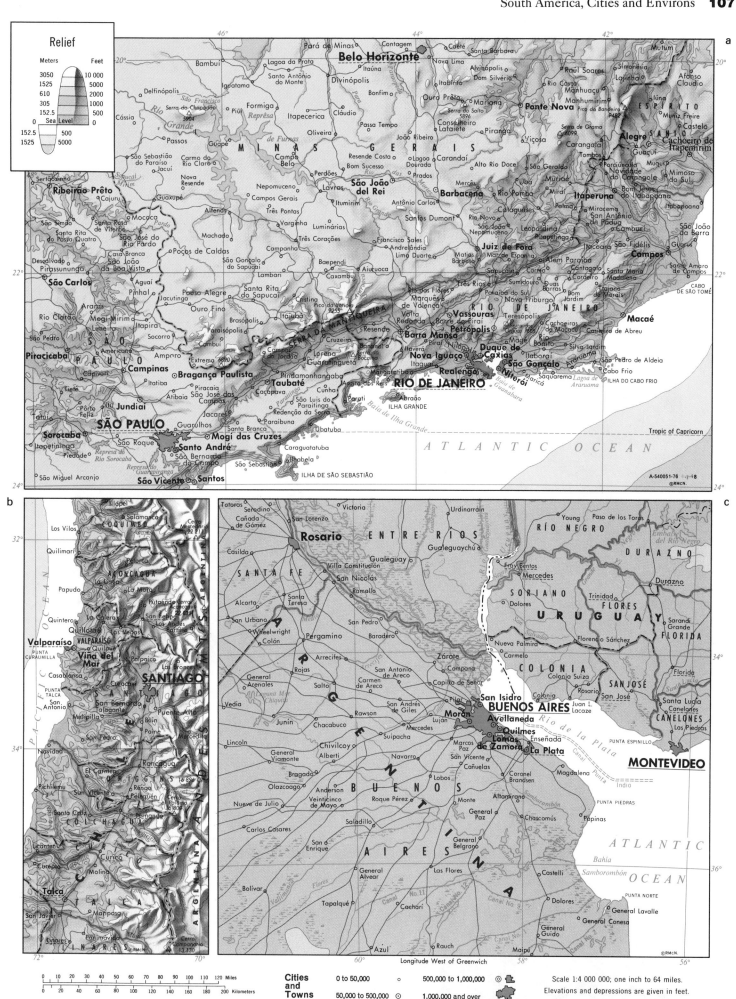

Relief

Meters	Feet
3050	10 000
1525	5000
610	2000
305	1000
152.5	500
0 Sea Level	0
152.5	500
1525	5000

a

Belo Horizonte

Ponte Nova

ESPÍRITO

Alegre

SANTO

Cachoeiro de Itapemirim

Ribeirão Prêto

M I N A S   G E R A I S

São João del Rei

Barbacena

Campos

CABO DE SÃO TOMÉ

São Carlos

Juiz de Fora

R I O   D E   J A N E I R O

Macaé

Piracicaba

S Ã O

Campinas

Bragança Paulista

Vassouras

Petrópolis

Barra Mansa

Duque de Caxias

Nova Iguaçu

São Gonçalo

P A U L O

Taubaté

RIO DE JANEIRO

Realengo

Niterói

ILHA DO CABO FRIO

Sorocaba

Jundiaí

SÃO PAULO

Mogi das Cruzes

Santo André

São Bernardo do Campo

ILHA GRANDE

Baía de Ilha Grande

Tropic of Capricorn

A T L A N T I C   O C E A N

São Vicente   **Santos**

ILHA DE SÃO SEBASTIÃO

A-540051-76   7·48   ©RMCN

24°

b

PACIFIC OCEAN

COQUIMBO

Valparaíso

VALPARAÍSO

Viña del Mar

SANTIAGO

SANTIAGO

A R G E N T I N A

O'HIGGINS

COLCHAGUA

CURICÓ

Talca

TALCA

LINARES

©RMCN

72°   70°

c

E N T R E   R I O S

Rosario

RÍO NEGRO

DURAZNO

SANTA FE

U R U G U A Y

SORIANO

FLORES

FLORIDA

COLONIA

SAN JOSÉ

CANELONES

A R G E N T I N A

BUENOS AIRES

San Isidro

Morón

Avellaneda

Quilmes

Lomas de Zamora

La Plata

MONTEVIDEO

Río de la Plata

B U E N O S

A I R E S

A T L A N T I C

O C E A N

Bahía Samborombón

PUNTA NORTE

60°   Longitude West of Greenwich   58°   56°

| 0 10 20 30 40 50 60 70 80 90 100 110 120 Miles |
| 0 20 40 60 80 100 120 140 160 180 200 Kilometers |

Cities and Towns

| 0 to 50,000 | ○ | 500,000 to 1,000,000 | ◎ |
| 50,000 to 500,000 | ⊙ | 1,000,000 and over | |

Scale 1:4 000 000; one inch to 64 miles.
Elevations and depressions are given in feet.

Europe

Europe is smaller than every other continent except Australia. In a sense, Europe is not really a continent at all, since it is part of the same vast landmass as Asia. Geographers sometimes refer to this landmass as a single continent, Eurasia. Europe occupies only about 18% of the land area of Eurasia.

Europe can be described as an enormous peninsula, stretching from the Ural Mountains, Ural River, and Caspian Sea in the east, to the Atlantic Ocean in the west; and from the Arctic Ocean in the north to the Mediterranean Sea, Black Sea, and Caucasus mountains in the south. The British Isles, Iceland, Corsica, Crete, and thousands of smaller islands that lie off the European mainland are usually considered as part of the continent.

A sweep of mountain ranges, including the Pyrenees, Alps and Carpathians, divides the colder, wetter north from the sun-drenched south.

Europe at a glance

Land area: 3,800,000 square miles (9,900,000 sq km)

Estimated population: 728,975,000

Population density: 192/square mile (74/sq km)

Mean elevation: 980 feet (300 m)

Highest point: Gora El' brus, Russia, 18,510 feet (5,642 m)

Lowest point: Caspian Sea, Asia-Europe, 92 feet (28 m) below sea level

Longest river: Volga, 2,194 mi (3,531 km)

Number of countries (incl. dependencies): 49

Largest independent country: Russia (Europe/Asia), 6,592,849 square miles (17,075,400 sq km)

Smallest independent country: Vatican City, 0.2 square miles (0.4 sq km)

Most populous independent country: Russia (Europe/Asia), 145,215,000

Least populous independent country: Vatican City, 1,000

Largest city: Moscow, pop. 8,368,449

Coldest place:
Ust'- Shchugor, Russia
-67°F (-55°C)

Driest place:
Astrakhan', Russia
6.4 inches (16 cm)

Lowest point:
Caspian Sea, Asia-Eur.
92 ft (28 m) below se

Highest point:
Gora El'brus, Russia
18,510 ft (5,642 m)

Wettest place:
Crkvice, Bosnia & Herzegovina
183 inches (465 cm)/year

Hottest place:
Sevilla, Spain
122°F (50°C)

Landforms

- Mountains
- Widely spaced mountains
- High tablelands
- Hills and low tablelands
- Plains
- Depresssions, basins
- High tablelands and ice caps
- Mountains and ice caps

© Rand McNally & Co.
M-550000-7C-EL1-1-1- -1

The Alps tower above a village in the Virgen Tal valley of western Austria.

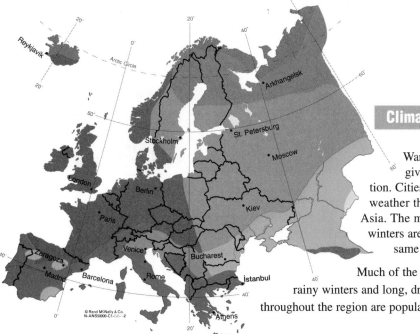

Climate

Warm, moist air masses flowing in from the Atlantic Ocean give much of Europe a mild climate and abundant precipitation. Cities like London, Paris and Rome all enjoy warmer weather than cities at similar latitudes in North America and Asia. The moderate winds don't reach eastern Europe, where the winters are long and cold and the summers short and cool. The same is true in the northern regions of Scandinavia.

Much of the south enjoys a Mediterranean climate, marked by short, rainy winters and long, dry summers. Indeed, the many beaches and islands found throughout the region are popular with vacationers year-round.

Tinted areas show temperature in degrees Fahrenheit. Vertical bars show precipitation in inches.

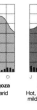   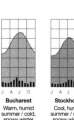 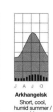

Zaragoza Semiarid | **Athens** Hot, dry summer / mild, rainy winter | **Venice** Warm, humid summer / mild winter | **Paris** Mild and rainy | **Bucharest** Warm, humid summer / cold, snowy winter | **Stockholm** Cool, humid summer / cold, snowy winter | **Arkhangelsk** Short, cool, humid summer / very cold, snowy winter | **Reykjavik** Cold and dry | **Extensive uplands** Climate varies with elevation and latitude

Population

Europe is the second most densely populated continent. Only Asia has a greater population density. However, Europe's density varies dramatically from country to country. The Netherlands, for instance, has a density of 991 people per square mile (383 per sq km), making it one of the most densely populated countries in the world. In contrast, Norway has only 30 people per square mile (12 per sq km).

A vast array of ethnic groups and cultures can be found in Europe's relatively small area. Throughout the centuries, this diversity has enriched European culture while also leading to many hostilities. Of the 60 languages spoken, the majority are derived from Latin, Germanic or Slavic roots. Most Europeans are Christian, either Protestant or Roman Catholic.

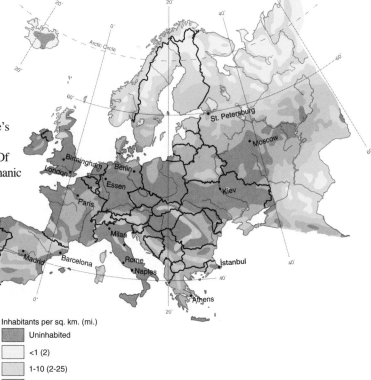

Fastest-Growing Countries
Croatia, 1.48% (annual rate of natural increase)
San Marino, 1.45%
Bosnia and Herzegovina, 1.38%

Slowest-Growing Countries
Bulgaria, -1.14%
Latvia, -0.81%
Ukraine, -0.78%

Inhabitants per sq. km. (mi.)
Uninhabited
<1 (2)
1-10 (2-25)
10-25 (25-60)
25-50 (60-125)
50-100 (125-250)
>100 (250)

© Rand McNally & Co.
M-550000-1P-EL1-|-|- -1

Environments and Land Use

Given the high population density of Europe, it is not surprising that evidence of human development can be seen in every part of the continent, with the exception of the northern reaches of Scandinavia. In Western Europe, small farms are surrounded by towns, cities and industrial areas. Only in the east, in areas such as the vast rolling steppes of the Ukraine, can large farms and unbroken natural vistas be found.

Harvesting grapes from vineyards in Burgundy, France

The heavily industrialized countries of Western Europe boast rich economies and high standards of living. Switzerland has a per capita Gross Domestic Product (GDP) approaching U.S. $22,000, the highest in the world. The figures are generally much lower in Eastern Europe. One of the continent's poorest countries is the tiny former Communist state of Albania, which has a per capita GDP of only U.S. $998.

Pollution is an unfortunate by-product of the continent's industry. One example is the scenic Rhine River: in the 1980s, large stretches were found to be so polluted that they were devoid of life. These findings sparked a 20-year program to clean up the river. In general, the countries of Eastern Europe suffer from the worst pollution, as economic development has in the past taken precedence over environmental policies.

The vast forests of Scandinavia support a large paper and wood-products economy. Where forests survive in countries farther to the south, they are often used for recreation. Along the Mediterranean, the warm and dry lands support olive and fruit orchards. In many of these areas, agriculture is being supplemented and even replaced by tourism.

Over-fishing has depleted the seas and ocean around Europe. The fleets of countries such as Spain and Great Britain must sail far into the North Atlantic to find the ever-dwindling stocks of fish.

Urban

Cropland

Cropland and woodland

Cropland and grazing land

Grassland, grazing land

Forest, woodland

Swamp, marsh

Tundra

Shrub, sparse grass, wasteland

Barren land

0 100 200 300 400 Miles
0 200 400 600 Kilometers

© Rand McNally & Co.
M-550000-8L-EL1-·-¹- -1

Political Changes Since 1989

Much of Europe lay in economic and physical ruin after World War II ended in 1945. Germany's cities and industrial centers had been ravaged by aerial bombardment and assaults by the Allied armies. Many other countries, such as Russia, Poland, Belgium, and the Netherlands suffered gravely from Nazi invasions and occupation.

After 1945, tensions among the victorious Allies grew, specifically between the western powers—the United States, Great Britain and France—and the Soviet Union. It became clear that the two sides had vastly different visions for post-war Europe. In 1946, former British prime minister Winston Churchill observed that an "Iron Curtain" had gone down across Europe. It was to stay in place for almost 45 years.

Germany and the city of Berlin were divided between the western powers and the Soviet Union. West Germany quickly joined the other countries of Western Europe in building a stable, affluent democratic society. East Germany became part of a bloc of Eastern European countries dominated by the Soviet Union. These included Poland, Czechoslovakia, Hungary, Romania, Albania, and Bulgaria (see map at right). The economies in these countries were tightly controlled and personal freedoms were severely limited by the Communist governments in power.

The two blocs faced each other in a tense, generally non-military standoff called "The Cold War," which lasted for four decades. However, in 1985 winds of reform began sweeping through Eastern Europe. In 1989, Hungary relaxed its borders with Austria, setting off a flow of refugees from the east who had been forbidden to travel to the west. Thus began a dizzying period of change: the next two years saw the collapse of the Soviet Union, the reunification of Germany, independence for the former Soviet republics, and freedom from Soviet influence for the former bloc countries.

Although much of the old east seems intent on adopting western ideals of democracy and freedom, the process is not without problems. Switching from communism to market economies has meant hardship for millions. It has also led to ethnic tensions that resulted in the peaceful break-up of Czechoslovakia and the violent civil wars in the former Yugoslavia.

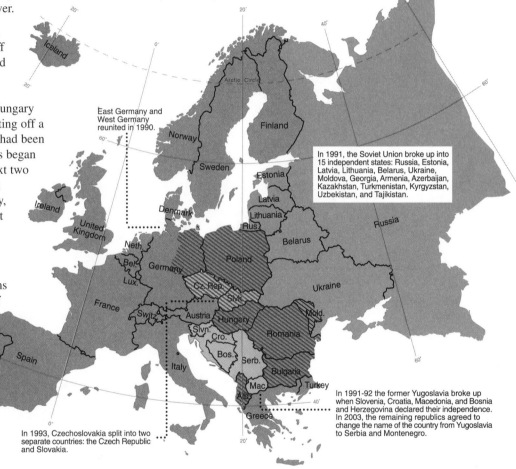

East Germany and West Germany reunited in 1990.

In 1991, the Soviet Union broke up into 15 independent states: Russia, Estonia, Latvia, Lithuania, Belarus, Ukraine, Moldova, Georgia, Armenia, Azerbaijan, Kazakhstan, Turkmenistan, Kyrgyzstan, Uzbekistan, and Tajikistan.

In 1993, Czechoslovakia split into two separate countries: the Czech Republic and Slovakia.

In 1991-92 the former Yugoslavia broke up when Slovenia, Croatia, Macedonia, and Bosnia and Herzegovina declared their independence. In 2003, the remaining republics agreed to change the name of the country from Yugoslavia to Serbia and Montenegro.

Political Change Since 1989

- Former Soviet Union
- Former Czechoslovakia
- Former Yugoslavia
- Former East and West Germany
- Former Soviet-bloc countries

© Rand McNally & Co.
M-550000-2P-EL1-·-·-·-2

Berlin Wall memorial

40,000 SQ MI
AREA

0   100   200
Miles

Scale 1: 16 000 000; one inch to 250 miles. Conic Projection
Elevations and depressions are given in feet

Longitude West of Greenwich   Longitude East of Greenwich

0   50 100   200   300   400   500 Miles
0   100   200   400   600   800 Kilometers

Relief

Meters		Feet
3050		10 000
1525		5000
610		2000
305		1000
152.5		500
0	Sea Level	0
152.5		Below Sea Level
1525	500	
3050	5000	
	10 000	

Scale 1: 16 000 000; one inch to 250 miles. Conic Projection
Elevations and depressions are given in feet

Longitude West of Greenwich   Longitude East of Greenwich

0   50   100   200   300   400   500 Miles
0   100   200   400   600   800 Kilometers

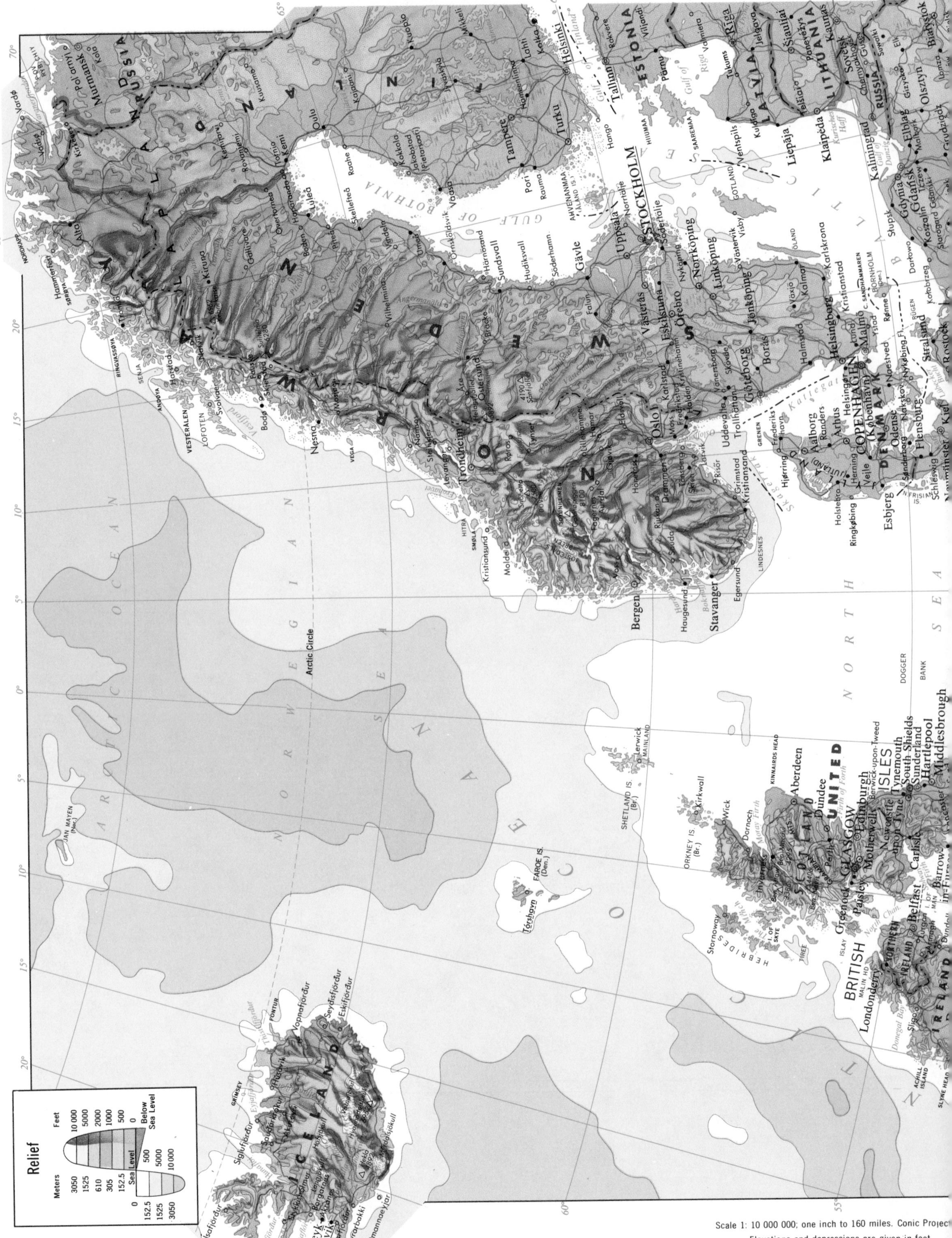

BELARU...

RUSSIA · Murmansk · Kola

L A P L A N D

F I N L A N D

S W E D E N

N O R W A Y

N O R W E G I A N   S E A

A R C T I C   O C E A N

Arctic Circle

ESTONIA · Tallinn
LATVIA · Riga
LITHUANIA
RUSSIA · Kaliningrad

Helsinki · Tampere · Turku

GULF OF BOTHNIA

Gulf of Finland

STOCKHOLM · Uppsala · Gävle · Västerås · Örebro · Norrköping · Linköping · Jönköping · Göteborg · Borås · Halmstad · Helsingborg · Malmö · Karlskrona · Kalmar

OSLO · Bergen · Stavanger · Haugesund · Egersund · Kristiansand · Trondheim · Kristiansund · Molde · Ålesund

Trondheim

GOTLAND · Visby
ÖLAND

DENMARK · COPENHAGEN (København) · Aalborg · Randers · Århus · Odense · Esbjerg · Herning

Skagerrak · Kattegat

GDAŃSK · Gdynia · Szczecin · RÜGEN

NORTH SEA

BALTIC SEA

JAN MAYEN (Nor.)

FAROE IS. (Den.) · Tórshavn

SHETLAND IS. · Lerwick · MAINLAND
ORKNEY IS. (Br.) · Kirkwall

DOGGER BANK

BRITISH ISLES

S C O T L A N D · Aberdeen · Dundee · EDINBURGH · GLASGOW · Greenock · Paisley · Perth · Inverness · Wick · Dornoch · Stornoway · HEBRIDES · ISLE OF SKYE · ISLAY · TIREE · Firth of Forth · Firth of Clyde

Newcastle upon Tyne · Tynemouth · South Shields · Sunderland · Hartlepool · Middlesbrough · Carlisle · Barrow-in-Furness · Lancaster

UNITED KINGDOM

NORTHERN IRELAND · Belfast · Londonderry · IRELAND · Sligo · ACHILL ISLAND · SLYNE HEAD · SLIGO BAY · DONEGAL BAY · MALIN HD · KINNAIRDS HEAD

I C E L A N D · Reykjavík · Hafnarfjörður · Vopnafjörður · Seyðisfjörður · Eskifjörður · Siglufjörður · Húsavík · Ísafjörður · Akureyri · FONTUR · Vestmannaeyjar

Relief

Meters	Feet
3050	10 000
1525	5000
610	2000
305	1000
152.5	500
0	0
Sea Level	Below Sea Level
152.5	500
1525	5000
3050	10 000

MEDITERRANEAN SEA

TYRRHENIAN SEA

ADRIATIC SEA

LIGURIAN SEA

IONIAN SEA

BAY OF BISCAY

ENGLISH CHANNEL

ATLAS MOUNTAINS

FRANCE · SPAIN · PORTUGAL · GERMANY · ITALY · POLAND · HUNGARY · CZECH REP. · AUSTRIA · SWITZERLAND · BELGIUM · NETHERLANDS · ENGLAND · CROATIA · SERBIA · BOSNIA · ALBANIA · TUNISIA · MOROCCO

LONDON · PARIS · MADRID · LISBON · ROME · NAPLES · MILAN · TURIN · MUNICH · VIENNA · PRAGUE · BUDAPEST · BRUSSELS · AMSTERDAM · BARCELONA · VALÈNCIA · BILBAO · SEVILLA · ALGIERS · TUNIS · PALERMO · CATANIA

A-559400-76-13-10-26
COPYRIGHT BY
RAND M⁹NALLY & COMPANY
MADE IN U.S.A.

Longitude East of Greenwich

Longitude West of Greenwich

50   100   150   200   250   300 Miles
100   200   300   400   500 Kilometers

Cities
and
Towns

0 to 50,000   500,000 to 1,000,000

50,000 to 500,000   1,000,000 and over

Relief

Feet	Meters
10000	3050
5000	1525
2000	610
1000	305
500	152.5
Sea Level	0 Sea Level
500	152.5
5000	1525
10000	3050

Below Sea Level

0 50 100 150 200 250 300 Miles

0 100 200 300 400 500 Kilometers

Scale 1:10 000 000; one inch to 160 miles. Conic Projection

Elevations and depressions are given in feet.

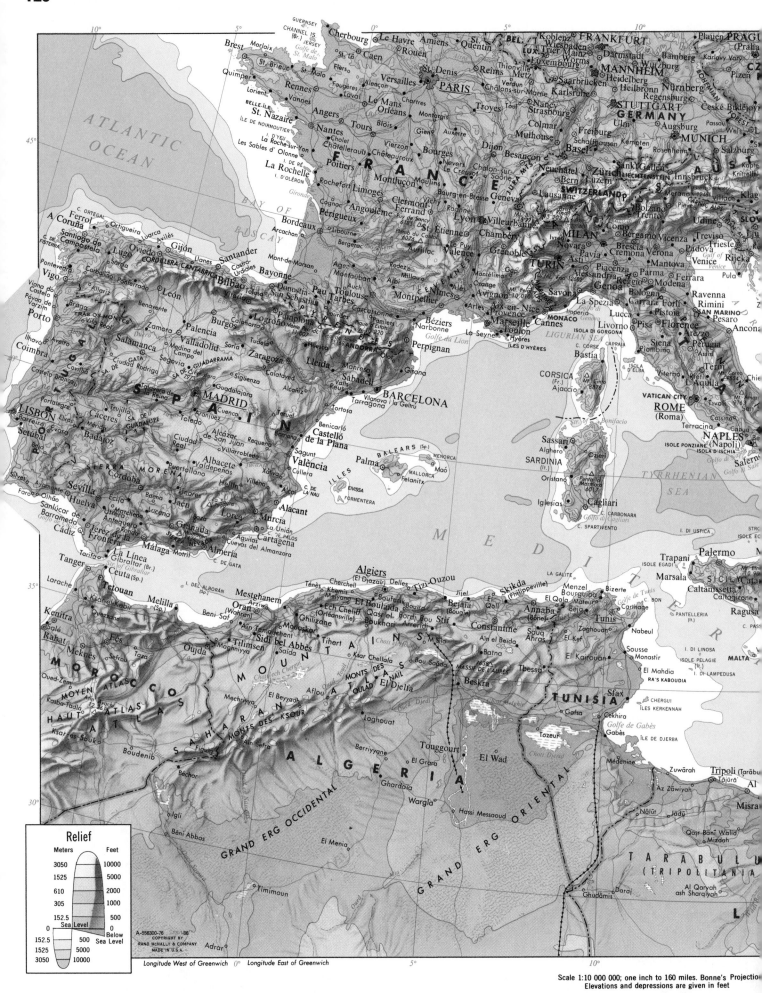

Relief

Meters	Feet
3050	10000
1525	5000
610	2000
305	1000
152.5	500
0 Sea Level	0 Below Sea Level
152.5	500
1525	5000
3050	10000

A-558300-76 8-1-86
COPYRIGHT BY
RAND MCNALLY & COMPANY
MADE IN U.S.A.

Longitude West of Greenwich 0° Longitude East of Greenwich

Scale 1:10 000 000; one inch to 160 miles. Bonne's Projection
Elevations and depressions are given in feet

20° 25° 30° 35° 40°

Zabrze **KATOWICE** Rzeszów Jarosław Brody Starokostiantyniv Smila Pavlohrad Synel'nykove **DONETS'K**
Ostrava Kraków **POLAND** Tarnów L'viv Ternopil' Khmel'nyts'kyi Vinnytsia Zvenyhorodka Shpola Kremenchuk Kirovohrad Dniprodzerzhyns'k **DNIPROPETROVS'K** Zaporizhzhia Novocherkassk Rostov-na-Donu
louc BESKID CARPATH MTS Ivano- Kamianets- **U K R A I N E** Uman Kryvyi Rih Voznesens'k Nikopol' Berdians'k Yeysk **RUSSIA**
SLOVAKIA Nové Zámky Košice Uzhhorod Frankivs'k Podil's'kyi Tul'chyn Haisyn Vovkuvainka Pervomais'k Chornomors'ke Primorsko- Tikhoretsk
Bratislava Banská Bystrica Prešov Mukacheve Khust Chernivtsi Radauti Kolomyia Soroka Balta Odesa Kherson Melitopol' KOSA Akhtarskaya Kropotkin Stavropol'
iener Neustadt Győr Miskolc Nyíregyháza Satu Mare Baia Mare Botoşani Iaşi Orhei Tiraspol Bilhorod- Mykolaïv Heniches'k BYRIUCHYI O. KRYMS'KYI Kerch Timashevsk Armavir Labinsk
Szombathely Székesfehérvár **BUDAPEST** Debrecen Simleu Dej Bistrita Piatra-Neamt Bacău Chişinău Tighina Dnistrovs'kyy Chornomors'ke M. TARKHANKUT PIVOSTRIV Anapa Maykop
Pápa Kecskemét Oradea Napoca Cluj Gheorgheni Husi **MOLDOVA** Comrat Bolhrad Dzhankoi (CRIMEAN PEN.) Feodosiia Krasnodar Novorossiysk
Nagykanizsa Szekszárd **HUNGARY** Békéscsaba Arad **R O M A N I A** Sighu Tecuci Vylkove Chornomors'ke Ievpatoriia Simferopol' Tuapse
Pécs Szeged Senta Timişoara Lugoj Deva Alba Iulia MERIDIONALI Braşov Râmnicu Sărat Galati Brăila Tulcea Sulina Yalta Sevastopol' Sochi
reb Sombor Vršac Sibiu Campulung Buzău Ploiesti M. SARYCH Sukhumi
OATIA Subotica Novi Sad CARPATII TRANSYLVANIAN ALPS Targu-Jiu Piteşti Constanta **GEORGIA**
isak Osijek Pančevo Craiova Bāilesti Turnu Slatina Magurele Rosiori de Vede **BUCHAREST** Călăraşi Silistra Dobrich N. KALIAKRA **B L A C K   S E A**
S. Brod Belgrade Drobeta-Turnu Corabia Tutrakan Razgrad
Gradacac (Beograd) Severin Vidin Lom Knezha Nikopol Svishtov Ruse Shumen Varna (Stalin)
Luka **BOSNIA AND** Sabac Loznica Paracin Vratsa Pleven Veliko-Turnovo Pomorie
Tuzla **HERZEGOVINA** Kragujevac Niš STARA PLANINA Sevlievo Sliven G. of Burgas
clivno Sarajevo Tirstenik BALKAN MTS Yambol Burgas KEREMPE BR Inebolu
Mostar Novi Pazar Pirot **Sofia** Stara Zagora Zonguldak Bartin INCE BR Sinop Trabzon Rize
SERBIA (Sofiya) **B U L G A R I A** Chirpan Kirklareli Ereğli Kastamonu Tosya Samsun Çarşamba Fatsa Giresun
stovo MLJET **AND MONTENEGRO** Cernik Kyustendil Pazardzhik Plovdiv Khaskovo Edirne Çorum Ünye Ordu Erzincan
ALAGRUŽA Dubrovnik Cetinje Skopje RHODOPE MTS Komotini Istanbul İzmit Adapazarı Amasya Merzifon Sivas Keban Gölü
Monte Sant'Angelo Ulcinj Tetovo MACEDON Drama Xánthi Alexandroupoli Tekirdağ İstanbul İznik Bolu Çankırı Sungurlu Zile Tokat Erzincan
arletta Tiranë Prilep Patršh Kavála **İSTANBUL** Bursa Bilecik Beypazarı Kızıl Tyana Yozgat A S I A Akşar
Molfetta Durrës **ALBANIA** Bitola Serres THÁSOS Gelibolu Balıkesir Mustafakemalpaşa **Ankara** Kırşehir Kayseri Elâziğ
Bari Elbasan Korçë Edessa Kavála Marmara Denizi (Angora) Erciyes Malatya
Altamura Vlore Flórina Thessaloníki LIMNOS Çanakkale Eskişehir Dağı
za Taranto SAZANIT Kastória Kozáni SAMOTHRÁKI Çanakkale Bandırma Kütahya Afyon Aksaray Niğde M I N O R Kahramanmaraş
Brindisi (Valona) Gjirokastër Thermaïkós Larisa Edremit Ayvalık Bergama Bolvadin Beyşehir T O R O S Gaziantep
Lecce Kólpos Vólos LIMNOS Mytilíni Manisa Akhisar Uşak Konya Karaman Ereğli Tarsus Adana Kilis
Golfo di PINDOS OROS LESVOS İzmir Kula Ödemiş Ulukışla Osmaniye Antakya Aleppo
Rossano Taranto Ioánnina Tríkala SKYROS Chíos Tire Aydın Söke Denizli Karaman İçel İskenderun Ladhiqiyah (Latakia)
za C.S. MARIA Kérkyra EÚVVOIA CHIOS Milas Antalya Silifke Alanya Antakya **SYRIA**
DI LEUCA KÉRKYRA **G R E E C E** Agrínio (Thívai) Chalkída SÁMOS Muğla Adalia Antalya Hamáh
Catanzaro IONIAN (Thebes) ÁNDROS Körfezi Körfezi Fethiye Homs
io di Calabria SEA **ATHENS** Peiraiás SÝROS TÍNOS Nicosia Famagusta Tartūs
ISLANDS (Athína) Larnaca Ţarābulus
KEFALLINÍA LÉFKADA Pátra Kórinthos PÁROS NÁXOS **CYPRUS** Limassol (Tripoli) Zahlah
ZÁKYNTHOS Pýrgos Trípoli SÝROS AMORGÓS SÝMI Ródos Nicosia **LEBANON** Beirut
Kyparissía Kalamáta Spárti MÍLOS ASTYPÁLAIA RÓDOS Şaydā (Sidon) Damascus
IONIAN SEA ÁKRA MALÉAS KÝTHIRA KÁRPATHOS Şūr (Tyre) (Dimashq) As Suwaydā
ÁKRA TAÍNARO ANTIKYTHIRA KÁSOS Acre Nablus Amman
Chaniá Irákleio Haifa **ISRAEL** Irbid
CRETE GÁVDOS Tel Aviv-Yafo **JORDAN**
Areas occupied by Israel since 1967 Jerusalem
Gaza Bethlehem
Dumyat Port Said Hebron
ALEXANDRIA Rashīd (Bûr Sa'îd) Al 'Arīsh Ma'ān
(Al Iskandariyah) Al Mahallah Al Mansūrah
RA'S AL KANĀIS Damanhūr Tanţā Al Ismā'īliyah
As Sallūm Sīdī Barrānī Al 'Amirīyah Banhā Zaqazīq Suez (As Suways)
Shibin al Kawm Al Qāhirah SINAI
Banghāzī Shahhāt Darnah Marsá Matrûh Al 'Alamayn Al Hammam **CAIRO** (Al Qāhirah) PEN.
Tulmaythah Tūkrah Tubruq (Tobruk) Al Jīzah Hulwān Gulf of Suez
AL JABAL AL AKHDAR Al Fayyūm Banī Suwayf SAUDI ARABIA
Surt Sulūq **EGYPT** ARABIA
An Nawfalīyah B A R Q A H MUNKHAFAD Al Fashn
Qasr al Burayqah (CYRENAICA) AL QATTĀRAH Banī Mazār
Ajdābiyah LIBYAN Al Minyā
Al 'Uqaylah PLATEAU Al Bawītī Mallawī
Maradah **L I B Y A** RED SEA
Awjilah (Oasis) D E S E R T

IONIAN SEA   **AEGEAN SEA**   **M E D I T E R R A N E A N   S E A**

S E A   O F   A Z O V   **B L A C K   S E A**

50 100 150 200 250 300 Miles
100 200 300 400 500 Kilometers

Africa

The Drakensberg Mountains in southern South Africa.

Africa, the second-largest continent, comprises about one-fifth of the world's land area. From the Equator, Africa extends roughly the same distance to the north as it does to the south.

A high plateau covers much of the continent. The edges of the plateau are marked by steep slopes, called escarpments, where the land angles sharply downward onto narrow coastal plains or into the sea. Many of the continent's great rivers plunge over these escarpments in falls or rapids, and therefore cannot be used as transportation routes from the coast into the continent's interior.

Among Africa's most significant mountain systems are the Atlas range in the far north and the Drakensberg range in the far south. A long string of mountain ranges and highlands running north-south through eastern Africa marks the course of the Great Rift Valley.

Africa at a glance

Land area: 11,700,000 square miles (30,300,000 sq km)

Estimated population: 832,590,000

Population density: 71/ square mile (27/sq km)

Mean elevation: 1,900 feet (580 m)

Highest point: Kilimanjaro, Tanzania, 19,340 feet (5,895 m)

Lowest point: Lac Assal, Djibouti, 515 feet (157 m) below sea level

Longest river: Nile, 4,145 mi (6,671 km)

Number of countries (incl. dependencies): 61

Largest independent country: Sudan, 967,500 square miles (2,505,813 sq km)

Smallest independent country: Seychelles, 176 square miles (455 sq km)

Most populous independent country: Nigeria, 128,285,000

Least populous independent country: Seychelles, 80,000

Largest city: Cairo, pop. 6,801,000

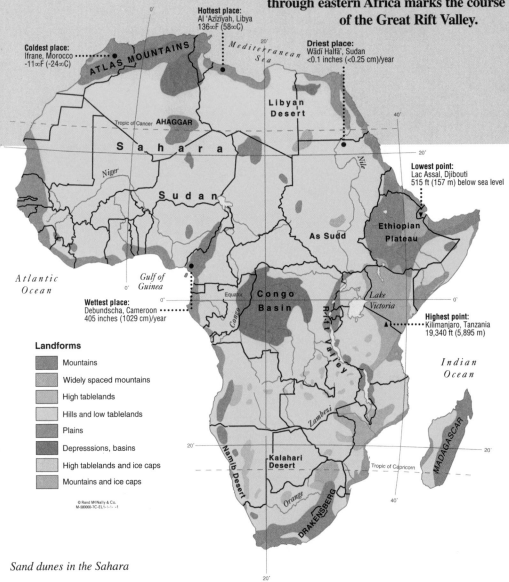

Coldest place:
Ifrane, Morocco
-11∞F (-24∞C)

Hottest place:
Al 'Azīzīyah, Libya
136∞F (58∞C)

Driest place:
Wādī Halfā', Sudan
<0.1 inches (<0.25 cm)/year

ATLAS MOUNTAINS

Mediterranean Sea

Libyan Desert

Tropic of Cancer   AHAGGAR

S a h a r a

Niger

S u d a n

Nile

Lowest point:
Lac Assal, Djibouti
515 ft (157 m) below sea level

As Sudd

Ethiopian Plateau

Atlantic Ocean

Gulf of Guinea

Equator

Congo Basin

Lake Victoria

Congo

Rift Valley

Wettest place:
Debundscha, Cameroon
405 inches (1029 cm)/year

Highest point:
Kilimanjaro, Tanzania
19,340 ft (5,895 m)

Indian Ocean

Zambezi

Namib Desert

Kalahari Desert

Tropic of Capricorn

MADAGASCAR

Orange

DRAKENSBERG

Landforms

- Mountains
- Widely spaced mountains
- High tablelands
- Hills and low tablelands
- Plains
- Depresssions, basins
- High tablelands and ice caps
- Mountains and ice caps

© Rand McNally & Co.
M-580000-7C-EL1-¹-¹- -1

Sand dunes in the Sahara

Climate

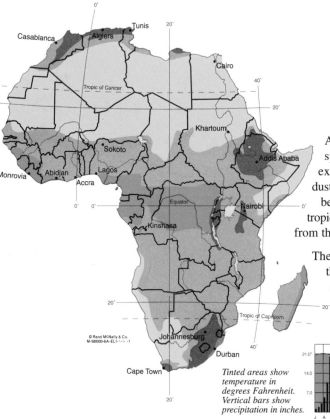

Africa's most prominent climatic region is the vast Sahara desert which spreads over much of the northern half of the continent. The Sahara experiences scorching daytime temperatures, minimal rainfall, and hot, dry, dust-laden winds that blow nearly continuously. South of the Sahara, the climate becomes increasingly humid, moving through zones of semiarid steppe and tropical savanna to the tropical rain forest that stretches across equatorial Africa from the Atlantic Ocean to the Rift Valley.

The climate patterns of northern Africa are repeated in reverse south of the Equator. The rain forest gives way to zones of decreasing humidity, and desert regions cover western South Africa and Namibia. Africa's mildest, most temperate climates are found along its Mediterranean coast, at its southwestern tip, and in eastern South Africa.

Tinted areas show temperature in degrees Fahrenheit. Vertical bars show precipitation in inches.

Monrovia
Hot and rainy

Kinshasa
Hot with rainy and dry seasons

Sokoto
Semiarid

Cairo
Very dry

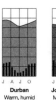
Tunis
Hot, dry summer / mild, rainy winter

Durban
Warm, humid summer / mild winter

Johannesburg
Mild and rainy

Extensive uplands
Climate varies with elevation and latitude

Population

About one-seventh of the world's people live in Africa. It is the second most populous continent. The population is almost evenly divided between the sub-Saharan countries and those bordering the Mediterranean. Large tracts of the Sahara are uninhabited. Despite recurring famines, disease, and warfare, the population is rapidly increasing.

The largest concentrations of people are generally found in regions in which one or more of the following conditions exist: moderate temperatures, ample water supply, and arable land. These regions include Egypt's fertile Nile Valley, the northern coast of the Gulf of Guinea, the highlands of East Africa, and the coastal regions of Morocco, Algeria, and Tunisia, north of the Atlas Mountains.

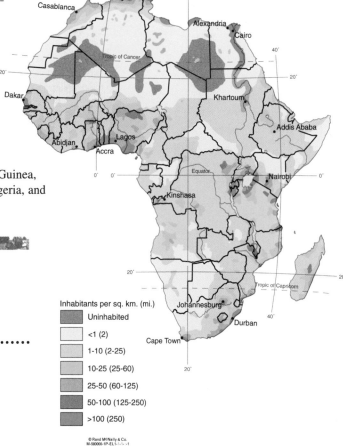

Inhabitants per sq. km. (mi.)

- Uninhabited
- <1 (2)
- 1-10 (2-25)
- 10-25 (25-60)
- 25-50 (60-125)
- 50-100 (125-250)
- >100 (250)

© Rand McNally & Co.
M-580000-1P-EL1-¹-¹-¹ -1

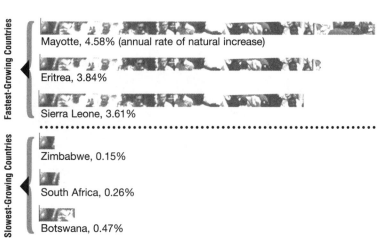

Fastest-Growing Countries

Mayotte, 4.58% (annual rate of natural increase)

Eritrea, 3.84%

Sierra Leone, 3.61%

Slowest-Growing Countries

Zimbabwe, 0.15%

South Africa, 0.26%

Botswana, 0.47%

Environments and Land Use

Deserts account for one-third of Africa's land area, and they claim new land every year. Drought, over-farming, and over-grazing can quickly turn marginal land, such as that of the Sahel region (also known as the Sudan), into barren waste-land. The huge Sahara desert has itself only existed a short time, in geological terms: cave paintings and other archeological evidence indicate that green pastureland covered the area just a few thousand years ago.

Shepherd with goats in the Sahel (Sudan)

Most Africans are subsistence farmers, growing sorghum, corn, millet, sweet potatoes, and other starchy foods. Commercial farms, most of which date from the colonial period, can be found throughout central and southern Africa, producing cash crops such as coffee, bananas, tobacco and cacao. One-quarter of the continent's land is suitable for grazing, but disease and drought have made raising animals difficult. Although three out of four Africans work in agriculture, Africa is the only continent that is not self-sufficient for food.

The great rain forests that cover much of equatorial Africa produce mahogany, ebony, and other valuable hardwoods. However, only limited areas of the forests are suitable for logging, and the lack of developed road networks makes it difficult and costly to transport the wood.

Vast mineral reserves are spread throughout the continent. Most are unexploited, but notable exceptions include the diamond mines of South Africa and Namibia, the copper mines of Zambia and Democratic Republic of the Congo, and the oil fields of Nigeria, Libya, and Algeria.

The great concentrations of wildlife for which Africa is famous can still be found in places such as Tanzania's Serengeti Plain and Botswana's Kalahari Desert. In many other parts of the continent, however, wildlife is quickly disappearing as humans encroach on habitat and poachers decimate entire species.

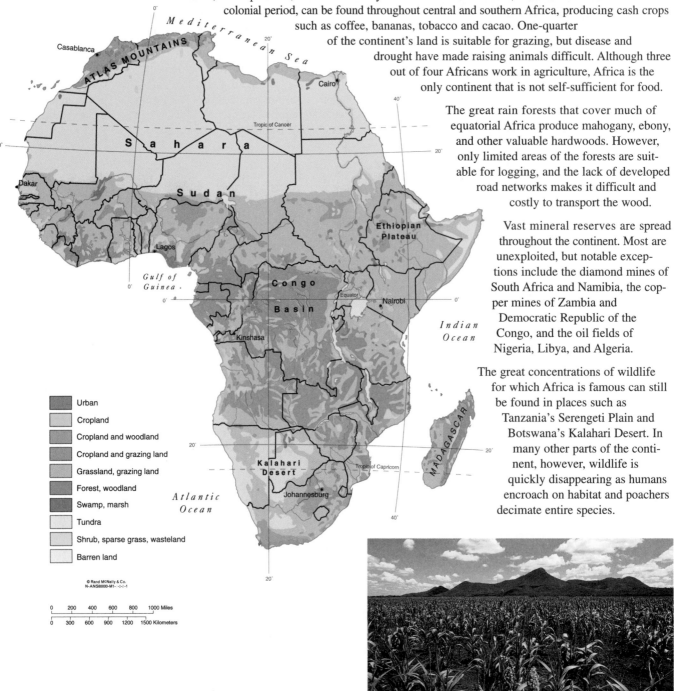

Urban

Cropland

Cropland and woodland

Cropland and grazing land

Grassland, grazing land

Forest, woodland

Swamp, marsh

Tundra

Shrub, sparse grass, wasteland

Barren land

© Rand McNally & Co.
N-ANS80000-M1- -≈-1

| 0 | 200 | 400 | 600 | 800 | 1000 Miles |
| 0 | 300 | 600 | 900 | 1200 | 1500 Kilometers |

Field of sorghum in Zimbabwe

Africa: from Colonial Rule to Independence

The origins of Europe's colonization of Africa can be traced back to the 1500s, when a lucrative slave trade developed to supply European settlers in the New World with laborers. Africa became the primary source for slaves: between the mid-1500s and the mid-1800s, 11 million Africans were captured and sold into slavery.

When the slave trade was banned across Europe in the early 1800s, commercial trade with Africa continued. In the second half of the century, competition for Africa's minerals and other raw materials intensified, and between 1880 and 1914, France, Britain, Italy, Portugal, Belgium, Spain, and Germany annexed large areas of Africa. Colonial rule was often characterized by racial prejudice and segregation.

In the late 19th and early 20th centuries, Egypt, Ethiopia, and South Africa began to break free from colonial influence. For most of Africa, however, colonial rule persisted through the mid-1900s, although it faced growing bitterness and nationalist sentiment. As the colonial powers struggled through two world wars, and as their international dominance declined, it became increasingly difficult for them to maintain their empires.

In 1951, Libya gained its independence, following a UN resolution that ended British and French control. Sudan peacefully won independence from Britain and Egypt in 1956. A year later, Britain granted independence to the Gold Coast, which became the new country of Ghana. Guinea separated from France in 1958, followed by all of the other French colonies in 1960. Anti-colonial movements gathered strength across Africa, and by the end of the 1970s, a total of 43 countries had become independent.

The end of colonial rule, however, has not brought peace and prosperity. Many of the newly freed countries were ill-prepared for independence. Their economies were oriented to fit the needs of the now-departed colonists, few transportation networks existed, and dictators and rival despots fought for power in civil wars.

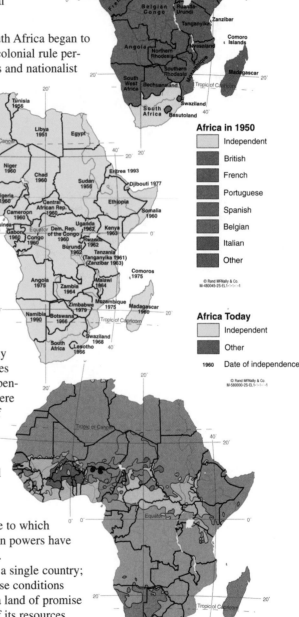

Africa in 1950

- Independent
- British
- French
- Portuguese
- Spanish
- Belgian
- Italian
- Other

© Rand McNally & Co.
M-480045-2S-EL1-·-·-·-·1

Africa Today

- Independent
- Other
- 1960   Date of independence

© Rand McNally & Co.
M-580000-2S-EL1-·-·-·-·1

People of the Samburu tribe

Further, most Africans identify themselves primarily with the tribe to which they belong. The political delineations established by the European powers have little meaning and often conflict with traditional tribal boundaries. In some cases, enemy tribes found themselves pushed together in a single country; in others, single tribes were divided among several countries. These conditions have already brought much warfare and hardship. Still, Africa is a land of promise and opportunity. The rich diversity of its people and abundance of its resources should inevitably enable the continent to realize its potential.

Ethno-linguistic Groups

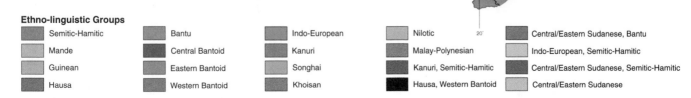

- Semitic-Hamitic
- Mande
- Guinean
- Hausa
- Bantu
- Central Bantoid
- Eastern Bantoid
- Western Bantoid
- Indo-European
- Kanuri
- Songhai
- Khoisan
- Nilotic
- Malay-Polynesian
- Kanuri, Semitic-Hamitic
- Hausa, Western Bantoid
- Central/Eastern Sudanese, Bantu
- Indo-European, Semitic-Hamitic
- Central/Eastern Sudanese, Semitic-Hamitic
- Central/Eastern Sudanese

© Rand McNally & Co.
M-580000-1D-EL1-·-·-·-·1

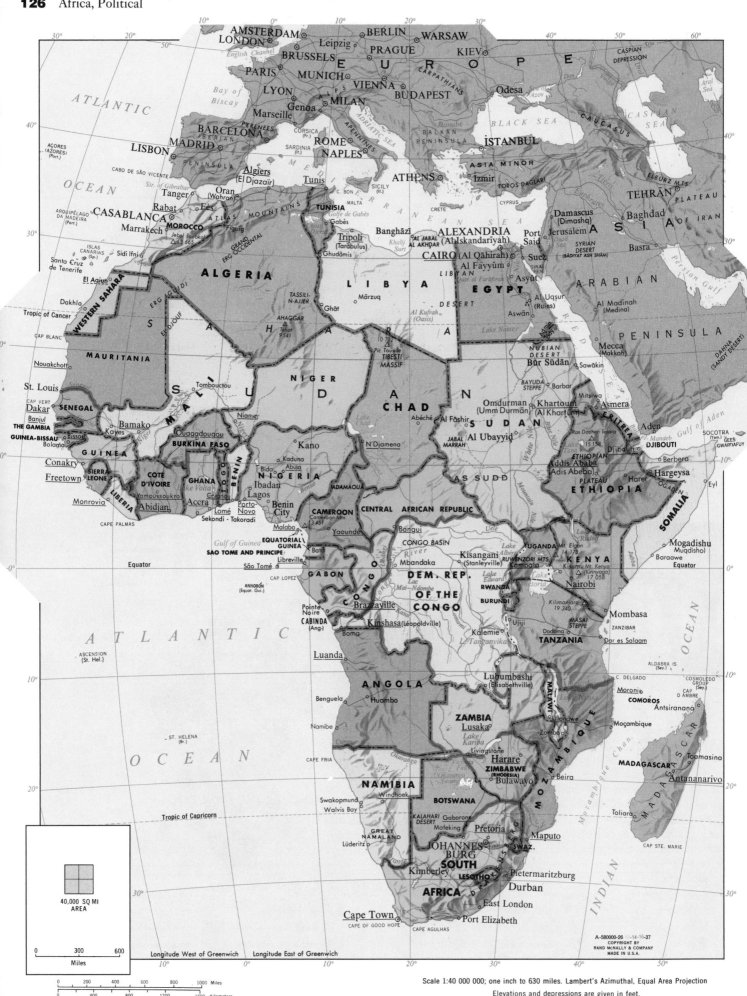

Scale 1:40 000 000; one inch to 630 miles. Lambert's Azimuthal, Equal Area Projection
Elevations and depressions are given in feet.

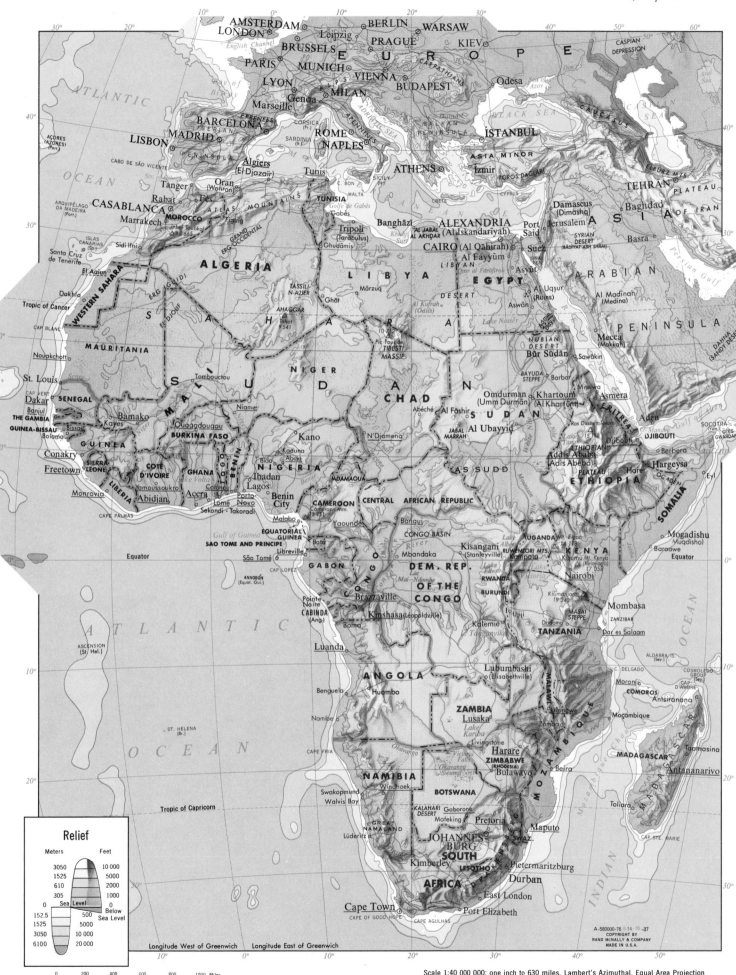

Relief

Meters		Feet
3050		10 000
1525		5000
610		2000
305		1000
0	Sea Level	0
152.5		500
1525		5000
3050		10 000
6100		20 000

Below Sea Level

Longitude West of Greenwich   Longitude East of Greenwich

0	200	400	600	800	1000 Miles
0	400		800	1200	1600 Kilometers

Scale 1:40 000 000; one inch to 630 miles. Lambert's Azimuthal, Equal Area Projection
Elevations and depressions are given in feet.

A-580000-76 8-14-16 -37
COPYRIGHT BY
RAND McNALLY & COMPANY
MADE IN U.S.A.

a

AÇORES (AZORES)
(Port.)
©RMCN.
FAIAL
GRACIOSA
PICO
TERCEIRA
SÃO JORGE
SÃO MIGUEL
Ponta Delgada
STA. MARIA
Same scale as main map

SPAIN
Cádiz
Sr. of Gibraltar
Gibraltar (U.K.)
Ceuta (Sp.)
Tanger (Tangier)
Larache
Ouezzane
Tetouan
Melilla (Sp.)
Beni Saf
Oran
Sidi bel Abbès
Saïda
Tilimsen
Ghilizane
Mestghanem
Mostaganem
Ech Cheliff
Tihert
Algiers (El-Djazaïr)
Cherchell
Delles
Tizi-Ouzou
Bejaïa (Bougie)
El Boulaïda
Stif
Millyya
Mauaskar
El Kseur
Bône
TUN
Skikda
Annaba
Guelma
Constantine
Batna
Beskra
El Djelfa
Laghouat
Aflou
El Aflou
Ghardaïa
Wargla
Touggourt
El Wad

Sala
Rabat
Casablanca
Azemmour
El Jadida
Settat
Oued-Zem
Fès
Taza
Meknès
Kasba-Tadla
Boudenib
Figuig
Igli
Béchar
Aïn-Sefra
MOROCCO
ATLAS MOUNTAINS
Safi (Asfi)
Marrakech
Essaouira
Demnat
Jebel Toubkal 13,665
Agadir
Taroudant
ANTI ATLAS
Tiznit
Sidi Ifni
Béni Abbès
GRAND ERG OCCIDENTAL
GRAND ERG ORIENTAL
Timimoun
El Menia
Hassi Messaoud
In Am
Ghur

ISLAS CANARIAS (Sp.)
LA PALMA
TENERIFE
San Sebastián
Sta. Cruz de Tenerife
GOMERA
HIERRO
GRAN CANARIA
Las Palmas de Gran Canaria
LANZAROTE
FUERTEVENTURA
CAP DRÄA
C. YUBY

El Aaiún
CABO BOJADOR
The Western Sahara is occupied by Morocco
WESTERN SAHARA

Adrar
In Salah
PLATEAU DU TADEMAIT
Bordj Omar Idriss
PLATEAU DU TINGHERT
Illizi

Dakhla
Tropic of Cancer
Fdérik
ERG IGUIDI
ERG CHECH
TIDIKELT
TASSILI-N-AJJER
Djanet

Tindouf
Chenachane
EL HANK
TANEZROUFT
Ouallene
Gh

S A H A R A
EL DJOUF
Taoudenni
AHAGGAR
Tahat 9,541
Tamenghest
Oued Tamenghi

Nouadhibou
CAP BLANC
CAP D'ARGUIN
Atar
Chinguetti
OUARANE
EL MREYYÉ
Mabrouk
Araouane
Kidal
ADRAR DES IFOGHAS
TUAREG
Mt. Gréboun 6,562
Iferouâne
Monts Tamgak 5,906

Nouâmrhar
CAP TIMIRIS
Akjoujt
VALLÉE DU TILEMSI
Monts Bagzane 6,300
AÏR
Agadez
Monts Bagzane

MAURITANIA
Nouakchott
Boutilimit
Tidjikdja
MALI
Tombouctou (Timbuktu)
Bamba
Gao
NIGER

Saint-Louis
Podor
Dagana
Aleg
Kiffa
Néma
Ouâlata
Gourma
Bourem
Tahoua

Louga
Matam
Sélibaby
Mbout
Nioro du Sahel
Nara
Niafounké
Goundam
Tessaoua
Zinder
Goure

Linguère
Kaédi
Bakel
Nioro du Sahel
Sokolo
Mopti
Tillabéry
Madaoua
Maradi

DAKAR
CAP VERT
Rufisque
Diourbel
Thiès
Kaolack
SENEGAL
Tambacounda
Kayes
Bafoulabé
Kita
Satadougou
Goumbou
Ségou
Djenné
San
Bandiagara
Dori
Niamey
Say
Dosso
Sokoto
Kaura Namoda
Birnin Kebbi
Katsina
Gumel
Hadejia
Nguru

THE GAMBIA
Banjul
Ziguinchor
GUINEA-BISSAU
Bissau
Bolama
Buba
Koumbia
FOUTA DJALLON
Labé
Mt. du Tomgué 5046
Siguiri
Bougouni
Sikasso
Bobo-Dioulasso
BURKINA FASO
Ouagadougou
Dédougou
Koudougou
Tenkodogo
Kaya
Ouahigouya
Fada N'gourma
Malanville
Kandi
Gusau
Gummi
Kano
Gaya
Zaria
Kontagora
Zungeru
Kaduna
Bauchi
Gombe

ARQUIPELAGO DOS BIJAGOS
Boké
Boffa
GUINEA
Timbo
Mamou
Kouroussa
Kankan
Koutiala
Gaoua
Gambaga
Sansanné-Mango
Natitingou
Illo
Minna
Jos
Boffao
Kindia
Forécariah

Conakry
Makeni
Kabala
Kissidougou
Beyla
Odienné
Korhogo
KONG
Kong
Tamale
Yendi
Sokode
Parakou
Jebba
NIGERIA
Abuja
Keffi
Ibi

SIERRA LEONE
Freetown
Moyamba
Bonthe
Pandembu
Kolahun
Kabala
Séguéla
Dabakala
Bouna
Bole
Savalou
Atakpamé
Baro
Iseyin
Oyo
Ilorin
Ogbomosho
Bida
Lokoja
Makurdi
Katsina Ala
GOTE

Bomi Hills
Moyamba
Mont Nimba 5748
Boyaké
Bouaflé
GHANA
Kintampo
TOGO
Savé
Pobé
Ibadan
Iwo
Oshogbo
Ilesha
Ife
Idah
Enugu

Robertsport
Monrovia
LIBERIA
Buchanan
COTE D'IVOIRE (IVORY COAST)
Yamoussoukro
Kumasi
Koforidua
Abomey
Palime
Anecho
Abeokuta
Ijebu Ode
Benin City
Onitsha
Sapele
Warri
Owerri
Aba
Port Harcourt
CAM

River Cess
Greenville
Abidjan
Port-Bouët
Tarkwa
Accra
Ada
Porto-Novo
Lagos
Forcados
Calabar
Kumba
Yao

CAPE PALMAS
Harper
Tabou
Grand Lahou
Grand Bassam
Assini
THREE POINTS
Cape Coast
Saltpond
Sekondi-Takoradi
Bignt of Benin
Brass
Bonny
Cameroon Mtn. 13,451
Limbé
Douala
Edéa

ATLANTIC OCEAN
GULF OF GUINEA
EQUATORIAL GUINEA
Bata
RIO MUNI
Malabo
BIOKO
SÃO TOMÉ AND PRINCIPE
ILHA DO PRINCIPE
Kribi
Campo
Ebo
ILHA DE SÃO TOMÉ
São Tomé
Bight of Biafra
Libreville

b

SANTA ANTÃO
SÃO VINCENTE
SÃO NICOLAU
SAL
BOA VISTA
CAPE VERDE
MAIO
SÃO TIAGO
FOGO
Praia
Same scale as main map
©RMCN.

A-589100-76
COPYRIGHT BY
RAND McNALLY & COMPANY
MADE IN U.S.A.

Longitude West of Greenwich
Longitude East of Greenwich

Scale 1:16 000 000; one inch to 250 miles. Sinusoidal Projection
Elevations and depressions are given in feet

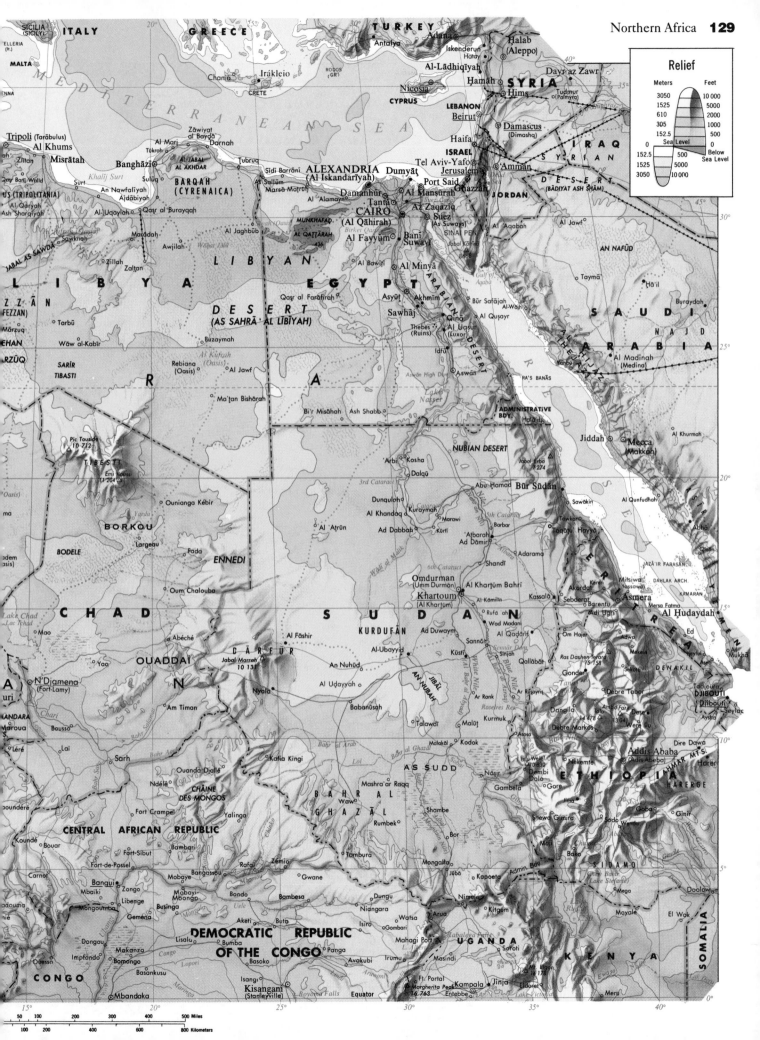

Relief

Meters	Feet
3050	10 000
1525	5000
610	2000
305	1000
152.5	500
Sea Level	0
	Below
152.5	500
1525	5000
3050	10 000
	Sea Level

SICILIA (SICILY)
ITALY
GREECE
TURKEY
MALTA
PANTELLERIA (It.)
ENNA

MEDITERRANEAN SEA

Antalya
Adana
Iskenderun
Ḥalab (Aleppo)
Hatay
Al-Lādhiqīyah
Dayr az Zawr
Ḥamāh
SYRIA
Ḥimş
Tudmur (Palmyra)
Chania
Irákleio
CRETE
RODOS (GR)
Nicosia
CYPRUS
LEBANON
Beirut
Damascus (Dimashq)
IRAQ

Tripoli (Tarābulus)
Al Khums
Misrātah
Zliten
Qaşr Bani Walid
US (TRIPOLITANIA)
Zāwiyat al Bayḍā
Al Marj
Tükroh
Darnah
AL JABAL AL AKHDAR
Ţubruq
Banghāzī
BARQAH (CYRENAICA)
Suluq
Sīdi Barrāni
As Sallūm
Marsá Maţrūḥ
ALEXANDRIA (Al Iskandarīyah)
Dumyāţ
Port Said
Az Zaqāzīq
Suez (As Suways)
Haifa
Tel Aviv-Yafo
Jerusalem
Ghazzah
ISRAEL
Amman
JORDAN
SYRIAN DESERT (BĀDIYAT ASH SHĀM)
Al 'Aqabah
Al Jawf
AN NAFŪD
SAUDI ARABIA
Ḥā'il
Buraydah
NAJD

An Nawfalīyah
Ajdābiyah
Surt
Qaşr al Burayqah
Al Uqaylah
Al Qāryah Ash Sharqīyah
Damanhūr
Tanta
Al Mansūrah
CAIRO (Al Qāhirah)
Al Fayyūm
Bani Suwayf
'Al 'Alamayn
Birket Qārūn
Jabal Kātrinā
SINAI PEN
JABAL AS SAWDA
Sawknah
Marādah
Awjilah
Wāḥat Jālū
Al Jaghbūb
MUNKHAFAD AL QAṬṬĀRAH 436
Al Baḥrīyah
Al Minyā
ARABIAN
Taymā
Zillah
Zaltan
LIBYAN
EGYPT
Qaşr al Farāfirah
Asyūṭ
Akhmīm
Sawhāj
Bür Safājah
Al-Wajh
DESERT
Al Madīnah (Medina)
Yanbu'
AL ḤIJAZ
Tarbū
Buzaymah
DESERT (AS SAHRĀ' AL LĪBĪYAH)
Qinā
Al Quşayr
Thebes (Ruins)
Al Uqşur (Luxor)
FEZZAN)
Mā/zuq
WĀW al-Kabīr
Idfū
RZŪQ
SARĪR TIBASTI
Rebiana (Oasis)
Al Jawf
Al Kufrah (Oasis)
Aswān High Dam
Aswān
RA'S BANĀS
Ma'ţan Bishārah
Lake Nasser
Bi'r Misāhah
Ash Shabb
ADMINISTRATIVE BDY.
Halā'ib
Jiddah
Mecca (Makkah)
Al Khurmah

Pic Toussidé 10 712
TIBESTI
Emi Koussi 11 204
Ouninanga Kébir
Yarda
BORKOU
BODELE
Largeau
FADA
ENNEDI
Oum Chalouba
'Arbi
Kosha
Dalqū
NUBIAN DESERT
Jabal 'Erba 7 274
3rd Cataract
4th Cataract
Abu Ḥamad
Bür Südän
Sawākin
Al Qunfudhah
Abhā
Dunqulah
Al Khandaq
Kuraymah
Marawi
5th Cataract
Tawkar
Ţaqaţu Ḥayyā
JAZĀ'IR FARASAN
Ad Dabbah
Kürti
Barbar
Kassalā
Adarama
KAMARAN
Lake Chad
Lac Tchad
Mao
CHAD
SUDAN
KURDUFĀN
Ad Duwaym
Shandī
6th Cataract
Omdurman (Umm Durmān)
Al Khartūm Bahrī
Akordat
Keren
Miţsiwa
Nassawa
DAHLAK ARCH.
Asmera
Al Ḥudaydah
BODELE
Abéché
DĀRFŪR
Al Fāshir
Jabal Marrah 10 131
Al-Ubayyid
An Nuhūd
Sannār
Al Qaḍārif
Ras Dashen Terara 15 158
Gonder
ERITREA
DENAKIL
DJIBOUTI
Djibouti
YEMEN
Al Mukhā
OUADDAÏ
Yao
N'Djamena (Fort-Lamy)
MANDARA
Maroua
Bousso
Léré
Laï
Sarh
Am Timan
Nyala
An Uḍayyah
Babanūsah
Talawdī
Kurmuk
Asosa
JIBĀL AN NUBAH
White Nile
Blue Nile
Sinjah
Sennar Dam
Qallābāt
Ar Rank
Roseires Res.
Kurmuk
Dangila
Debre Tabor
Debre Markos
Amba Farit 13 042
Dese
Were llu
Dire Dawa
Harer
HARERGE
ADDIS ABABA (Adis Abeba)
ETHIOPIA
Malakāl
Kodok
Nāşir
Gambela
Gore
Jima
Sodo
Wendo
Ginir
Goba
SIDAMO
CHAÎNE DES MONGOS
Ndélé
Yalinga
BAHR AL GHAZĀL
Mashra'ar Raqq
Shambe
Rumbek
Bor
AS SUDD
Juba
Kapoeta
Admin. Bdy.
Mega
Moyale
El Wak
CENTRAL AFRICAN REPUBLIC
Bouar
Fort-Sibut
Fort-de-Possel
Carnot
Bambari
Rafaï
Zémio
Gwane
Mongalla
Mega
Bangui
Mbaïki
Zongo
Mobaye
Bangassou
Bondo
Bambesa
Dungu
Niangara
Isiro
Watsa
Gombari
Arua
Kitgum
Lake Stefanie
Koundé
Mongoumba
Businga
Gemena
Aketi
Buta
Mahagi Port
UGANDA
Soroti
SOMALIA
KENYA
Doolow
Bomongo
Basankusu
Lisala
Bumba
Panga
Avakubi
Irumu
Masindi
Moyale
DEMOCRATIC REPUBLIC OF THE CONGO
Mt. Elgon 14 178
CONGO
Dongou
Makanza
Impfondo
Bomongo
Ouesso
Mbandaka
Isangi
Kisangani (Stanleyville)
Boyoma Falls
Equator
Ft. Portal
Margherita Peak 16 763
Kampala
Jinja
Lake Victoria
Entebbe
Eldoret
Meru

50 100 200 300 400 500 Miles
100 200 400 600 800 Kilometers

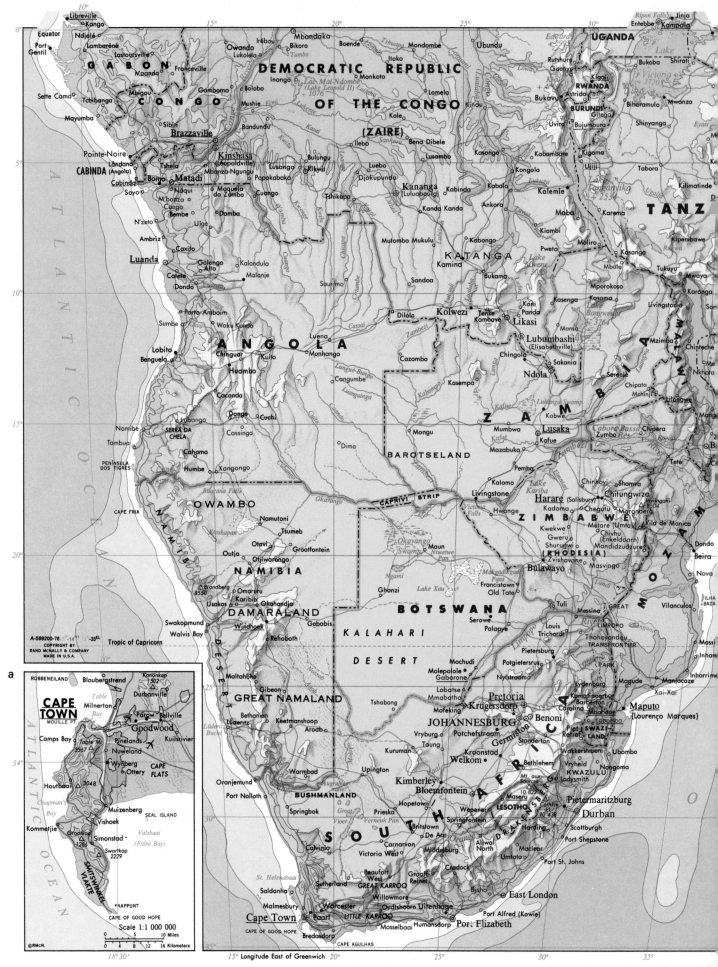

Scale 1:16 000 000; one inch to 250 miles. Sinusoidal Projection
Elevations and depressions are given in feet

b

Mt. Kenya
(Kirinyaga)
r.Hall 17058
airobi

SOMALIA
Kismaayo
Buur Gaabo
Witu
Lamu
Malindi
Takaungu
Mombasa
Tanga
Vanga
PEMBA ISLAND
Pangani
ZANZIBAR
Zanzibar
Bagamoyo
Dar es Salaam
Kisaki
Morogoro
MAFIA
Utete
Kilwa Kivinje
Lindi
Mikindani
CABO DELGADO
Masasi
Moçimboa
da Praia
Ibo
Pemba
Lúrio
Memba
Nacala
Moçambique
ILHA ANGOCHE
Angoche

COMOROS
Moroni
NJAZIDJA
MWALI
NZWANI
ALDABRA IS.
(Sey.)
COSMOLEDO GROUP
(Sey.)
ÎLES GLORIEUSES
(Fr.)
Antsiranana
CAP D'AMBRE
Dzaoudzi
MAYOTTE
(Fr.)
NOSY BE
Iharana

Mahajanga
Mandritsara
Maroantsetra
NOSY BORAHA
CAP SAINT-ANDRÉ
Besalampy
Ambatondrazaka
Fenoarivo
Atsinanana
MADAGASCAR
ÎLE JUAN DE NOVA
(Fr.)
Maintirano
Moramanga
Toamasina
Antananarivo
Tsiafajavona
8671
Vatomandry
NOSY BARREN
Antsirabe
Mahanoro
Morondava
Ambositra
BASSAS DA INDIA
(Fr.)
Fianarantsoa
Mananjary
EUROPA
(Fr.)
Morombe
Manakara
Ihosy
Ivohibe
Parafangana
Betroka
Toliara
Mahaly
Trafonomby
8547
Farafafay
CAP STE. MARIE

Equator

Continued on main map of Africa

Longitude East of Greenwich
ERITREA
Red Sea
YEMEN
Al Mukha
Madinat
ash Sha'b
Aden ('Adan)
SOCOTRA
(Yemen)
Hadibu
Aseb
ABD AL-KURI
GEES GWARDAFUY
Obock
Tadjoura
Calula
DJIBOUTI
Djibouti
Seylac
Boosaaso
MAYD
Laas
Qoray
RAS HAFUN
Aysha
Berbera
Karin
Hurdiyo
Shimbiris
7897
Borraan
Booraana
Bender Beyla
Dire Dawa
AHMAR MTS.
Harer
Jijiga
Hargeysa
Laas Caanood
Burco
Degeh Bur
Buuhoodle
NOGAL VALLEY
Eyl
ETHIOPIA
OGADEN
Gaalkacyo
AUDO RANGE
Kelafo
Hobyo
Doolow
Ceel Buur
KENYA
Xuddur
Bulo Berde
Luuq
Cadale
El Wak
Baydhabo
(Baidoa)
Baardheere
(Bardera)
Marka
Afgooye
Saranley
Baraawe
Baadheere
Mogadishu
(Múqdisho)

Location of area shown on the map

EUROPE
ASIA
AFRICA
©RMCN.

Scale 1:16 000 000;
one inch to 250 miles.
A-580051-76

c

NATAL
Clocolan
Pitseng
Estcourt
Kranskop
Eshowe
Teyateyaneng
Mokhotlong
Catkin Pk.
10438
Mooirivier
Greytown
Mapumulo
Machache
9464
Mt. Gilboa
5803
New Hanover
Dalton
Stanger
LESOTHO
Thabana
Ntlenyana
11425
Howick
Wartburg
Roma
Impendle
Pietermaritzburg
Nishoni
5851
Camper
down
Verulam
10159
Bulwer
Richmond
Pinetown
Mohale's
Hoek
8326
Donnybrook
Mid Illovo
Durban
The Twins
8820
Swartberg
7619
Creighton
Isipingo
Zastron
Qacha's Nek
Franklin
Ixopo
Quthing
Matatiele
EASTERN
Umkomaas
9684
Cedarville
Kokstad
Umzinto
Scottburgh
Witberg
2853
Mount
Fletcher
7426
Mt. Currie
7291
Harding
Park Rynie
Herschel
Ben Macdhui
9846
CAPE
Sezela
Lady Grey
Rhodes
Mount Frere
Mount Ayliff
Umtentweni
Port Shepstone
Barkly East
Maclear
Bizana
Uvongo Beach
Margate
Jamestown
Qumbu
Flagstaff
Port Edward
Rossouw
Ugie
8430
Elliot
Tabankulu
Lusikisiki
EASTERN
Molteno
Dordrecht
Indwe
Cala
Tsolo
Libode
Port St. Johns
STORMBERG
Umtata
Ngqeleni
Sterkstroom
Lady Frere
Engcobo
RAME HEAD
Mqanduli
SOUTH
Waverly
Tarkastad
Queenstown
Tsomo
Elliotdale
Tylden
Cofimvaba
Idutywa
Cradock
Whittlesea
Naamakwe
Willowvale
BANKBERG
6606
WINTERBERG
7778
Seymour
Stutterheim
Frankfort
Komga
Butterworth
Kentani
AFRICA
Pearston
Adelaide
Keiskammahoek
Macleantown
Kei Mouth
Somerset East
Bedford
Fort
Beaufort
Bisho
King William
Town
Berlin
Morgan's Bay
Breidbach
East London
Gonubie
Riebeek-Oos
Alicedale
Fort Alice
Peddie
Kidd's Beach
SUURBERGE
Kirkwood
Salem
Bathurst
Hamburg
Addo
Grahamstown
Alexandria
Uitenhage
Port Alfred (Kowie)
SAINT CROIX
ISLAND
BIRD ISLAND
Port Elizabeth
KAAP RECIFE

INDIAN
OCEAN

Scale 1:4 000 000
0 10 20 30 40 Miles
0 10 20 30 40 50 60 Kilometers

Longitude East of Greenwich

Relief

Meters		Feet
3050		10 000
1525		5000
610		2000
305		1000
152.5		500
0	Sea Level	0
152.5		500
1525		5000
3050		10 000

©RMCN.

Asia

Covering nearly one-third of the Earth's land surface, Asia is by far the largest of the seven continents. It is a land of extremes and dramatic physical contrasts, containing nearly every type of landform, and many of them on a vast scale. It boasts the world's lowest point (the Dead Sea), its highest point (Mt. Everest), its highest and largest plateau (the Plateau of Tibet), and its largest inland body of water (the Caspian Sea).

Wide belts of mountain systems cover much of Asia. The Himalayas, which form a great 1,500-mile (2,400-km) arc south of Tibet, are the highest mountains in the world: more than 90 Himalayan peaks rise above 24,000 feet (7,320 m).

The beginnings of civilization can be traced to three distinct areas of Asia: Mesopotamia, around 4000 BC; the Indus River valley, around 3000 BC; and China, around 2000 BC. Eight of the world's major religions—Buddhism, Christianity, Confucianism, Hinduism, Islam, Judaism, Shinto, and Taoism—originated in Asia.

Asia at a glance

Land area:
17,300,000 square miles
(44,900,000 sq km)

Estimated population:
3,761,165,000

Population density:
217/square mile (84/sq km)

Mean elevation: 3,000 feet
(910 m)

Highest point: Mt. Everest,
China (Tibet)-Nepal, 29,028
feet (8,848 m)

Lowest point: Dead Sea,
Israel-Jordan, 1,339 feet
(408 m) below sea level

Longest river: Yangtze
(Chang), 3,900 mi (6,300 km)

Number of countries
(incl. dependencies): 49

Largest independent country:
Russia (Europe/Asia),
6,592,849 square miles
(17,075,400 sq km)

Smallest independent country:
Maldives, 115 square miles
(298 sq km)

**Most populous independent
country:** China, 1,278,720,000

**Least populous independent
country:** Maldives, 315,000

Largest city: Mumbai, India,
pop. 11,914,398

Map labels

Coldest place:
Verkhoyansk, Russia
-90°F (-68°C)

Lowest point:
Dead Sea, Israel-Jordan
1,339 ft (408 m) below sea level

Hottest place:
Tirat Zvi, Israel
129°F (54°C)

Driest place:
Aden, Yemen
1.8 inches (4.6 cm)/year

Wettest place:
Cherrapunji, India
450 inches (1143 cm)/year

Highest point:
Mt. Everest, China (Tibet)-Nepal
29,028 ft (8,848 m)

Poluostrov Kamchatka, Sea of Okhotsk, Siberia, Western Siberian Lowland, Ob', Yenisey, Amur, Sea of Japan, HONSHU, Pacific Ocean, East China Sea, Huang, Yangtze, URALS, Kirghiz Steppe, CAUCASUS, ALTAI MTS., Gobi Desert, TIEN SHAN, PAMIRS, KUNLUN SHAN, Plateau of Tibet, ZAGROS MTS., Plateau of Iran, HIMALAYAS, Indus, Ganges, Arabian Peninsula, Arabian Sea, Deccan, Bay of Bengal, South China Sea, LUZON, Malay Pen., SUMATRA, BORNEO, NEW GUINEA, Equator

Landforms

- Mountains
- Widely spaced mountains
- High tablelands
- Hills and low tablelands
- Plains
- Depresssions, basins
- High tablelands and ice caps
- Mountains and ice caps

Annapurna, one of the highest mountains in the Himalayas

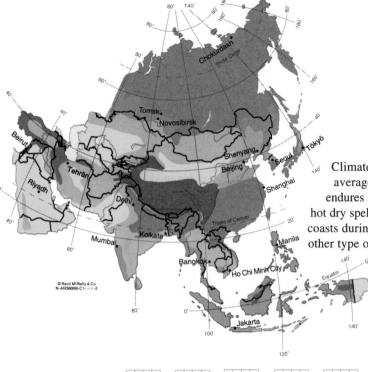

© Rand McNally & Co.
N-ANS60000-C1- -- -3

Climate

Climates vary greatly across Asia. In much of Siberia, temperatures average below -5°F (-20°C) in January, while the Persian Gulf region endures summer temperatures as high as 122°F (50°C). Monsoons interrupt hot dry spells with much-needed rain along the southeast and Indian Ocean coasts during the summer months. Between these extremes, almost every other type of climate on Earth can be found in Asia.

This climatic diversity can be explained by the continent's great expanse, from the Arctic to the tropics, and its great range in elevations.

Tinted areas show temperature in degrees Fahrenheit. Vertical bars show precipitation in inches.

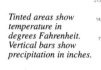

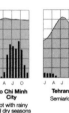
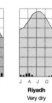

| **Jakarta** Hot and rainy | **Ho Chi Minh City** Hot with rainy and dry seasons | **Tehran** Semiarid | **Riyadh** Very dry | **Beirut** Hot, dry summer / mild, rainy winter | **Shanghai** Warm, humid summer / mild winter | **Shenyang** Warm, humid summer / cold, snowy winter | **Novosibirsk** Cool, humid summer / cold, snowy winter | **Tomsk** Short, cool, humid summer / very cold, snowy winter | **Chokurdakh** Cold and dry | **Extensive uplands** Climate varies with elevation and latitude |

Population

With close to 3.8 billion people, Asia is nearly five times as populous as any other continent and is home to more than one out of every two people in the world. If its current annual growth rate continues, Asia's population will exceed 5 billion by the year 2030. The continent contains the two most populous countries in the world, China and India, as well as the most populous metropolitan area, Tōkyō-Yokohama, Japan.

Great concentrations of people are found in India, eastern China, Japan, Vietnam, and on the Indonesian island of Java. In contrast, vast stretches of northern Siberia, Mongolia, western China, and the Arabian Peninsula are only sparsely populated. Numerous desert regions, including Arabia's Rub' al Khālī and China's Takla Makān, are uninhabited.

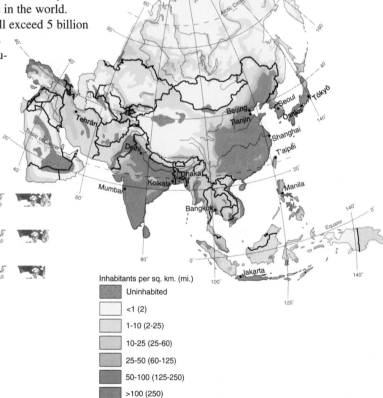

Inhabitants per sq. km. (mi.)

	Uninhabited
	<1 (2)
	1-10 (2-25)
	10-25 (25-60)
	25-50 (60-125)
	50-100 (125-250)
	>100 (250)

© Rand McNally & Co.
N-ANS60000-T1- -- -3

Fastest-Growing Countries

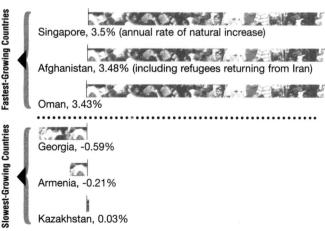

Singapore, 3.5% (annual rate of natural increase)

Afghanistan, 3.48% (including refugees returning from Iran)

Oman, 3.43%

Slowest-Growing Countries

Georgia, -0.59%

Armenia, -0.21%

Kazakhstan, 0.03%

Environments and Land Use

Despite rapid industrialization in Japan, Korea, and Singapore, feeding the enormous and fast-growing population remains Asia's primary economic focus. In China, India, and Indonesia, two-thirds of the work force is engaged in farming. Where arable land exists, it is generally cultivated intensively. Rice is the most commonly grown crop: the continent produces more than 90% of the world's total. Other important crops include wheat, sorghum, millet, maize, and barley.

Asia's major agricultural regions are found in the fertile alluvial valleys, floodplains, and deltas of some of its greatest rivers, such as the Ganges and Brahmaputra in northern India, the Indus in Pakistan, the Huang (Yellow) and Yangtze in eastern China, the Irawaddy in Myanmar (Burma), the Mekong in Cambodia and Vietnam, and the Tigris and Euphrates in Iraq.

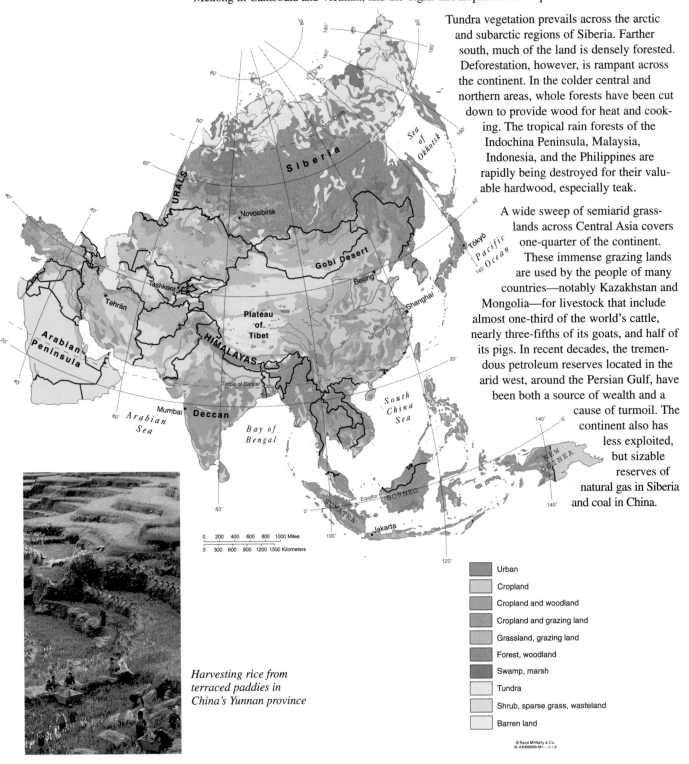

Tundra vegetation prevails across the arctic and subarctic regions of Siberia. Farther south, much of the land is densely forested. Deforestation, however, is rampant across the continent. In the colder central and northern areas, whole forests have been cut down to provide wood for heat and cooking. The tropical rain forests of the Indochina Peninsula, Malaysia, Indonesia, and the Philippines are rapidly being destroyed for their valuable hardwood, especially teak.

A wide sweep of semiarid grasslands across Central Asia covers one-quarter of the continent. These immense grazing lands are used by the people of many countries—notably Kazakhstan and Mongolia—for livestock that include almost one-third of the world's cattle, nearly three-fifths of its goats, and half of its pigs. In recent decades, the tremendous petroleum reserves located in the arid west, around the Persian Gulf, have been both a source of wealth and a cause of turmoil. The continent also has less exploited, but sizable reserves of natural gas in Siberia and coal in China.

Harvesting rice from terraced paddies in China's Yunnan province

	Urban
	Cropland
	Cropland and woodland
	Cropland and grazing land
	Grassland, grazing land
	Forest, woodland
	Swamp, marsh
	Tundra
	Shrub, sparse grass, wasteland
	Barren land

© Rand McNally & Co.
N-ANS60000-M1- -3-7-3

Asia and the Ring of Fire

"Ring of Fire" is the dramatic name given to the volcanoes that nearly encircle the Pacific Ocean. Its existence is explained by plate tectonic theory. According to the theory, Earth's thin crust is broken into sections or plates that move relative to each other. (See Plate Tectonics, pages 12 and 13.)

The giant Pacific plate submerges beneath other plates and plunges into Earth's hot interior, creating deep ocean trenches and causing magma to rise to the surface and erupt as volcanoes. The moving plates also trigger thousands of earthquakes that rumble along the Ring of Fire every year.

The Asian section of the Ring of Fire starts in the north on the Kamchatka Peninsula; swings down through the Kuril Islands; and includes Japan, Taiwan, the Philippines, and Indonesia.

The Kamchatka Peninsula, about the size of California, has more than 100 volcanoes. About 20 of these are active. Klyuchevskaya, the largest active volcano in Kamchatka, and in Eurasia, puts out about 60 million tons of basalt a year.

Japan is one of the most earthquake-prone regions in the world. Four plates come together at Japan, and their movement against each other creates constant strain on the earth's crust. In 1995, an earthquake at Kōbe resulted in 5,500 fatalities. Japan's most deadly quake was in 1923, when more than 140,000 lives were lost.

Mt. Pinatubo, Philippines

The largest volcanic eruption in recorded history occurred in Indonesia. In 1815, Mt. Tambora spewed a column of ash 28 miles into the air. The fallout ruined crops, causing widespread famine. 82,000 people died as a result of Tambora's eruption, most of them from starvation. Gases from Tambora circled the globe and lowered world temperatures by as much as 5°. In 1816, the "year without summer", killing frosts during summer months destroyed crops in Europe and North America.

The 1991 eruption of Mt. Pinatubo in the Philippines was the second largest volcanic eruption of the 20th century, and approximately ten times as large as Mt. St. Helen's. Pinatubo blew an ash column about 21 miles into the sky. Although Pinatubo is near a heavily populated area not far from Manila, authorities were able to warn and evacuate residents in advance, preventing what could have been a major disaster.

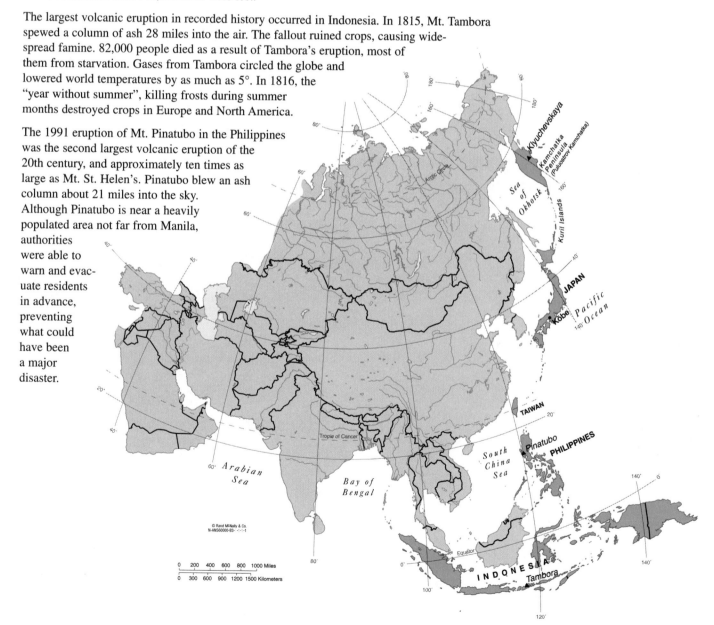

© Rand McNally & Co.
N-ANS60000-B3- -!-:-1

0 200 400 600 800 1000 Miles
0 300 600 900 1200 1500 Kilometers

Scale 1:40 000 000; one inch to 630 miles. Lambert's Azimuthal, Equal Area Projection
Elevations and depressions are given in feet

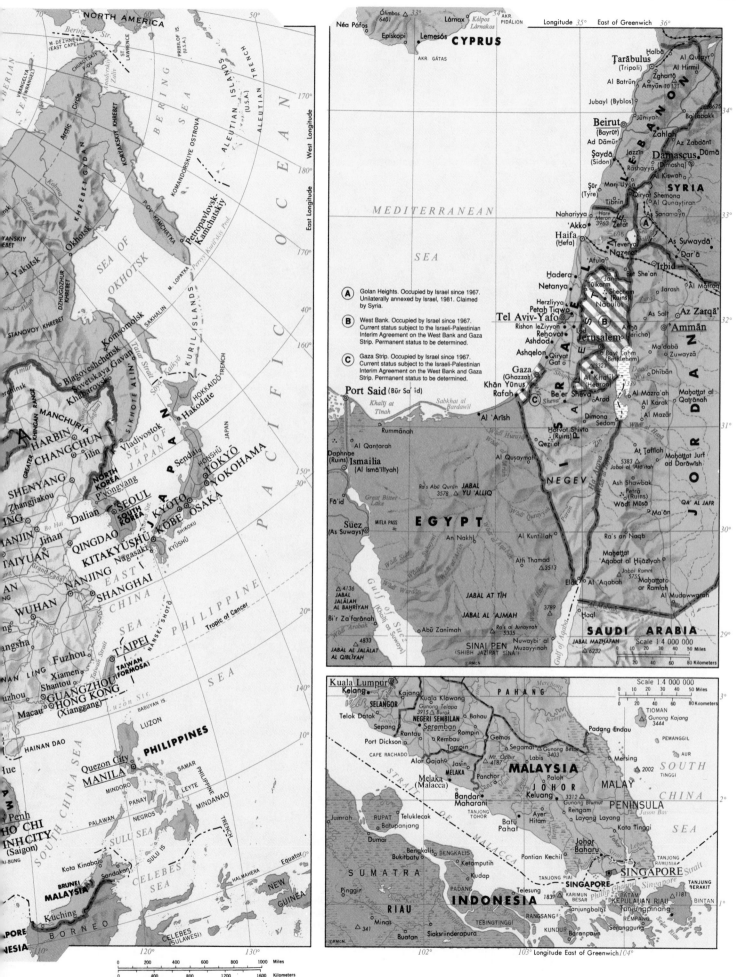

Relief

Meters		Feet
3050		10 000
1525		5000
610		2000
305		1000
0	Sea Level	0
		Below
152.5		Sea Level
		500
1525		5000
3050		10 000
6100		20 000

A-519695-76   '84 26 46
COPYRIGHT BY
RAND McNALLY & COMPANY
MADE IN U.S.A.

Scale 1:40 000 000; one inch to 630 miles. Lambert's Azimuthal, Equal Area Projection
Elevations and depressions are given in feet

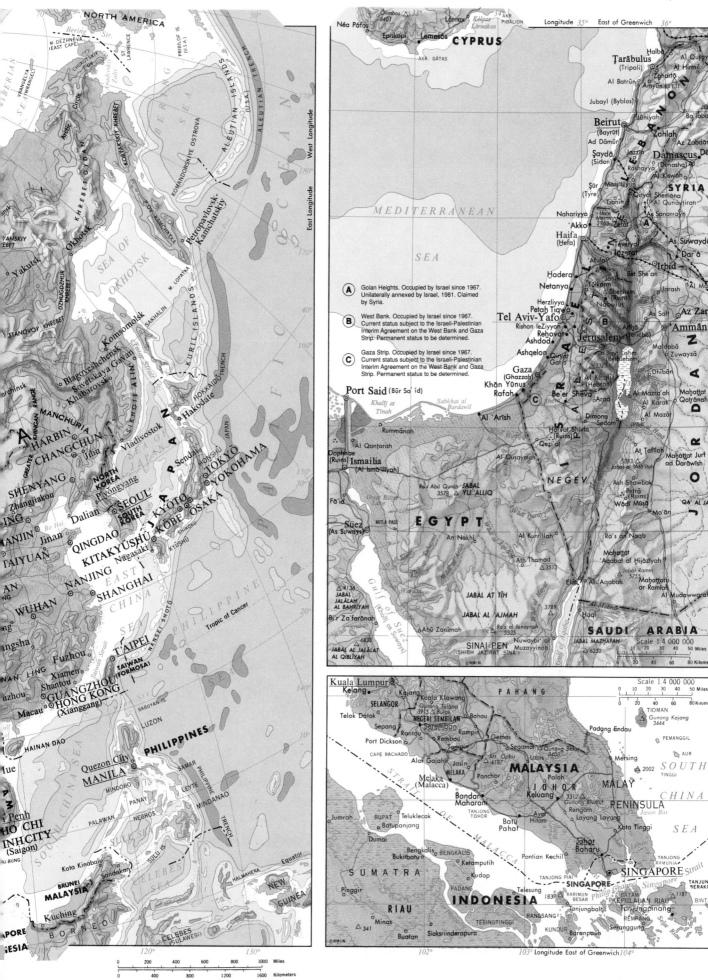

a

NORTH AMERICA

CYPRUS

MEDITERRANEAN

SEA

(A) Golan Heights. Occupied by Israel since 1967. Unilaterally annexed by Israel, 1981. Claimed by Syria.

(B) West Bank. Occupied by Israel since 1967. Current status subject to the Israeli-Palestinian Interim Agreement on the West Bank and Gaza Strip. Permanent status to be determined.

(C) Gaza Strip. Occupied by Israel since 1967. Current status subject to the Israeli-Palestinian Interim Agreement on the West Bank and Gaza Strip. Permanent status to be determined.

Ţarābulus (Tripoli)

Beirut (Bayrūt)

LEBANON

Damascus (Dimashq)

SYRIA

Tel Aviv-Yafo

Jerusalem

Amman

JORDAN

Port Said (Būr Saʿīd)

Ismailia (Al Ismāʿīlīyah)

Suez (As Suways)

EGYPT

NEGEV

SAUDI ARABIA

SINAI PEN (SHIBH JAZĪRAT SĪNĀʾ)

Scale 1:4 000 000
0   20   40   50 Miles
0 20 40 60 80 Kilometers

SIBERIA

Bering Str.

BERING SEA

ALEUTIAN ISLANDS (U.S.A.)

SEA OF OKHOTSK

KURIL ISLANDS

PACIFIC OCEAN

Petropavlovsk-Kamchatskiy

Vladivostok

JAPAN

TOKYO
YOKOHAMA
KYŌTO
OSAKA
KOBE

MANCHURIA

HARBIN
CHANGCHUN
SHENYANG

NORTH KOREA
Pyongyang

SOUTH KOREA
SEOUL

Dalian
QINGDAO

NANJING
SHANGHAI

WUHAN

EAST CHINA SEA

Tropic of Cancer

T'AIPEI
TAIWAN (FORMOSA)

GUANGZHOU
HONG KONG (Xianggang)
Macau

HAINAN DAO

PHILIPPINES

Quezon City
MANILA

LUZON

SAMAR
LEYTE

PALAWAN
PANAY
NEGROS
MINDANAO

PHILIPPINE TRENCH

SOUTH CHINA SEA

HO CHI MINH CITY (Saigon)

BRUNEI
MALAYSIA
Kuching

BORNEO

CELEBES (SULAWESI)

NEW GUINEA

0   200   400   600   800   1000 Miles
0   400   800   1200   1600 Kilometers

b

Kuala Lumpur
Kelang

SELANGOR

PAHANG

NEGERI SEMBILAN
Seremban

MELAKA
Melaka (Malacca)

MALAYSIA

JOHOR

MALAY PENINSULA

Johor Baharu

SINGAPORE

SUMATRA

INDONESIA

RIAU

KEPULAUAN RIAU

STRAIT OF MALACCA

SOUTH CHINA SEA

Scale 1:4 000 000
0   10   20   40   50 Miles
0 20 40 60 80 Kilometers

Cities
and
Towns

0 to 50,000   o

50,000 to 500,000   ⊙

500,000 to 1,000,000   ⊚

1,000,000 and over

85° Longitude East of Greenwich   90°

Scale 1:16 000 000; one inch to 250 miles Conic Project
Elevations and depressions are given in feet.

Relief

Meters		Feet
3050		10 000
1525		5000
610		2000
305		1000
152.5		500
0	Sea Level	0
152.5		500
1525		5000
3050		10 000

BLACK SEA

İstanbul Boğazı (Bosporus)
Marmara Denizi
Troy (Ruins)
Mytilini
İZMİR
Bergama
Kütahya
Bursa
Eskişehir
İstanbul
Zonguldak
Kastamonu
Çankırı
Sinop
Samsun
Çorum
Yozgat
Mazirgan
Giresun
Trabzon
Tokat
Sivas
Erzincan
RUSSIA
CAUCASUS
Vladikavkaz
Groznyy
Kutaisi
Pot'i
Batumi
GEORGIA
Tbilisi
Derbent
Makhachkala
Aqtaū
Fort-Shevchenko
UST-URT PLATEAU
KAZA
UZBEKIST
Kungrad
Chimbay
Nukus
KYZY
TURKESTAN
'KARA-KUM (DESERT)
Khiva
Turtkul'
Charje

T U R K E Y
Ankara
Afyon
Aydın
Muğla
Fethiye
Denizli
Konya
Kahramanmaraş
Kayseri
Malatya
Erzurum
Ağrı
Kars
Gyumri
ARMENIA
Yerevan
AZERBAIJAN
BAKU (Bakı)
Gänca
AZER.
Tabrīz
Ardabīl
Lānkārān
Khvoy
Orūmīyeh
Bandar-e Anzali
Rasht
Bandar-e Torkeman
Chekishler
Nebitdag
Turkmenbashy
Zal. Kara-Bogaz-Gol
CASPIAN SEA
Surface 92 feet below Sea Level
TURKMENISTAN
Ashgabat
KOPPEH DAGH
Bojnūrd
Gushgy
Mary
Charje

Rodos
Antalya
TOROS DAĞLARI
İçel
Tarsus
Adana
İskenderun
Hatay
Gaziantep
Şanlıurfa
Siverek
Mardin
Diyarbakır
Cizre
KÜRDISTAN
Van
Bitlis
Mt. Ararat 16,946
Zanjan
Mianeh
Qazvīn
ELBURZ MTS.
Qolleh-ye Damāvand
Gorgān
Dāmghān
Emāmshahr
Neyshābūr
MASHHAD
Herāt
AFG

CYPRUS
Nicosia
MEDITERRANEAN SEA
Tarābulus (Tripoli)
Al Lādhiqīyah (Latakia)
Ḥimṣ
Ḥamāh
Aleppo
Dayr az Zawr
Al Mawsil
Nineveh
As Sulaymānīyah
Arbīl
Kangāvar
Hamadān
Sanandaj
Kermānshāh
TEHRĀN
Qom
Arāk
DASHT-E KAVIR DESERT
Bajestān
Ferdows
Qāyen
Bīrjand
Qāen

LEBANON
Sayda (Sidon)
Beirut
Haifa
ISRAEL
Tel Aviv-Yafo
Jerusalem
Gaza
Rashīd
Damietta
Port Said
ALEXANDRIA (Al Iskandarīyah)
CAIRO (Al Qāhirah)
Suez (As Suways)
Damascus (Dimashq)
As Suwaydā
Palmyra (Ruins)
Abū Kamāl
Tikrīt
Ar Ramādī
BAGHDAD
Karbalā
An Najaf
Babylon (Ruins)
Karkūk
Bakhtarān
Borūjerd
Qom
Kāshān
Qomsheh
Eşfahān
Daryācheh-ye Namak
DASHT-E LUT (DESERT)
Yazd
Bāfq
PLATEAU OF IRAN
Ţabas
Rīgān
Khāsh
I R A N
Zāhedān
Farāh

Areas occupied by Israel since 1967
JORDAN
Amman
Suez Canal
SINAI PEN
Jabal Kātrīnā 8,690
EGYPT
Būr Safājah
Al Qusayr
At Turayf
SYRIAN DESERT
Al Jawf
Sakākah
Rafḥā
Badanah
An Nāṣirīyah
Al Başrah
Bandar-e Khomeynī
Khorramshahr
Ahvāz
Abādān
KUWAIT
Kuwait (Al Kuwayt)
Dezfūl
Shūshtar
Masjed Soleymān
Kakar
Shīrāz
Kāzerūn
Borāzjān
Bandar-e Būshehr
Jahrom
Lār
Persepolis (Ruins)
Rafsanjān
Kermān
Zāhedān
Bampūr

GULF OF SUEZ
GULF OF AQABA
Al 'Aqabah
Ma'ān
RED SEA
Al Wajh
Khaybar
Taymā
AN NAFŪD
Ḥā'il
JABAL SHAMMAR
Buraydah
'Unayzah
Sudayr
Ash Shaqrā
AD DAHNĀ
AL HASĀ
Al Qaṭīf
Az Zahrān (Dhahran)
Ad Dammām
BAHRAIN
Al Manāmah
QATAR
Ad Dawhah
Abū Ẓaby
UNITED ARAB EMIRATES
RA'S AL KHAYMAH
Al Buraymī
Dubayy
Ajman
OMAN
RA'S AT TANNŪRAH
Al Jubayl
Bandar-e tengeh
Qeshm
Bandar-e 'Abbās
Sīr of Hormuz
QESHM
Jāsk
Bandar Beheshtī
Gwādar

SAUDI ARABIA
NAJD
Al Madīnah (Medina)
Yanbu'
Jabal Radwā 5,000
Riyadh (Ar Riyāḍ)
Al Aflāj
Ad Dilam
Al Hufūf
Al Khurmah
Mubarraz
NAFŪD
AD DAHY
JABAL ṬUWAYQ
AR RUB' AL KHĀLĪ
OMAN
JABAL AL AKHDAR 9,957
Jabal ash Shām
Muscat
Maṭraḥ
Al Khābūrah
Sūr
RA'S AL ḤADD

EGYPT
SUDAN
Būr Sūdān
Sawākin
Ṭawkar
Jiddah
Mecca (Makkah)
Aţ Ṭā'if
Al Qunfudhah
Abha
Qizān
Abū 'Arīsh
Jabal Ibrāhīm
Wādī ad Dawāsir
Al Lidām
Qal'at Bīshah
ARABIA
NAJRAN
Ṣa'dah
Shibām
Tarīm
Sayūn
HADRAMAWT
Mirbāṭ
KHŪRYĀN-MŪRYĀN (Oman)
RA'S AL MADRAKAH
AR

ERITREA
Kassalā
Kereng
Sebderat
Akordat
Mitsiwa (Massawa)
Asmera
Adi Ugri
JAZĀ'IR FARASĀN
DAHLAK ARCH.
KAMARĀN
Al Luhayyah
Hodar Shu'ayb 12,008
Ṣan'ā
RAMLAT AS SAB'ATAYN
Ṭarim
Al Ḥawtah
San'ā
Ḥajjah
Al Ḥudaydah
YEMEN
Ash Shiḥr
Al Mukallā
Sayḥūt
RA'S FARTAK

ETHIOPIA
DENAKIL
Ed
Beylul
Madinat ash Sha'b
Al Mukhā (Mocha)
Jabal Ḥamd 10,729
Aden ('Adan)
Bāb al Mandab
GULF OF ADEN
SUQUTRA (SOCOTRA) (Yemen)
Hadibū
Caluula
GEES GWARDAFUY

DJIBOUTI
Tadjoura
Djibouti
Aysha
Ḥarer
Seylac
Berbera
Lass Qoray
SOMALIA
A-569400-76 11-24-21-43
COPYRIGHT BY
RAND McNALLY & COMPANY
MADE IN U.S.A.

Relief		
Meters		Feet
3050		10 000
1525		5000
610		2000
305		1000
152.5		500
0	Sea Level	0
152.5		500	Below Sea Level
1525		5000
3050		10 000

Longitude East of Green

Scale 1:16 000 000; one inch to 250 miles. Polyconic Projecti
Elevations and depressions are given in feet

Scale 1:4 000 000

Scale 1:40 000 000

1-TRIPURA
2-MANIPUR
3-LAKSHADWEEP
4-DELHI
5-DĀDRA AND NAGAR HAVELI
6-PONDICHERRY
7-GOA, DAMĀN, AND DIU

INDIA · POLITICAL

Area occupied by Pakistan and claimed by India.

Area claimed and occupied by India; status disputed by Pakistan.

Area occupied by China and claimed by India.

Area occupied by India and claimed by China.

SRI LANKA (CEYLON)

Same scale as main map

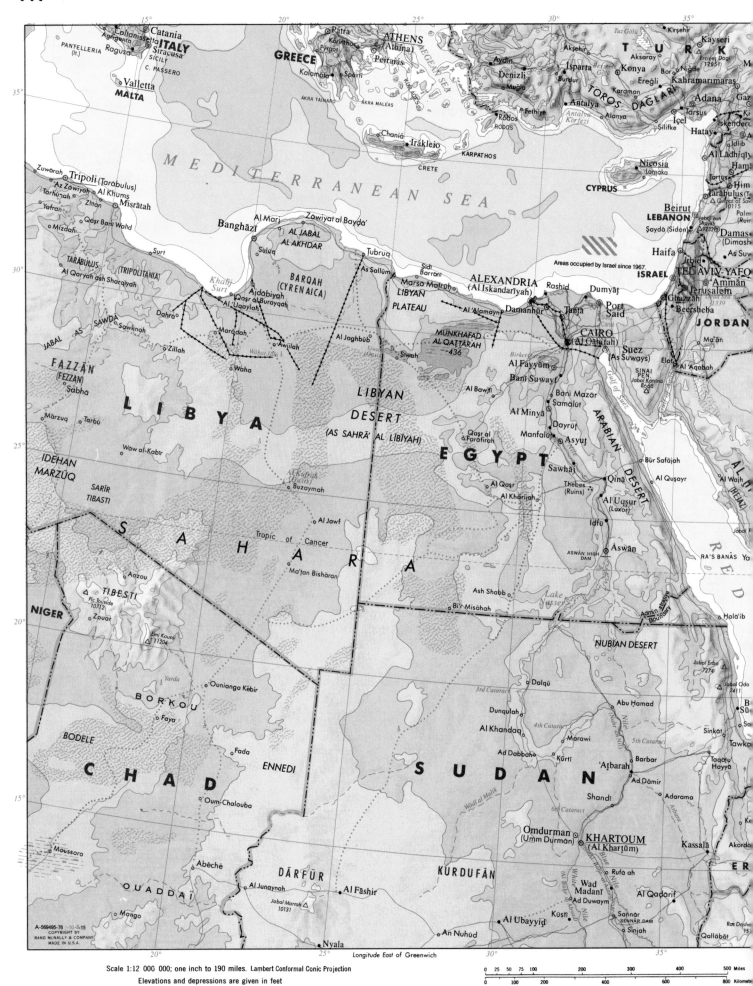

AZERBAIJAN
Yerevan
Erzurum
Mt. Ararat 16854 △
AZER.
BAKU (Bakı)
Turkmenbashy
Celeken
Nebitdag
Gyzylorbat
Kaka
TURKMENISTAN
Ashgabat
KOPPEH DAGH
Mary
Yoloten
Andkhvoy
Naxsıvan
Xankändi (Stepanakert)
Salyan
Länkäran
Astara
CASPIAN SEA
Surface 92 Feet Below Sea Level
Quchan
Meymaneh
Mus
Tatvana
Bitlis
Van
Khvoy
Marand
Ahar
Ardabil
Bandar-e Anzali
Lähijän
Bandar-e Torkeman
Gorgan
Bojnürd
Quchan
Binalud 11208
Neyshabur
Mashhad
Saragt
Tagtabazar

Diyarbakir
KURDISTAN
Orümiyeh
Maragheh
Mianeh
Rasht
Chälüs
Babol
Emämshahr
Sabzevar
Torbat-e Heydariyeh
Torbat-e Jäm
Ghurián
Herät

rfa
Mardin
Zakho
Al Mawsil
Arbil
Tabriz
Zanjan
Qazvin
Qelleh-ye Damgvand 18386
ELBURZ MTS
Kashmar
Ferdows
Qäyen
Birjand
Shindand
AFGHANISTAN

As Sulaymäniyah
Sanandaj
TEHRAN
Rey
Söveh
Qom
DASHT-E KAVIR DESERT
Bejestän
Faräh

Zawr
Abū Kamāl
Hadithah
Tikrit
Samarra
Bayji
Karkūk
Bakhtarän
Arak
Khorramabad
Kashan
I R A N
Na'in
PLATEAU OF IRAN
DASHT-E LUT (DESERT)
Nehbandän
Zaranj

Ar Ramādi
BAGHDAD
Babylon (Ruins)
Al Kūt
Dezfül
Shushtar
Esfahan
Qomsheh
Yazd
Birjand
Chār Borjak

Karbala
An Najaf
As Samāwah
An Nasiriyah
Masjed Soleymän
Haft Gel 14100 △
Surmaq
Rafsanjan
Kerman
Zähedän
CHAGAI HILLS
PAKISTAN

SYRIAN
I R A Q
MESOPOTAMIA
Ahväz
Behbehän
Persepolis (Ruins)
Gachsärän
Kazerün
Shiräz
Daryächeh-ye Bakhtegän
Firgun 10760
Lädiz
Hamūn-i Mäshkel

DESERT
Badanah
Al Başrah
Khorramshahr
Abadan
Bandar-e Khomeyni
Jahrom
Lar
Bandar-e 'Abbäs
Strait of Hormuz
Jäsk
Bampür
Gwädar

Sakākah
Rafha'
KUWAIT
Kuwait (Al Kuwayt)
Bandar-e Büshehr
Daryächeh-ye
Bandar Beheshti
Gwädar

AN NAFÜD
Ha'il
JABAL SHAMMAR
Buraydah
Unayzah
Al Qaysümah
AD DAHNA
AL HASA
Ra's at Tannürah
Al Qatif
Ad Dammäm
Az Zahrän (Dhahran)
BAHRAIN
Al Manämah
QATAR
Dukhän
Bandar-e Lengeh
OMAN
Ash Shäriqah
GULF OF OMAN
At Khäbürah
Muscat

SAUDI
NAJD
Ash Shaqrä'
Al Hufuf
Ad Dawhah
Abū Zaby
UNITED ARAB EMIRATES
Dubayy
JABAL ASH SHAM 2 9957
AL JABAL AL AKHDAR
Shür
RA'S AL HADD

Riyadh (Ar Riyad)
As Sulaymäniyah
AL AFLAJ
AD DAHY
ARABIA
Al Madinah (Medina)
Mahd adh Dhahab
NAFŪD AD DAHY
JABAL TUWAYQ
Al Mubarraz
Al 'Ubaylah
OMAN
AL MASIRAH

Mecca (Makkah)
Al Ta'if
ARABIA
Al Lidäm
AR RUB' AL KHALI
RA'S AL MADRAKAH
Al Jawärah

Al Lith
Qal'at Bishah
KHURYAN MURYAN

ASIR
Al Qunfudhah
Abha
NAJRAN
Mirbat
ARABIAN SEA

JĀZA'IR FARASĀN
Qizän
Sa'dah
RAMLAT AS SAB'ATAYN
Shibam
Say'ün
Al Ghaydah
RA'S FARTAK

Ithwa
DAHLAK ARCH.
cera
KAMARAN
Al Luhayyah
Şan'ä
San'a
YEMEN
HADRAMAWT
Sayhüt
SUQUTRA (SOCOTRA) (Yemen)
Hadibu

Al Hudaydah
Ibb
Ta'izz
Shuqrah
Al Hawrah
Ash Shihr
Al Mukalla

Mekele
Ramfu 6988
DENAKIL
Al Makha (Mocha)
Aseb
Aden ('Adan)
Madinat ash Sha'b
GULF OF ADEN
Calula
GEES GWARDAFUY
Qandala

OPIA
DJIBOUTI
Tadjoura
Obock
Seylac
SOMALIA

Relief		
Meters		Feet
3050		10 000
1525		5000
610		2000
305		1000
152.5		500
	Sea Level	
152.5		500 Below Sea Level
1525		5 000
3050		10 000
6100		20 000

Scale 1:16 000 000; one inch to 250 miles. Polyconic Projection
Elevations and depressions are given in feet

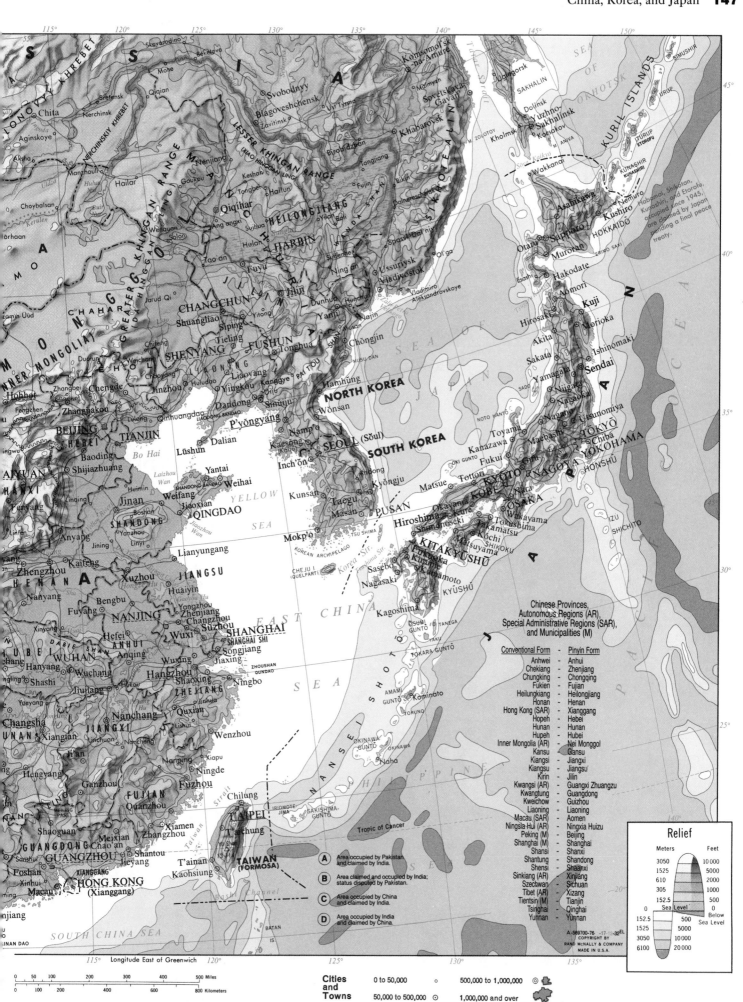

Chinese Provinces,
Autonomous Regions (AR),
Special Administrative Regions (SAR),
and Municipalities (M)

Conventional Form	Pinyin Form
Anhwei	Anhui
Chekiang	Zhenjiang
Chungking	Chongqing
Fūkien	Fujian
Heilungkiang	Heilongjiang
Honan	Henan
Hong Kong (SAR)	Xianggang
Hopeh	Hebei
Hunan	Hunan
Hupeh	Hubei
Inner Mongolia (AR)	Nei Monggol
Kansu	Gansu
Kiangsi	Jiangxi
Kiangsu	Jiangsu
Kirin	Jilin
Kwangsi (AR)	Guangxi Zhuangzu
Kwangtung	Guangdong
Kweichow	Guizhou
Liaoning	Liaoning
Macau (SAR)	Aomen
Ningsia-Hui (AR)	Ningxia Huizu
Peking (M)	Beijing
Shanghai (M)	Shanghai
Shansi	Shanxi
Shantung	Shandong
Shensi	Shaanxi
Sinkiang (AR)	Xinjiang
Szechwan	Sichuan
Tibet (AR)	Xizang
Tientsin (M)	Tianjin
Tsinghai	Qinghai
Yunnan	Yunnan

Ⓐ Area occupied by Pakistan and claimed by India.

Ⓑ Area claimed and occupied by India; status disputed by Pakistan.

Ⓒ Area occupied by China and claimed by India.

Ⓓ Area occupied by India and claimed by China.

Habomai, Shikotan, Kunashiri, and Etorofu, occupied since 1945, are claimed by Japan pending a final peace treaty.

A-569700-76 -17- -30 EL
COPYRIGHT BY
RAND McNALLY & COMPANY
MADE IN U.S.A.

Relief

Meters		Feet
3050		10 000
1525		5000
610		2000
305		1000
152.5		500
0	Sea Level	Sea Level
		Below
152.5		500
1525		5000
3050		10 000
6100		20 000

0 50 100 200 300 400 500 Miles

0 100 200 400 600 800 Kilometers

Longitude East of Greenwich

Cities and Towns

0 to 50,000 ∘

50,000 to 500,000 ⊙

500,000 to 1,000,000 ◎

1,000,000 and over

148

Scale 1:16 000 000; one inch to 250 miles. Polyconic Projection
Elevations and depressions are given in feet

a

PHILIPPINE SEA

PHILIPPINE SEA

SOUTH CHINA SEA

PHILIPPINES

LUZON

MANILA

Quezon City
Pasig
Cavite

POLILLO IS.
POLILLO

Lamon Bay

Laguna
Bay

MINDORO

TABLAS

SIBUYAN SEA

MASBATE

BURIAS

CALAGUAS ISLAND

MARINDUQUE ISLAND

Scale 1:4 000 000

0   10   20   30   40 Miles
0 10 20 30 40 50 60 Kilometers

©RMcN

PHILIPPINES

PHILIPPINE SEA

PHILIPPINE TRENCH

SAMAR
Tacloban
LEYTE
DINAGAT ISLAND

BOHOL

MINDANAO
Davao

PALAU

SONSOROL
ISLANDS

KEPULAUAN
TALAUD

PULAU SANGIHE

PULAU SIAU

MOROTAI

HALMAHERA

KEPULAUAN
MAPIA

PULAU
WAIGEO

Laut
Maluku
(Moluca Sea)

PULAU BACAN

PULAU
TALIBU

PULAU
MANGOLE

KEPULAUAN
SULA

PULAU SANANA

MALUKU
(MOLUCCAS)

CERAM
(SERAM)

SALAWATI

PULAU
MISOOL

JAZIRAH
DOBERAI

Manokwari

Sorong

BIAK

PULAU NUMFOOR

PULAU YAPEN

Teluk Berau

Fakfak

Teluk
Cenderawasih

TG. PERKAM

Jayapura
(Sukarnapura)

PEGUNUNGAN VAN REES

NINIGO GROUP

HERMIT IS.

ADMIRALTY ISLANDS

MANUS
ISLAND

MUSSAU
ISLAND

EMIRA
ISLAND

NEW HANOVER

Kavieng

BISMARCK
ARCH.

NEW
IRELAND

BURU

Ambon

PULAU AMBON

Piru

Bula

PULAU ADI

KEPULAUAN
BANDA

KEPULAUAN
KAI

KAI KECIL

Kaimana

PEGUNUNGAN MAOKE

Puncak Jaya
16 503

Puncak Trikora
15 584

NEW GUINEA

Mt. Wilhelm 14 793

KARKAR ISLAND

LONG ISLAND

Madang

Talasea

WITU
ISLANDS

Rabaul

Kokopo

BISMARCK SEA

BISMARCK

The Father
7546

NEW BRITAIN

I A N

KEPULAUAN
LUCIPARA

Laut Banda
(BANDA SEA)

Dobo

KEPULAUAN
ARU

PULAU
TRANGAN

PULAU
WETAR

DE ATAURO

PULAU
ALOR

PULAU
MOA

PULAU
DAMAR

PULAU
BABAR

YAMDENA

KEPULAUAN
TANIMBAR

PULAU
SELARU

PULAU
YOS
SUDARSA

TANJUNG VALS

Merauke

PAPUA
NEW GUINEA

Mt. Giluwe 14 330

Mt. Bangeta
13 520

Loe

Morobe

Mt. Albert Edward
13 090

Gulf
of Papua

OWEN STANLEY RA.

Buna

Mt. Victoria
13 238

Port Moresby

TROBRIAND IS

WOODLARK
ISLAND

D'ENTRECASTEAUX IS

Samarai

CORAL SEA

Dili

EAST TIMOR

TIMOR

ARAFURA SEA

Daru

Torres Strait

C. YORK

CAPE YORK PEN

GREAT BARRIER REEF

TIMOR
SEA

MELVILLE
ISLAND

COBOURG
PEN

CROKER ISLAND

WESSEL IS

BATHURST
ISLAND

Van
Diemen Gulf

Darwin

C. ARNHEM

AUSTRALIA

Gulf of Carpentaria

Equator

0°

10°

50 100   200   300   500 Miles
100   200   400   600   800 Kilometers

Oceania (including Australia and New Zealand)

Oceania is comprised of Australia, New Zealand, eastern New Guinea, and approximately 25,000 other islands in the South Pacific, most of which are uninhabited. Many of the islands are coral atolls, formed by microscopic creatures over scores of centuries, while others are the result of volcanic action.

Bay of Islands, North Island, New Zealand

Oceania's largest landmass is Australia, which at three million square miles (7.7 million sq km) is the world's smallest continent. In fact, it is smaller than five countries—Russia, Canada, China, Brazil, and the United States. Australia is generally flat and dry. The interior is sparsely populated, with most people living in coastal cities such as Sydney.

The next-largest part of Oceania is Papua New Guinea, the country occupying the eastern half of the island of New Guinea, which has some of the most forbidding and remote terrain in the world. New Zealand, Oceania's third-largest country, is known for its natural beauty and its huge herds of sheep.

Oceania at a glance

Land area: 3,300,000 square miles (8,500,000 sq km)

Estimated population: 31,415,000

Population density: 9.5/square mile (3.7/sq km)

Mean elevation: 1,000 feet (305 m)

Highest point: Mt. Wilhelm, Papua New Guinea, 14,793 feet (4,509 m)

Lowest point: Lake Eyre, South Australia, 52 feet (16 m) below sea level

Longest river: Murray-Darling, 2,330 mi (3,750 km)

Number of countries (incl. dependencies): 33

Largest independent country: Australia, 2,969,910 square miles (7,692,030 sq km)

Smallest independent country: Nauru, 8.0 square miles (21 sq km)

Most populous independent country: Australia, 19,455,000

Least populous independent country: Tuvalu, 11,000

Largest city: Brisbane, pop. 806,746

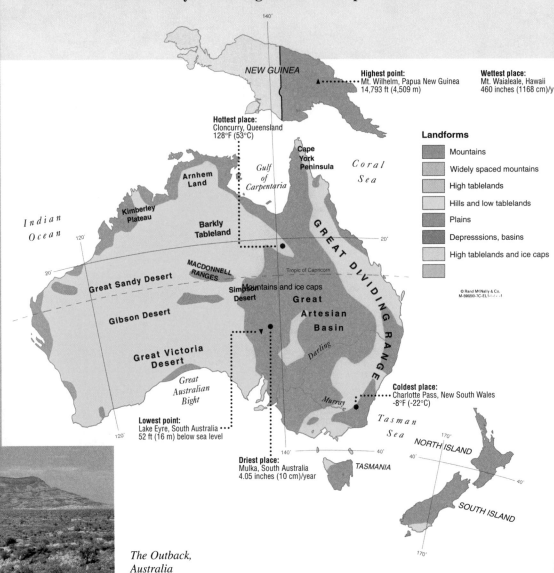

Highest point:
Mt. Wilhelm, Papua New Guinea
14,793 ft (4,509 m)

Wettest place:
Mt. Waialeale, Hawaii
460 inches (1168 cm)/y

Hottest place:
Cloncurry, Queensland
128°F (53°C)

NEW GUINEA

Cape York Peninsula

Coral Sea

Arnhem Land

Gulf of Carpentaria

Kimberley Plateau

Indian Ocean

Barkly Tableland

GREAT DIVIDING RANGE

MACDONNELL RANGES

Great Sandy Desert

Tropic of Capricorn

Simpson Desert

Gibson Desert

Great Artesian Basin

Great Victoria Desert

Darling

Landforms

Mountains
Widely spaced mountains
High tablelands
Hills and low tablelands
Plains
Depresssions, basins
High tablelands and ice caps
Mountains and ice caps

© Rand McNally & Co.
M-590200-7C-EL1-¹-¹-- -1

Great Australian Bight

Murray

Coldest place:
Charlotte Pass, New South Wales
-8°F (-22°C)

Lowest point:
Lake Eyre, South Australia
52 ft (16 m) below sea level

Tasman Sea

NORTH ISLAND

Driest place:
Mulka, South Australia
4.05 inches (10 cm)/year

TASMANIA

SOUTH ISLAND

The Outback, Australia

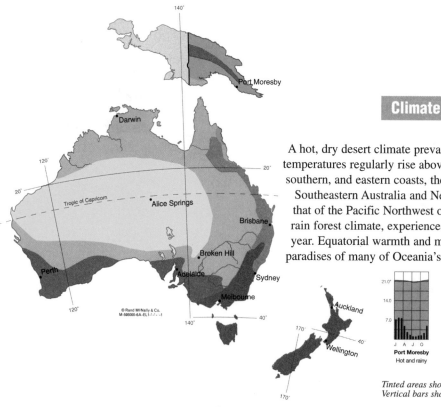

© Rand McNally & Co.
M-595000-6A-EL1-1-1-1

Climate

A hot, dry desert climate prevails in central and western Australia, where summer temperatures regularly rise above 100°F (40°C). Toward the continent's northern, southern, and eastern coasts, the climate becomes more temperate and less arid.

Southeastern Australia and New Zealand enjoy a milder, rainier climate similar to that of the Pacific Northwest of the United States. New Guinea, which has a tropical rain forest climate, experiences heavy rainfall and high temperatures throughout the year. Equatorial warmth and moderating tradewinds combine to make tropical paradises of many of Oceania's islands.

Port Moresby
Hot and rainy

Darwin
Hot with rainy and dry seasons

Broken Hill
Semiarid

Alice Springs
Very dry

Perth
Hot, dry summer / mild, rainy winter

Brisbane
Warm, humid summer / mild winter

Tinted areas show temperature in degrees Fahrenheit. Vertical bars show precipitation in inches.

Wellington
Mild and rainy

Extensive uplands
Climate varies with elevation and latitude

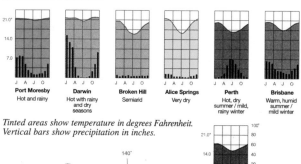

Population

Australia's population is concentrated in the coastal regions, especially along the stretch of southeastern coast that includes Adelaide, Melbourne, Sydney, and Brisbane. Almost all Australians speak English and are descendants of British settlers. In recent years, many immigrants have arrived from Asia, especially Hong Kong. Aboriginal people account for only about 1% of Australia's population. New Zealand has a similar ethnic make-up, but its indigenous people, the Maori, represent about 10% of the population. The North Island is home to approximately three out of four New Zealanders; the South Island, which is more mountainous and heavily forested, is sparsely populated.

Centuries of isolation have given rise to many distinctive cultures among the island groups of Oceania. There has been little immigration from other parts of the world.

Inhabitants per sq. km. (mi.)

- Uninhabited
- <1 (2)
- 1-10 (2-25)
- 10-25 (25-60)
- 25-50 (60-125)
- 50-100 (125-250)
- >100 (250)

© Rand McNally & Co.
M-595000-1P-EL1-1-1-1

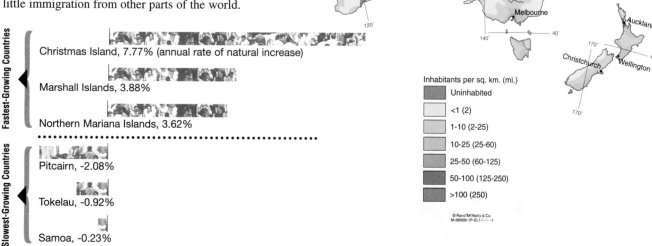

Fastest-Growing Countries

Christmas Island, 7.77% (annual rate of natural increase)

Marshall Islands, 3.88%

Northern Mariana Islands, 3.62%

Slowest-Growing Countries

Pitcairn, -2.08%

Tokelau, -0.92%

Samoa, -0.23%

Environments and Land Use

Much of central and western Australia is a dry, inhospitable land of sand, rocks, and scrub vegetation. Surrounding this desert region is a broad band of semiarid grassland that covers more than half of the continent and supports a huge livestock industry. Australia has more sheep—132 million—than any other country in the world, as well as sizable herds of cattle. The dry climate and sparse plant life, however, mean that each animal requires a dozen or more acres to survive. Six percent of the continent is suitable for crops; most of the arable land is found on fertile plains in the southeast. Major crops include wheat, sugar cane, oats, barley, sorghum, and rice.

Farmland on North Island, New Zealand

Tourism plays an important role in Australia's economy. Among the continent's major attractions are its unusual wildlife, such as kangaroos, koalas, wombats, and platypuses; the Great Barrier Reef, which stretches for 1,250 miles (2,000 km) along the northeastern coast; and the ruggedly beautiful Outback, with its dramatic rock formations such as Ayers Rock (Uluru) and the Olga Rocks.

Thanks to its fertile land and temperate climate, New Zealand has a thriving livestock industry and is a leading world exporter of dairy products and lamb. Thinly populated and with little industry, it is one of the world's least polluted countries. Its pristine beauty encompasses a variety of scenery, including mountains, fjords, glaciers, rain forests, beaches and geysers. Only the country's relative isolation restrains its growing tourism industry.

Dense tropical rain forests blanket much of Papua New Guinea. These forests have thus far escaped the large-scale deforestation that is taking place in other tropical forests around the world.

Tourism is central to the economies of many of the islands throughout Oceania. Abundant sunshine, pleasant temperatures, and beautiful beaches draw millions of visitors each year to islands such as Tahiti and Fiji. For islands with little or no tourism, the economic scene is less promising: many islanders rely on subsistence fishing and foreign aid from former colonial powers.

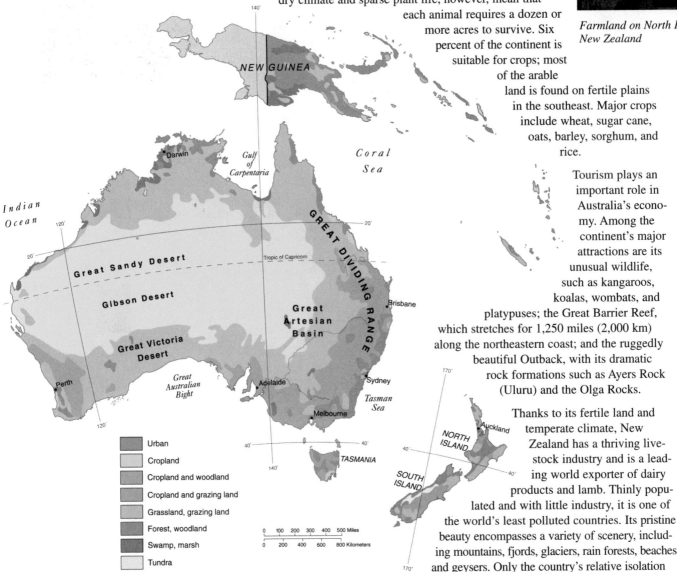

NEW GUINEA

Darwin
Gulf of Carpentaria
Coral Sea

Indian Ocean

Great Sandy Desert
Tropic of Capricorn

Gibson Desert

GREAT DIVIDING RANGE

Brisbane

Great Artesian Basin

Great Victoria Desert

Great Australian Bight

Perth

Adelaide
Sydney
Tasman Sea
Melbourne

TASMANIA

▣	Urban
▣	Cropland
▣	Cropland and woodland
▣	Cropland and grazing land
▣	Grassland, grazing land
▣	Forest, woodland
▣	Swamp, marsh
▣	Tundra
▣	Shrub, sparse grass, wasteland
▣	Barren land

© Rand McNally & Co.
N-ANS95000-M1- -3-3-1

0 100 200 300 400 500 Miles
0 200 400 600 800 Kilometers

NORTH ISLAND
Auckland

SOUTH ISLAND

Herding sheep near Goulburn, New South Wales

The Original Australians and New Zealanders

Many anthropologists believe that Australia's Aborigines are the oldest race of people on Earth. During the 40,000 years since they migrated to the island continent from Asia, they have developed a rich culture with an intricate spiritual and social life.

The original New Zealanders, the Maoris, arrived from other Polynesian islands in the 10th century. At the beginning of large-scale immigration from Britain in the 1800s, the British government signed a treaty with the Maoris which granted them full rights as citizens. With the exception of some disputes over land, this agreement has paved the way for the historically harmonious relations between the races in New Zealand.

Aboriginal boy with elders, Western Australia

Relations between the Aborigines and whites in Australia have been less harmonious. The arrival of the first European colonists in 1788 set in motion a chain of events that decimated the Aborigines and threatened their unique culture. Disease and skirmishes killed Aborigines along the coast, and thousands of others were forced from their lands by settlers. Some sought refuge with Aborigines already living in Australia's interior, the Outback. Alcoholism and other social problems became common among the Aborigines as they found themselves confronted by a society they did not understand.

Australia was slow to recognize the rights of its first inhabitants. In the early 1960s, official attitudes began to change as public embarrassment grew over the decades of discrimination. A significant step occurred in 1962 when full rights of citizenship were extended to the Aborigines.

Questions of land ownership, however, remain problematic for both

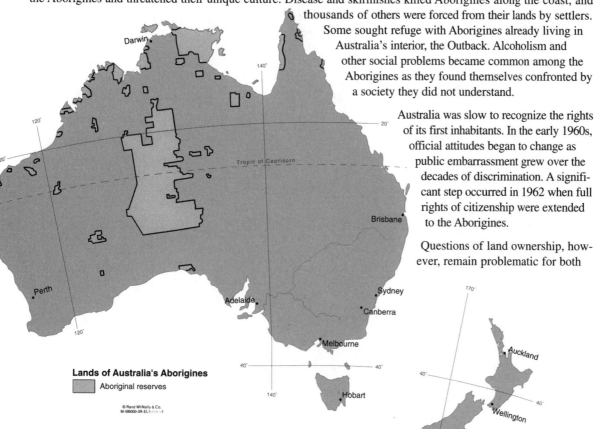

Lands of Australia's Aborigines

Aboriginal reserves

© Rand McNally & Co.
M-595000-3R-EL1-·-·-·-·-1

sides. The government has set aside large reserves for the Aborigines, but much of the land is in the continent's hostile interior (see map above). Only in the past two decades has an agreement been reached allowing Aborigines to share in the vast mineral wealth of their northern lands. Recent court decisions have awarded individual Aborigines rights to ancestral lands which were seized by settlers, but many local governments continue to fight these decisions.

In the face of indifference and hostility, there has recently been an upsurge of interest in cultural traditions among the approximately 240,000 Australians of aboriginal descent. Still, many of the traditions of the 500 different tribes that were present 200 years ago have been lost.

154

Pasuruan
G. Mahameru 12 060
G. Raung
Singaraja
G. Rinjani 225
Sumbawa Besar
Baturi
Lombok Selat
LOMBOK
SUMBAWA
FLORES
Waingapu
SUMBA
SAWU
ROTI
Kupang
TIMOR
Dili
ALOR
LOMBLEN PANTAR
EAST TIMOR

I N D O N E S I A

SELARU
TANJUNG VALS

A R A F U R A   S E A

S U N D A   I S L A N D S

SAVU SEA

TIMOR SEA

SUNDA TRENCH

I N D I A N

O C E A N

CAPE LONDONDERRY

C. VAN DIEMEN
CROKER
MELVILLE
Van Diemen Gulf
BATHURST
Darwin
Clarence Str.
Dundas
COBURG PEN.
WESSEL IS.
CAPE ARNHEM

Joseph Bonaparte Gulf
Anson Bay
Blue Mud Bay
GROOTE EYLANDT
Limmen Bight

ARNHEM LAND
Pine Creek
Katherine

GULF
CARPENTA

SIR EDWARD PELLEW GROUP
WELLES

Wyndham
Mt. Hann 2800
KING LEOPOLD RANGES
BUCCANEER ARCH.
CAPE LEVEQUE
King
Sunday Str.
Collier Bay
Queen Chan.
Victoria
Roper
Woods

Birdum
Victoria River Downs
Borroloola
Newcastle Waters

N O R T H E R N

Burketown

DAMPIER LAND
Broome
Derby
GEIKIE RANGE
Fitzroy Crossing
Halls Creek
Roebuck Bay
LaGrange
Fitzroy
Sturt Cr.

Tanami
Daly Waters
Tennant Creek

Alexandria
Camooweal
Mount Isa
Doi
Dajo
Q

T E R R I T O R Y

EIGHTY MILE BEACH
LARREY POINT
RIPON
Port Hedland
DAMPIER ARCH.
MONTE BELLO IS.
BARROW
Roebourne
Marble Bar
Nullagine
De Grey

Barrow Creek

GREAT SANDY DESERT
Mackay

NORTH WEST CAPE
Onslow
Millstream
HAMERSLEY RANGE
Mt. Bruce 4052
Jiggalong
Fortescue
Ashburton

Mt. Ziel 4955
MACDONNELL RANGES
Arltunga
Alice Springs
JAMES RANGE
Hay

POINT CLOATES
Disappointment
Macdonald
Amadeus

SIMPSON

W E S T E R N

GIBSON DESERT

Uluru (Ayers Rock)
Finke
DESERT

Birdsville

Tropic of Capricorn
CAPE FARQUHAR
Carnarvon
Peak Hill
Nabberu
Carnegie
Wells
Gillen

Charlotte Waters

MUSGRAVE RANGES
Mt. Woodroffe 4724
EVERARD RANGES

Oodnadatta

Geographe
BERNIER
DORRE
Shark Bay
DIRK HARTOG
STEEP POINT
Gascoyne

Meekatharra
Nannine
Cue
Sandstone
Austin

Wiluna
Yeo

STUART RANGE
William Creek
Marree
Farin

Ajana
Northampton
Mount Magnet
Laverton
Carey

S O U T H   A U S T R A L I A

Woomera
Pimba
Paratoo
FLI

HOUTMAN ROCKS
Geraldton
Mingenew
Dongara
Barlee
Moore

Menzies
Ballard
Lefroy
Rebecca
GREAT VICTORIA DESERT

Ooldea Station

Whyalla
Port Pirie
Port Aug
Pet
Glads

A U S T R A L I A

Pithara
Miling
Moora
Lake Brown
Southern Cross
Coolgardie
Kalgoorlie-Boulder
Goldards Soak

Rawlinna
Hughes
Penong
Ceduna

EYRE PENINSULA
Moonta
Wallaroo
Part Wi
Ga
Ac

DARLING RANGE
Perth
Fremantle
Northam
York
SWANLAND
Narrogin
Collie
Bunbury
Busselton
CAPE NATURALISTE
CAPE LEEUWIN
Nornalup
Albany
Katanning
Hopetoun
Ravensthorpe
Esperance
Norseman
Salmon Gums
Dundas
Cowan
Eyre
Eucla
NULLARBOR PLAIN
POINT FOWLER

Penong

Port Lincoln

KANGAROO
King
CAPE JAF
Mt.

Geographe Bay
PT. D'ENTRECASTEAUX
WEST CAPE HOWE
King George Sd.
ARCHIPELAGO OF THE RECHERCHE

GREAT AUSTRALIAN BIGHT

Gulf St. Vincent
Encounter

I N D I A N   O C E A N

40,000 SQ MI AREA

0   100   200
Miles

Longitude 115° East of Greenwich

Scale 1:16 000 000; one inch to 250 miles. Lambert's Azimuthal, Equal Area Project
Elevations and depressions are given in feet

PAPUA NEW GUINEA

W GUINEA

Mt. Albert Edward
11100
Buna
Mt. Victoria
13 363
Port Moresby

Torres Strait
BANKS
HORN
CAPE YORK

TROBRIAND IS.
WOODLARK
D'ENTRECASTEAUX ISLANDS

OWEN STANLEY RA.

SOUTH CAPE
Samarai
LOUISIADE ARCHIPELAGO

TAGULA
ROSSEL

CHOISEUL
VELLA LAVELLA
NEW GEORGIA
RENDOVA
SANTA ISABEL
FLORIDA
RUSSELL IS.
TULAGI
Honiara
GUADALCANAL

SOLOMON ISLANDS

MALAITA

SAN CRISTÓBAL

RENNELL

SANTA CRUZ ISLANDS

TORRES IS.
BANKS ISLANDS

ESPÍRITU SANTO
MAEWO
NEW
PENTECOST
MALEKULA
AMBRIM
HEBRIDES
EPI
VANUATU
EFATE
Port Vila
EROMANGA
TANA

ÎLES BÉLEP
OUVÉA
LIFOU
ÎLES LOYAUTÉ
(French)
ANEITYUM
NEW CALEDONIA
(Fr.)
MARÉ
Noumea
ÎLE DES PINS

ÎLES CHESTERFIELD (Fr.)

Tropic of Capricorn

C O R A L   S E A

P A C I F I C   O C E A N

OSPREY REEF
CAPE MELVILLE
HOLMES REEFS
WILLIS IS.
FLINDERS REEFS
LIHOU REEF
TREGROSSE IS.
MARION REEF
SWAIN REEFS
WRECK REEFS

CAPE YORK PENINSULA

Princess Charlotte Bay

Laura
Cooktown
Palmerville
ATHERTON Cairns
Mungana
Mt. Bartle Frere 5322
PLATEAU
Croydon
Forsayth
Inaham
HINCHINBROOK
Halifax Bay
Townsville
Charters Towers
Bowen
WHITSUNDAY
CUMBERLAND IS.
Repulse Bay
Mt. Dalrymple 4190
Mackay
NORTHUMBERLAND IS.

Richmond
Hughenden
Kynuna
Winton

Gilbert
GREGORY RANGE
Buchanan
Galilee

QUEENSLAND

Longreach
Barcaldine
Jericho
Blackall
Tambo
BUCKLAND TABLELAND
Yaraka

Clermont
Emerald
Dingo
Rockhampton
Mount Morgan
CURTIS
Gladstone

Quilpie
Charleville
Roma
Bundaberg
Hervey Bay
SANDY CAPE
FRASER
Maryborough
Gympie

Thargomindah
St. George
DARLING DOWNS
Dalby
Toowoomba
Ipswich
Brisbane
N. STRADBROKE I.
Southport

Cunnamulla
Dirranbandi
Mungindi
Warwick
Mt. Roberts 3495
Lismore

NEW SOUTH WALES

Hungerford
Brewarrina
Bourke
Walgett
Moree
Narrabri
Inverell
Glen Innes
NEW ENGLAND RANGE
Grafton

Wilcannia
Cobar
Coonamble
Nyngan
Coonabarabran
WARRUMBUNGLE RA.
Tamworth
The Round Mountain
Armidale

Broken Hill
Nymagee
Dubbo
LIVERPOOL RA.
Kempsey
Port Macquarie

Wentworth
Hay
Forbes
Orange
Bathurst
BLUE MTS.
Cessnock
Maitland
Newcastle

RIVERINA
West Wyalong
Cowra
Lithgow
SYDNEY
Botany Bay
Wollongong

Narrandera
Wagga Wagga
Goulburn
Jervis Bay
Canberra
AUSTL. CAP. TER.

MURRAY
Deniliquin
Albury
Mt. Kosciusko 7316

Swan Hill
Kerang
Benalla
Cooma
Bega
Bombala
CAPE HOWE

Echuca
VICTORIA
GREAT
Bendigo
Maryborough
MELBOURNE

Ballarat
Geelong
Bairnsdale
NINETY MILE BEACH

CAPE OTWAY
Warrnambool
Wonthaggi
WILSON'S PROMONTORY

Port Phillip
KING

FLINDERS
FURNEAUX GROUP
CAPE BARREN

HUNTER IS.
Burnie
Ulverstone
Devonport
Launceston

TASMANIA
Mt. Ossa 5305
Strahan
New Norfolk
Risdon
Hobart
BRUNY
SOUTH EAST CAPE

T A S M A N   S E A

LORD HOWE
(NEW S. WALES)

a

NEW ZEALAND

NORTH CAPE
Kaitaia
Russell
GREAT BARRIER
HauraKi Gulf
Devonport
Auckland
NORTH ISLAND
Hamilton
Bay of Plenty
EAST CAPE

North Taranaki Bight
New Plymouth
C. EGMONT
Mt. Egmont
South Taranaki Bight
Wanganui
Gisborne
Hawke Bay
Napier
Hastings
Palmerston North

CAPE FAREWELL
Tasman Bay
Cook Strait
Nelson
Lower Hutt
Wellington

Karamea Bight
CAPE FOULWIND

Greymouth
Hokitika
SOUTHERN ALPS
Pegasus Bay
Christchurch
Canterbury Bight

SOUTH ISLAND
Mt. Cook 12349
Timaru

CASCADE PT.
RESOLUTION ISLAND
Dunedin
CAPE SAUNDERS

Foveaux Str.
Invercargill
STEWART ISLAND
SOUTHWEST CAPE

P A C I F I C   O C E A N

T A S M A N   S E A

Same scale as main map

Cities and Towns

o 0 to 50,000	◉ 500,000 to 1,000,000
⊙ 50,000 to 500,000	1,000,000 and over

0 50 100 200 300 400 500 Miles
0 100 200 400 600 800 Kilometers

Relief

Meters		Feet
3050		10 000
1525		5000
610		2000
305		1000
152.5		500
0	Sea Level	0
152.5		500	Below
1525		5000	Sea Level
3050		10 000
6100		20 000

A-590200-76 7 18EL
COPYRIGHT BY
RAND McNALLY & COMPANY
MADE IN U.S.A.

Longitude 115° East of Greenwich

Scale 1:16 000 000; one inch to 250 miles. Lambert's Azimuthal, Equal Area Projec
Elevations and depressions are given in feet

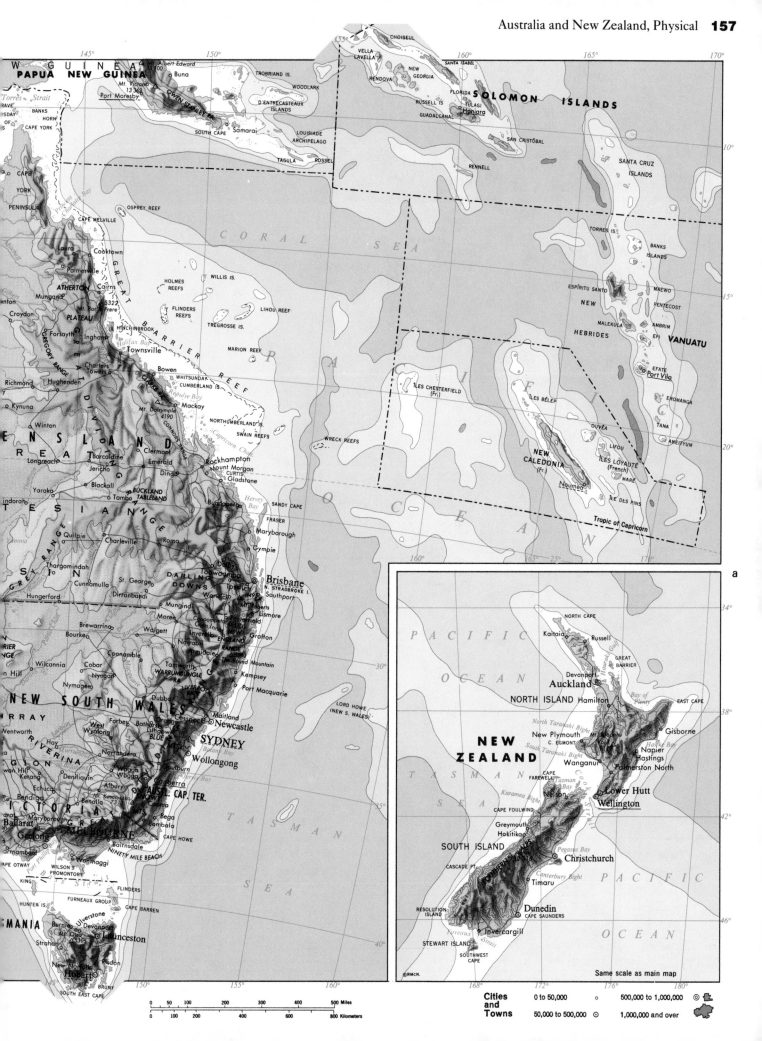

Main Map

W GUINEA
PAPUA NEW GUINEA
Torres Strait
RAVE
SDAY
OF
S
BANKS
HORN
CAPE YORK
Mt. Victoria 13,363
Port Moresby
Mt. Albert Edward 13,100
Buna
OWEN STANLEY RA.
TROBRIAND IS.
WOODLARK
D'ENTRECASTEAUX ISLANDS
SOUTH CAPE
Samarai
LOUISIADE ARCHIPELAGO
TAGULA
ROSSEL

CHOISEUL
VELLA LAVELLA
RENDOVA
NEW GEORGIA
SANTA ISABEL
FLORIDA
RUSSELL IS.
TULAGI
Honiara
GUADALCANAL
SOLOMON ISLANDS
SAN CRISTÓBAL
RENNELL
SANTA CRUZ ISLANDS

CAPE YORK PENINSULA
OSPREY REEF
CAPE MELVILLE

CORAL SEA

TORRES IS.
BANKS ISLANDS

ESPÍRITU SANTO
NEW HEBRIDES
MAEWO
PENTECOST
AMBRIM
EPI
MALEKULA
VANUATU
EROMANGA
EFATE
Port Vila
TANA
ANEITYUM

Laura
Cooktown
Palmerville
ATHERTON
Mungana
Cairns
Mt. Bartle Frere 5,322
Croydon
Forsayth
PLATEAU
Ingham
HINCHINBROOK I.
Halifax Bay
Townsville
HOLMES REEFS
WILLIS IS.
FLINDERS REEFS
LIHOU REEF
TREGROSSE IS.
MARION REEF

ÎLES CHESTERFIELD (Fr.)
ÎLES BÉLEP
OUVÉA
LIFOU
ÎLES LOYAUTÉ (French)
MARÉ
NEW CALEDONIA (Fr.)
Nouméa
ÎLE DES PINS

Richmond
Hughenden
Kynuna
Charters Towers
Bowen
WHITSUNDAY
CUMBERLAND IS.
Repulse Bay
Mackay
Mt. Dalrymple 4,190
NORTHUMBERLAND IS.
SWAIN REEFS
Clermont
Emerald
Dingo
Rockhampton
Mount Morgan
CURTIS I.
Gladstone
CAPRICORN CHAN.

PACIFIC OCEAN

WRECK REEFS

QUEENSLAND
GREAT DIVIDING RANGE
Winton
Longreach
Barcaldine
Jerico
Blackall
BUCKLAND TABLELAND
Tambo
Yaraka
GREGORY RANGE
Quilpie
Charleville
Roma
BUNDABERG
Bundaberg
Hervey Bay
SANDY CAPE
FRASER I.
Maryborough
Gympie
Thargomindah
St. George
DARLING DOWNS
Dalby
Toowoomba
Ipswich
BRISBANE
N. STRADBROKE I.
Southport
Cunnamulla
Dirranbandi
Mungindi
Moree
Warwick
Mt. Roberts 4,495
Lismore
Hungerford

Tropic of Capricorn

GREY RANGE
Thargomindah
Cunnamulla
Brewarrina
Bourke
Walgett
Narrabri
Tamworth
Inverell
Glen Innes
Tenterfield
Grafton
NEW ENGLAND RANGE
Armidale
Round Mountain
BARRIER RANGE
Wilcannia
Cobar
Nyngan
Coonamble
WARRUMBUNGLE RA.
Kempsey
Port Macquarie
Broken Hill
Nymagee
NEW SOUTH WALES
Nyngan
Dubbo
Tamworth
LIVERPOOL
Newcastle
MURRAY
Wentworth
RIVERINA
Hay
West Wyalong
Forbes
Bathurst
Lithgow
Cessnock
Maitland
BLUE MTS.
Hill
Wilcannia
Narrandera
Wagga Wagga
Goulburn
SYDNEY
Wollongong
Botany Bay
swan Hill
Kerang
Deniliquin
Albury
Benalla
Mt. Kosciusko 7,316
AUSTL. CAP. TER.
Canberra
Jervis Bay
Echuca
Bendigo
VICTORIA
Maryborough
GREAT DIVIDING RANGE
Bega
Bombala
CAPE HOWE
Ballarat
MELBOURNE
Geelong
Bairnsdale
NINETY MILE BEACH
CAPE OTWAY
Port Phillip
Wonthaggi
WILSON'S PROMONTORY
KING I.
FLINDERS I.
HUNTER IS.
FURNEAUX GROUP
CAPE BARREN
TASMAN SEA
LORD HOWE (NEW S. WALES)
TASMANIA
Burnie
Ulverstone
Devonport
Mt. Ossa 5,305
Strahan
New Norfolk
Risdon
HOBART
BRUNY I.
SOUTH EAST CAPE

New Zealand Inset

NORTH CAPE
Kaitaia
Russell
PACIFIC OCEAN
Devonport
Auckland
NORTH ISLAND
Hamilton
GREAT BARRIER
Bay of Plenty
EAST CAPE
North Taranaki Bight
New Plymouth
Mt. Egmont
C. EGMONT
South Taranaki Bight
Gisborne
NEW ZEALAND
Napier
Hastings
Wanganui
Palmerston North
CAPE FAREWELL
Tasman Bay
Nelson
Karamea Bight
Hawke Bay
Lower Hutt
Wellington
TASMAN SEA
CAPE FOULWIND
Greymouth
Hokitika
SOUTHERN ALPS
SOUTH ISLAND
Pegasus Bay
Christchurch
CASCADE PT.
Canterbury Bight
Timaru
PACIFIC OCEAN
RESOLUTION ISLAND
Foveaux Strait
Dunedin
CAPE SAUNDERS
Invercargill
STEWART ISLAND
SOUTHWEST CAPE

©RMcN.
a

Same scale as main map

Cities and Towns		
0 to 50,000 ○	500,000 to 1,000,000 ◉
50,000 to 500,000 ⊙	1,000,000 and over

Scale:
0 50 100 200 300 400 500 Miles
0 100 200 400 600 800 Kilometers

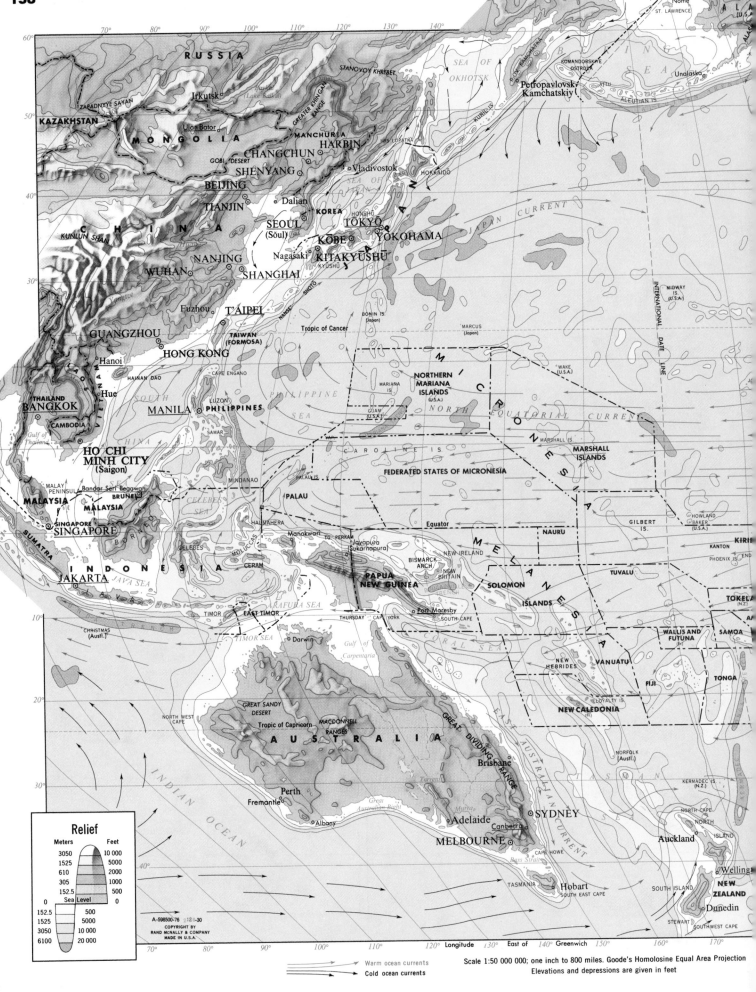

RUSSIA

ZAPADNYYE SAYAN
Irkutsk
(Lake Baikal)
KAZAKHSTAN
MONGOLIA
Ulan Bator
GOBI DESERT
GREATER KHINGAN RANGE
STANOVOY KHREBET
SEA OF OKHOTSK
MYS LOPATKA
KURILS
Petropavlovsk-Kamchatskiy
KOMANDORSKIYE OSTROVA
BERING SEA
Unalaska
ATTU
ALEUTIAN IS.
Nome
ST. LAWRENCE
ALASKA (U.S.)

CHANGCHUN
HARBIN
MANCHURIA
SHENYANG
BEIJING
TIANJIN
Dalian
Vladivostok
KOREA
HOKKAIDO
HONSHU
SEOUL (Sŏul)
TOKYO
KOBE
YOKOHAMA
Nagasaki
KITAKYUSHU
KYUSHU
JAPAN CURRENT

KUNLUN SHAN
CHINA
WUHAN
NANJING
SHANGHAI
Fuzhou
T'AIPEI
GUANGZHOU
HONG KONG
TAIWAN (FORMOSA)
NANSEI SHOTO
Tropic of Cancer
BONIN IS. (Japan)
MARCUS (Japan)
MIDWAY IS. (U.S.A.)
INTERNATIONAL DATE LINE

Hanoi
Hue
HAINAN DAO
CAPE ENGANO
PHILIPPINE SEA
M I C R O N E S I A
NORTHERN MARIANA ISLANDS (U.S.A.)
MARIANA IS.
GUAM (U.S.A.)
WAKE (U.S.A.)
NORTH EQUATORIAL CURRENT

THAILAND
BANGKOK
CAMBODIA
VIETNAM
LAOS
Gulf of Thailand
SOUTH CHINA SEA
MANILA
PHILIPPINES
LUZON
SAMAR
MINDANAO
CAROLINE IS.
MARSHALL IS.
MARSHALL ISLANDS

HO CHI MINH CITY (Saigon)
MALAY PENINSULA
MALAYSIA
Bandar Seri Begawan
BRUNEI
MALAYSIA
PALAU IS.
PALAU
HALMAHERA
CELEBES SEA
FEDERATED STATES OF MICRONESIA

SINGAPORE
SUMATRA
BORNEO
CELEBES
MOLUCCAS
CERAM
Manokwari
TG. PERRAM
Jayapura (Sukarnapura)
Equator
NAURU
GILBERT IS.
HOWLAND BAKER (U.S.A.)
KANTON
KIRI
PHOENIX IS.

INDONESIA
JAKARTA
JAVA SEA
JAVA
BISMARCK ARCH.
NEW IRELAND
NEW BRITAIN
M E L A N E S I A
TUVALU
TOKELAU (N.Z.)

CHRISTMAS (Austl.)
TIMOR
EAST TIMOR
ARAFURA SEA
PAPUA NEW GUINEA
BOUGAINVILLE
NEW GUINEA TRENCH
Port Moresby
SOLOMON ISLANDS
WALLIS AND FUTUNA
SAMOA

TIMOR SEA
Darwin
Gulf of Carpentaria
THURSDAY
CAPE YORK
SOUTH CAPE
CORAL SEA
NEW HEBRIDES
VANUATU
FIJI
TONGA

NORTH WEST CAPE
GREAT SANDY DESERT
Tropic of Capricorn
MACDONNELL RANGES
AUSTRALIA
GREAT DIVIDING RANGE
EAST AUSTRALIAN CURRENT
NEW CALEDONIA (Fr.)
LOYALTY IS.

Perth
Fremantle
Albany
Great Australian Bight
Adelaide
Canberra
SYDNEY
Brisbane
NORFOLK (Austl.)
NORTH CAPE
NORTH ISLAND
Auckland

INDIAN OCEAN
MELBOURNE
CAPE HOWE
Bass Strait
TASMANIA
Hobart
SOUTH EAST CAPE
TASMAN SEA
KERMADEC IS. (N.Z.)
SOUTH ISLAND
Dunedin
STEWART
SOUTHWEST CAPE
Wellington
NEW ZEALAND

Relief

Meters	Feet
3050	10 000
1525	5000
610	2000
305	1000
152.5	500
Sea Level	0
152.5	500
1525	5000
3050	10 000
6100	20 000

A-598500-76   2129-30
COPYRIGHT BY
RAND McNALLY & COMPANY
MADE IN U.S.A.

70° 80° 90° 100° 110° 120° **Longitude** 130° East of 140° Greenwich 150° 160° 170°

→ Warm ocean currents
→ Cold ocean currents

Scale 1:50 000 000; one inch to 800 miles. Goode's Homolosine Equal Area Projection
Elevations and depressions are given in feet

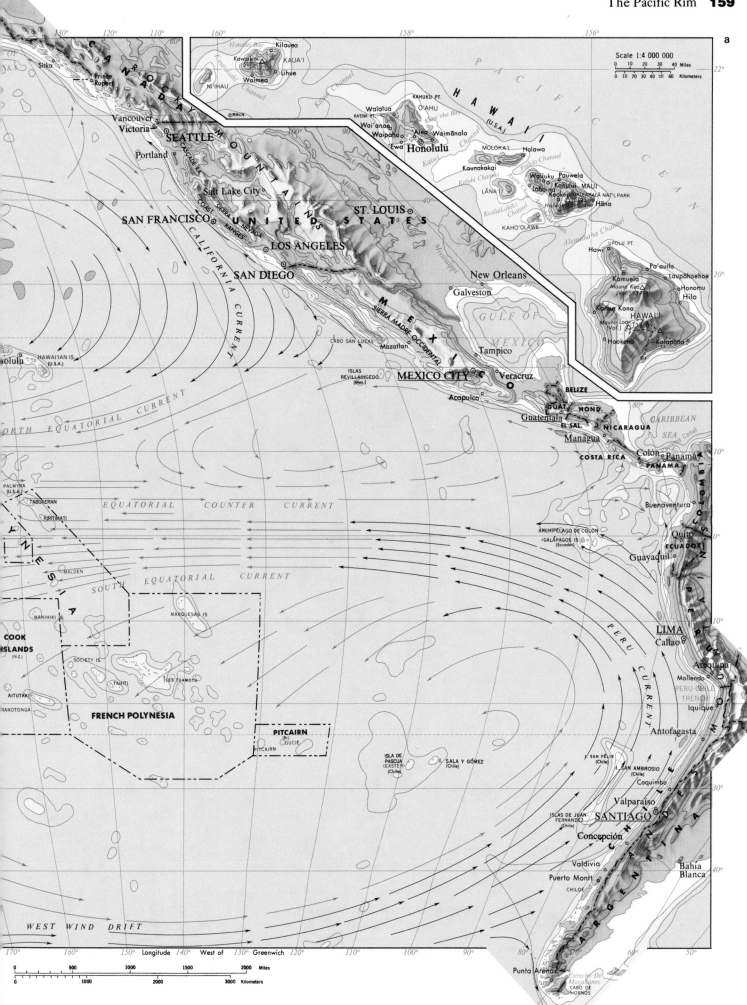

a

Scale 1:4 000 000

0 10 20 30   40 Miles
0 10 20 30 40   60 Kilometers

PACIFIC   OCEAN

HAWAII
(U.S.A.)

Hanalei Bay
Kilauea
Kawaikini
5170
KAUA'I
Lihue
Waimea
NI'IHAU
Kaukakahi Channel

KAHUKU PT.
O'AHU
Waialua
KA'ENA PT.
Wai'anae
Waipahu
Ewa
Honolulu
Aiea
Waimanalo
Kane'ohe Bay
Kailu
Kaiwi Channel

MOLOKA'I
Kaunakakai
Halawa
Wailuku Pauwela
LANA'I
Kahului MAUI
Lahaina Ha'iku HALEAKALA NAT'L PARK
Kaoko Haleakala Crater Hana
KAHO'OLAWE
Alenuihaha Channel

UPOLU PT.
Hawi Pa'auilo Laupahoehoe
Kamuela Honomu
Mauna Kea Hilo
(Vol.) 13,796
Kailua Kona HAWAII
Mauna Loa 13,680
(Vol.)
Hookena Kalapana

CANADA
SKA
Sitka
Prince Rupert

ROCKY   MOUNTAINS

Vancouver
Victoria
SEATTLE
Portland

Salt Lake City

CASCADE RA.
COAST RANGES
SIERRA NEVADA

SAN FRANCISCO

UNITED   STATES
ST. LOUIS

LOS ANGELES

SAN DIEGO

CALIFORNIA   CURRENT

MEXICO
SIERRA MADRE OCCIDENTAL

CABO SAN LUCAS
Mazatlan
ISLAS REVILLAGIGEDO
(Mex.)

MEXICO CITY
Acapulco

New Orleans
Galveston

GULF OF

MEXICO

Tampico
Veracruz

BELIZE
GUAT. HOND.
Guatemala
EL SAL. NICARAGUA
Managua
COSTA RICA
CARIBBEAN
SEA
Colon Panama
PANAMA

olulu
HAWAI'IAN IS.
(U.S.A.)

NORTH   EQUATORIAL   CURRENT

PALMYRA
(U.S.A.)
TABUAERAN
KIRITIMATI

EQUATORIAL   COUNTER   CURRENT

ARCHIPELAGO DE COLON
(GALAPAGOS IS.)
(Ecuador)

Buenaventura

COLOMBIA

Quito
ECUADOR
Guayaquil

MALDEN

SOUTH   EQUATORIAL   CURRENT

MANIHIKI IS.
COOK
ISLANDS
(N.Z.)

SOCIETY IS.
AITUTAKI
TAHITI
ILES TUAMOTU
RAROTONGA

FRENCH POLYNESIA

MARQUESAS IS.

PERU

LIMA
Callao

PITCAIRN
(Br.)
DUCIE
PITCAIRN

ISLA DE PASCUA
(EASTER)
(Chile)
I. SALA Y GOMEZ
(Chile)

I. SAN FELIX
(Chile)
I. SAN AMBROSIO
(Chile)
Coquimbo

Arequipa
Mollendo
PERU-CHILE
TRENCH
Iquique
Antofagasta

Valparaiso
ISLAS DE JUAN FERNANDEZ
(Chile)
SANTIAGO
Concepcion
Valdivia
Puerto Montt
CHILOE

ANDES
CHILE
ARGENTINA

Bahia
Blanca

WEST   WIND   DRIFT

Punta Arenas
Estrecho De Magallanes
CABO DE HORNOS

170°   160°   150°   Longitude 140°   West of   130°   Greenwich 120°   110°   100°   90°   80°   70°   60°   50°

0   500   1000   1500   2000 Miles
0   1000   2000   3000 Kilometers

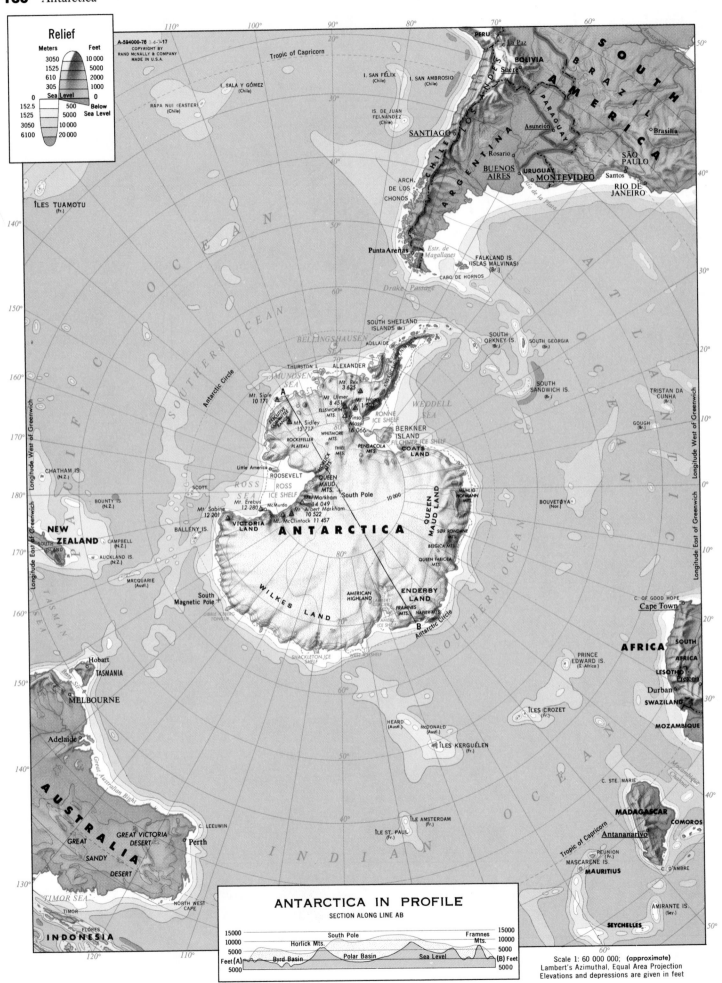

Relief

Meters		Feet
3050		10 000
1525		5000
610		2000
305		1000
0	Sea Level	0
152.5		500
	Sea Level	Below
1525		5000
3050		10 000
6100		20 000

A-594000-76 3-4-7-17
COPYRIGHT BY
RAND McNALLY & COMPANY
MADE IN U.S.A.

Tropic of Capricorn

ANTARCTICA IN PROFILE
SECTION ALONG LINE AB

Scale 1: 60 000 000; (approximate)
Lambert's Azimuthal, Equal Area Projection
Elevations and depressions are given in feet

Glossary

Foreign Geographical Terms

Afk. Afrikaans
Ara. Arabic
Ber. Berber
Blg. Bulgarian
Bur. Burmese
Cbd. Cambodian
Ch. Chinese
Czech Czech
Dan. Danish
Du. Dutch
Est. Estonian
Finn. Finnish
Fr. French
Gae. Gaelic
Ger. German
Gr. Greek
Heb. Hebrew
Ice. Icelandic
Indon. Indonesian
It. Italian
Jpn. Japanese
Kor. Korean
Lao. Laotian
Lapp. Lappish
Mal. Malay
Mong. Mongolian
Nor. Norwegian
Pas. Pashto
Per. Persian
Pol. Polish
Port. Portuguese
Rom. Romanian
Rus. Russian
S./C. Serbo-Croatian
Slo. Slovak
Sp. Spanish
Swe. Swedish
Thai Thai
Tib. Tibetan
Tur. Turkish
Ukr. Ukranian
Viet. Vietnamese

-å, Dan., Nor., Swe. ... river
āb, Per. ... river
ada(lar), Tur. ... island(s)
adrar, Ber. ... mountains
ákra, akrotírion, Gr. ... cape
altos, Sp. ... mountains, hills
-älv,-älven, Swe. ... river
-ån, Swe. ... river
archipel, Fr. ... archipelago
archipiélago, Sp. ... archipelago
arquipélago, Port. ... archipelago
arroyo, Sp. ... brook
-ås,-åsen, Swe. ... hills
baai, Du. ... bay
bab, Ara. ... strait
Bach, Ger. ... brook, creek
-backen, Swe. ... hill
bælt, Dan. ... strait
bahía, Sp. ... bay
bahr, baḩr, Ara. ... river, sea
baía, Port. ... bay
baie, Fr. ... bay
-bana, Jpn. ... cape
banco, Sp. ... bank
bandao, Ch. ... peninsula
bassin, Fr. ... basin
batang, Indon. ... river
bātlāq, Per. ... marsh
ben, Gae. ... mountain
Berg, Ger. ... mountain, hill
-berg, Afk. ... mountains
Berge, Ger. ... mountains
bi'r, Ara. ... well
birkat, Ara. ... lake
bocca, It. ... river mouth, pass
boğazı, Tur. ... strait
bogd, Mong. ... range
bolsón, Sp. ... enclosed basin
-breen, Nor. ... glacier
Brücke, Ger. ... bridge
Bucht, Ger. ... bay
bugt, Dan. ... bay
bukit, Indon., Mal. ... mountain, hill
-bukten, Swe. ... bay
bulu, Indon. ... mountain
Burg, Ger. ... castle
burn, Gae. ... brook
burnu, burun, Tur. ... cape
cabezas, Sp. ... peaks
cabo, Port., Sp. ... cape
campo, It. ... plain
cap, Fr. ... cape
capo, It. ... cape
catena, Sp. ... range
cayo(s), Sp. ... cay(s), islet(s)
cerro(s), Sp. ... mountain(s), hill(s)
chaîne, Fr. ... range
château, Fr. ... castle
chiang, Ch. ... harbor, harbour
chott, Ara. ... intermittent lake, salt marsh
cima, It., Sp. ... peak
città, It. ... city
ciudad, Sp. ... city
co, Tib. ... lake
co., cerro, Sp. ... mountain, hill
col, Fr. ... pass
colina(s), Sp. ... hill(s)
colline, It. ... hills
collines, Fr. ... hills
con, Viet. ... islands
cord., cordillera, Sp. ... range
costa, Sp. ... coast
côte, Fr. ... coast, hills
cuchilla, Sp. ... hills, ridge
dağ, dağı, Tur. ... mountain
dāgh, Per. ... mountains
-dake, Jpn. ... mountain
-dal, -dalen, Nor., Swe. ... valley
danau, Indon. ... lake
dao, Ch., Viet. ... island
daryācheh, Per. ... lake
dasht, Per. ... desert
deniz, denizi, Tur. ... sea
desierto, Sp. ... desert
détroit, Fr. ... strait
dijk, Du. ... dike
distrito, Sp. ... district
djebel, Ara. ... mountain(s)
-do, Kor. ... island
-elv,-elva, Nor. ... river
embalse, Sp. ... reservoir
erg, Ara. ... sand desert
estrecho, Sp. ... strait
étang, Fr. ... pond
-ey, Ice. ... island
fjäll(en), Swe. ... mountain(s)
fjället, Swe. ... mountain
fjärden, Swe. ... fjord
-fjell, -fjellet, Nor. ... mountain
-fjord, Nor. ... fjord
-fjorden, Nor., Swe. ... fjord, lake
-fjörur, Ice. ... fjord, bay
-flói, Ice. ... bay
foce, It. ... river mouth, pass
forêt, Fr. ... forest
-forsen, Swe. ... waterfall
Forst, Ger. ... forest
-foss, Ice. ... waterfall
-fossen, Nor. ... waterfall
g., gora, Rus. ... mountain, hill
g., gunong, Mal. ... mountain
gang, Ch. ... bay
-gang, Kor. ... river
gave, Fr. ... mountain torrent
gebergte, Du. ... range
Gebirge, Ger. ... range
Gipfel, Ger. ... peak
göl, Tur. ... lake
golfe, Fr. ... gulf
golfete, Sp. ... bay
golfo, It., Sp. ... gulf
gölü, Tur. ... lake
gora, Rus. ... mountain, hill
gora, S. \C. ... mountains
góra, Pol. ... mountain
gory, Rus. ... mountains, hills
góry, Pol. ... mountains
gr'ada, Rus. ... ridge
guba, Rus. ... bay
gunong, Mal. ... mountain
gunung, Indon. ... mountain
-guntō, Jpn. ... islands
Haff, Ger. ... lagoon
hai, Ch. ... sea, lake
-hama, Jpn. ... beach
hamada, Ara. ... desert
hāmūn, Per. ... lake, marsh
-hantō, Jpn. ... peninsula
hare, Heb. ... mountains, hills
-hav, Swe. ... sea, bay
havre, Fr. ... harbor, harbour
he, Ch. ... river
ho, Ch. ... river
-ho, Kor. ... reservoir
-holm, Dan. ... island
hora, Czech, Slo. ... mountain
Horn, Ger. ... point, peak
hu, Ch. ... lake, reservoir
Hügel, Ger. ... hill
-huk, Swe. ... cape
ig., igarapé, Port. ... river
île(s), Fr. ... island(s)
ilet(s), Fr. ... islet(s)
ilha(s), Port. ... island(s)
ilhéu(s), Port. ... islet(s)
Insel(n), Ger. ... island(s)
isla(s), Sp. ... island(s)
isola, It. ... island
isole, It. ... islands
istmo, Sp. ... isthmus
jabal, Ara. ... mountain(s)
järv, Est. ... lake
-järvi, Finn. ... lake
jazā'ir, Ara. ... islands
jazirah, Indon. ... peninsula
jiang, Ch. ... river
-jima, Jpn. ... island
-joki, Finn. ... river
-jökull, Ice. ... glacier
-kai, Jpn. ... sea
-kaikyō, Jpn. ... strait
-kaise, Lapp. ... mountain
kali, Indon. ... brook
kandao, Pas. ... pass
-kang, Kor. ... river
-kapp, Nor. ... cape
kepulauan, Indon. ... islands
khalīj, Ara. ... gulf
khrebet, Russ., Ukr. ... range
-ko, Jpn. ... lake, lagoon
-kō, Jpn. ... harbor, harbour
kólpos, Gr. ... bay
Kopf, Ger. ... peak
körfezi, Tur. ... gulf, bay
kosa, Rus., Ukr. ... spit
kou, Ch. ... bay, pass
kuala, Mal. ... bay
kūh(ha), Per. ... mountain(s)
la, Tib. ... pass
lac(s), Fr. ... lake(s)
lag., laguna, Sp. ... lagoon, lake
lago, It., Port., Sp. ... lake
lagoa, Port. ... lake, lagoon
laguna, Sp. ... lagoon, lake
lagune, Fr. ... lagoon
laht, Est. ... bay
-lahti, Finn. ... gulf
län, Swe. ... county
laut, Indon. ... sea
liedao, Ch. ... islands
liman, Rus. ... estuary
ling, Ch. ... mountain(s), peak
llano(s), Sp. ... plain(s)
loch, Gae. ... lake, inlet
lomas, Sp. ... hills
lough, Gae. ... lake
lyman, Ukr. ... estuary
-maa, Est. ... island
-man, Kor. ... bay
mar, Sp., It. ... sea
marais, Fr. ... marsh
mare, It. ... sea
massif, Fr. ... massif
Meer, Ger. ... sea, lake
mer, Fr. ... sea
mesa, Sp. ... mesa
meseta, Sp. ... plateau
-misaki, Jpn. ... cape
mont, Fr. ... mount
montagna, It. ... mountain
montagne(s), Fr. ... mountain(s)
montaña(s), Sp. ... mountain(s)
monte, It., Port., Sp. ... mount
montes, Port., Sp. ... mountains
monti, It. ... mountains
monts, Fr. ... mountains
more, Rus., Ukr. ... sea
morne, Fr. ... mountain
morro, Port., Sp. ... hill, mountain
mui, Viet. ... point
munkhafad, Ara. ... depression
munţii, Rom. ... mountains
-nada, Jpn. ... sea, gulf
nafūd, Ara. ... desert
nagor'ye, Rus. ... plateau, mountains
-näs, Swe. ... peninsula
ness, Gae. ... promontory
nos, Blg. ... cape
nuruu, Mong. ... mountains
nuur, Mong. ... lake
-ø, Dan., Nor. ... island
-ö, Swe. ... island
o., ostrov, Rus. ... island
óros, Gr. ... mountain(s)
ostriv, Ukr. ... island
ostrov(a), Rus. ... island(s)
otok, S. \C. ... island
ouadi, Ara. ... wadi
oued, Ara. ... wadi
-øy, -øya, Nor. ... island
oz., ozero, Rus., Ukr. ... lake
pampa, Sp. ... plain
pas, Fr. ... strait
paso, Sp. ... pass
Pass, Ger. ... pass
passe, Fr. ... passage
passo, It. ... pass
peg., pegunungan, Indon. ... mountains
pélagos, Gr. ... sea
peña, Sp. ... peak, rock
península, Sp. ... peninsula
pertuis, Fr. ... strait
peski, Rus. ... sand desert
phnum, Cbd. ... mountain
phou, Lao. ... mountain
pic, Fr. ... peak
pico(s), Port., Sp. ... peak(s)
-piggen, Nor. ... mountain
pik, Rus. ... peak
pique, Fr. ... peak
piton(s), Fr. ... peak(s)
pivostriv, Ukr. ... peninsula
planalto, Port. ... plateau
planina, S. \C. ... mountain, range
plato, Afk., Blg., Rus. ... plateau
playa, Sp. ... beach
pointe, Fr. ... point
polje, S. \C. ... plain, basin
poluostrov, Rus. ... peninsula
pont, Fr. ... bridge
ponta, pontal, Port. ... point
porto, It. ... port
presa, Sp. ... reservoir, dam
presqu'île, Fr. ... peninsula
proliv, Rus. ... strait
puerto, Sp. ... port
pulau, Indon., Mal. ... island
puncak, Indon. ... peak
punta, It., Sp. ... point, peak
qundao, Ch. ... islands
rāo., ribeirāo, Port. ... river
ras, ra's, Ara. ... cape
rās, Per. ... cape
récif, Fr. ... reef
represa, Port. ... dam, reservoir
-retto, Jpn. ... islands
ría, Sp. ... ria (inlet)
rib., ribeira, Port. ... brook
ribeirão, Port. ... river
rio, Port. ... river
río, Sp. ... river
riviera, It. ... coast
rivière, Fr. ... river
roca, Sp. ... rock
rocca, It. ... rock, mountain
rt, S. \C. ... cape
sa., serra, Port. ... range
sahrā', Ara. ... desert
-saki, Jpn. ... cape
salar, Sp. ... salt flat
salina(s), Sp. ... salt marsh, salt flat
salto(s), Port., Sp. ... waterfall
-sammyaku, Jpn. ... range
-san, Jpn., Kor. ... mountain
-sanmaek, Kor. ... mountains
Schloss, Ger. ... castle
sebkha, Ara. ... salt flat
See(n), Ger. ... lake(s)
selat, Indon. ... strait
seno, Sp. ... sound
serra, Port. ... range, mountain
serranía(s), Sp. ... ridge(s)
shan, Ch. ... mountain(s), island
shanmo, Ch. ... mountains
-shima, Jpn. ... island
-shotō, Jpn. ... islands
sierra, Sp. ... range, ridge
-sjø, Nor. ... lake
-sjön, Swe. ... lake, bay
-sø, Dan. ... lake
Spitze, Ger. ... peak
sta., santa, Port., Sp. ... saint
ste., sainte, Fr. ... saint
step', Rus. ... steppe
štít, Slo. ... peak
sto., santo, Port., Sp. ... saint
stretto, It. ... strait
Strom, Ger. ... stream
-ström, -strömmen, Swe. ... stream
-su, Kor. ... river
-suidō, Jpn. ... channel
Sund, Ger. ... sound
-sund, Swe. ... sound
-take, Jpn. ... mountain
Tal, Ger. ... valley
tanjong, Mal. ... cape
tanjung, Indon. ... cape
tao, Ch. ... island
teluk, Indon. ... bay
thale, Thai ... lagoon
-tō, Jpn. ... island
tônlé, Cbd. ... lake
-tunturi, Finn. ... hill, mountain
ujung, Indon. ... cape
-umi, Jpn. ... lagoon
-ura, Jpn. ... lake
valle, It., Sp. ... valley
vallée, Fr. ... valley
vârful, Rom. ... mountain
-vatn, Ice., Nor. ... lake
vdkhr., vodokhranilishche, Rus. ... reservoir
-vesi, Finn. ... lake
-viken, Swe. ... gulf
vodokhranilishche, Rus. ... reservoir
vodoskhovyshche, Ukr. ... reservoir
vol., volcán, Sp. ... volcano
wādī, Ara. ... wadi
wāhat, wāhāt, Ara. ... oasis
wan, Ch., Jpn. ... bay
-yama, Jpn. ... mountain
yarımadası, Tur. ... peninsula
yoma, Bur. ... mountains
yumco, Tib. ... lake
yunhe, Ch. ... canal
-zaki, Jpn. ... point
zaliv, Rus. ... gulf, bay
zatoka, Ukr. ... gulf, bay
zee, Du. ... sea, lake

Abbreviations of Geographical Names and Terms

Ab., Can. .... Alberta, Can.
Afg. .... Afghanistan
Afr. .... Africa
Ak., U.S. .... Alaska, U.S.
Al., U.S. .... Alabama, U.S.
Alb. .... Albania
Alg. .... Algeria
Ang. .... Angola
Ant. .... Antarctica
Ar., U.S. ...... Arkansas, U.S.
Arg. .... Argentina
Arm. .... Armenia
Aus. .... Austria
Austl. .... Australia
Az., U.S. ...... Arizona, U.S.
Azer. .... Azerbaijan
B. .... Bay
Bah. .... Bahamas
Bahr. .... Bahrain
Barb. .... Barbados
B.C., Can. .... British
Columbia, Can.
Bdi. .... Burundi
Bel. .... Belgium
Bela. .... Belarus
Bhu. .... Bhutan
Bngl. .... Bangladesh
Bol. .... Bolivia
Bos. .... Bosnia
and Herzegovina
Bots. .... Botswana
Braz. .... Brazil
Bul. .... Bulgaria
Burkina............ Burkina Faso
C. .... Cape
Ca., U.S. .... California,
U.S.
Camb. .... Cambodia
Can. .... Canada
C.A.R. .... Central
African Republic
Cay. Is. .... Cayman Islands
C. Iv. .... Cote d'Ivoire
Co., U.S. ..... Colorado, U.S.
Col. .... Colombia
C.R. .... Costa Rica

Cro. .... Croatia
Ct., U.S. .... Connecticut, U.S.
Ctry. .... Country
C.V. .... Cape Verde
Cyp. .... Cyprus
Czech Rep. . Czech Republic
D.C., U.S. .... District of
Columbia, U.S.
De., U.S. ...... Delaware, U.S.
Den. .... Denmark
Dep. .... Dependency
Des. .... Desert
Dji. .... Djibouti
D.R.C. .... Democratic
Republic of the Congo
Ec. .... Ecuador
El Sal. .... El Salvador
Eng., U.K. ..... England, U.K.
Eq. Gui. .. Equatorial Guinea
Erit. .... Eritrea
Est. .... Estonia
Eth. .... Ethiopia
Eur. .... Europe
Falk. Is. ..... Falkland Islands
Fin. .... Finland
Fl., U.S. .... Florida, U.S.
Fr. .... France
Fr. Gu. .... French Guiana
G. .... Gulf
Ga., U.S. ...... Georgia, U.S.
Gam. .... The Gambia
Gaza Str. .... Gaza Strip
Geor. .... Georgia
Ger. .... Germany
Grc. .... Greece
Guad. .... Guadeloupe
Guat. .... Guatemala
Gui. .... Guinea
Gui.-B. .... Guinea-Bissau
Guy. .... Guyana
Hi., U.S. .... Hawaii, U.S.
Hond. .... Honduras
Hung. .... Hungary
I. .... Island
Ia., U.S. .... Iowa, U.S.
Ice. .... Iceland

Id., U.S. .... Idaho, U.S.
Il., U.S. .... Illinois, U.S.
In., U.S. .... Indiana, U.S.
Indon. .... Indonesia
Ire. .... Ireland
Is. .... Islands
Isr. .... Israel
Jam. .... Jamaica
Jord. .... Jordan
Kaz. .... Kazakhstan
Ks., U.S. .... Kansas, U.S.
Kuw. .... Kuwait
Ky., U.S. ...... Kentucky, U.S.
Kyrg. .... Kyrgyzstan
L. .... Lake
La., U.S. ..... Louisiana, U.S.
Lat. .... Latvia
Leb. .... Lebanon
Leso. .... Lesotho
Lib. .... Liberia
Lith. .... Lithuania
Lux. .... Luxembourg
Ma., U.S. ... Massachusetts,
U.S.
Mac. .... Macedonia
Madag. .... Madagascar
Malay. .... Malaysia
Mart. .... Martinique
Maur. .... Mauritania
Mb., Can. ...... Manitoba, Can.
Md., U.S. ... Maryland, U.S.
Me., U.S. .... Maine, U.S.
Mex. .... Mexico
Mi., U.S. ... Michigan, U.S.
Mn., U.S. .. Minnesota, U.S.
Mo., U.S. ... Missouri, U.S.
Mol. .... Moldova
Mong. .... Mongolia
Monts. .... Montserrat
Mor. .... Morocco
Moz. .... Mozambique
Ms., U.S. ... Mississippi, U.S.
Mt. .... Mountain
Mt., U.S. .... Montana, U.S.
Mts. .... Mountains
Mwi. .... Malawi

Myan. .... Myanmar
N.A. .... North America
N.B., Can. .... New
Brunswick, Can.
N.C., U.S. .... North
Carolina, U.S.
N. Cal. .... New Caledonia
N.D., U.S. .... North
Dakota, U.S.
Ne., U.S. ... Nebraska, U.S.
Neth. .... Netherlands
Neth. Ant. ... Netherlands
Antilles
N.H., U.S. .... New
Hampshire, U.S.
Nic. .... Nicaragua
Nig. .... Nigeria
N. Ire., U.K. .... Northern
Ireland, U.K.
N.J., U.S. .. New Jersey, U.S.
N. Kor. .... North Korea
N.L., Can. .... Newfoundland
and Labrador, Can.
N.M., U.S. .... New
Mexico, U.S.
Nmb. .... Namibia
Nor. .... Norway
N.S., Can. .... Nova
Scotia, Can.
N.T., Can. .... Northwest
Territories, Can.
Nu., Can. ..... Nunavut, Can.
Nv., U.S. ...... Nevada, U.S.
N.Y., U.S. .. New York, U.S.
N.Z. .... New Zealand
Oc. .... Oceania
Oh., U.S. .... Ohio, U.S.
Ok., U.S. ... Oklahoma, U.S.
On., Can. ...... Ontario, Can.
Or., U.S. .... Oregon, U.S.
Pa., U.S. . Pennsylvania, U.S.
Pak. .... Pakistan
Pan. .... Panama
Pap. N. Gui. .... Papua
New Guinea
Para. .... Paraguay

P.E., Can. .... Prince Edward
Island, Can.
Pen. .... Peninsula
Phil. .... Philippines
Pk. .... Peak
Plat. .... Plateau
Pol. .... Poland
Polit. Reg. ... Political Region
Port. .... Portugal
P.R. .... Puerto Rico
Prov. .... Province
Qc., Can. ... Quebec, Can.
R. .... River
Ra. .... Range
Reg. .... Region
Res. .... Reservoir
R.I., U.S. .... Rhode
Island, U.S.
Rom. .... Romania
Rw. .... Rwanda
S.A. .... South America
S. Afr. .... South Africa
Sau. Ar. .... Saudi Arabia
S.C., U.S. .... South
Carolina, U.S.
Scot., U.K. .... Scotland, U.K.
S.D., U.S. .... South
Dakota, U.S.
Sen. .... Senegal
Serb. .... Serbia and
Montenegro
Sk., Can. .... Saskatchewan,
Can.
S. Kor. .... South Korea
S.L. .... Sierra Leone
Slvk. .... Slovakia
Slvn. .... Slovenia
Som. .... Somalia
Sp. N. Afr. .... Spanish
North Africa
Sri L. .... Sri Lanka
Str. .... Strait
St. Vin. .... St. Vincent
and the Grenadines
Sur. .... Suriname
Swaz. .... Swaziland

Swe. .... Sweden
Switz. .... Switzerland
Tai. .... Taiwan
Taj. .... Tajikistan
Tan. .... Tanzania
Ter. .... Territory
Thai. .... Thailand
Tn., U.S. .... Tennessee, U.S.
Trin. .... Trinidad and Tobago
Tun. .... Tunisia
Tur. .... Turkey
Turk. .... Turkmenistan
Tx., U.S. ...... Texas, U.S.
U.A.E. .... United
Arab Emirates
Ug. .... Uganda
U.K. .... United Kingdom
Ukr. .... Ukraine
Ur. .... Uruguay
U.S. .... United States
Ut., U.S. .... Utah, U.S.
Uzb. .... Uzbekistan
Va., U.S. ..... Virginia, U.S.
Ven. .... Venezuela
Viet. .... Vietnam
V.I.U.S. .... Virgin
Islands (U.S.)
Vol. .... Volcano
Vt., U.S. .... Vermont, U.S.
Wa., U.S. .. Washington, U.S.
Wal./F. ... Wallis and Futuna
W.B. .... West Bank
Wi., U.S. ... Wisconsin, U.S.
W. Sah. ...... Western Sahara
W.V., U.S. .... West
Virginia, U.S.
Wy., U.S. ..... Wyoming, U.S.
Yk., Can. .... Yukon
Territory, Can.
Zam. .... Zambia
Zimb. .... Zimbabwe

Index

This universal index includes in a single alphabetical list approximately 4,100 names of features that appear on the reference maps. Each name is followed by geographical coordinates and a page reference.

Abbreviation and Capitalization

Abbreviations of names on the maps have been standardized as much as possible. Names that are abbreviated on the maps are generally spelled out in full in the index. Periods are used after all abbreviations regardless of local practice. The abbreviation "St." is used only for "Saint". "Sankt" and other forms of this term are spelled out."

Most initial letters of names are capitalized, except for a few Dutch names, such as "'s-Gravenhage." Capitalization of non-initial words in a name generally follows local practice.

Alphabetization

Names are alphabetized in the order of the letters of the English alphabet. Spanish *ll* and *ch*, for example, are not treated as distinct letters.

Furthermore, diacritical marks are disregarded in alphabetization. German or Scandinavian *ä* or *ö* are treated as *a* or *o*.

The names of physical features may appear inverted, since they are always alphabetized under the proper, not the generic, part of the name, thus: "Gibraltar, Strait of." Otherwise every entry, whether consisting of one word or more, is alphabetized as a single continuous entity. "Lakeland," for example, appears after "Lake Forest" and before "La Línea." Names beginning with articles (Le Havre, Al Manāmah, Ad Dawhah) are not inverted. Names beginning "St.," "Ste.'" and "Sainte" are alphabetized as though spelled "Saint."

In the case of identical names, towns are listed first, then political divisions, then physical features.

Generic Terms

Except for cities, the names of all features are followed by terms that represent broad classes of features, for example, *Mississippi, R.* or *Alabama, State.*

Country names and names of features that extend beyond the boundaries of one country are followed by the name of the continent in which each is located. Country designations follow the names of all other places in the index. The locations of places in the United States, Canada, and the United Kingdom are further defined by abbreviations that indicate the state, province, or political division in which each is located.

Page References and Geographical Coordinates

The geographical coordinates and page references are found in the last columns of each entry.

Latitude and longitude coordinates for point features, such as cities and mountain peaks, indicate the locations of the symbols. For extensive areal features, such as countries or mountain ranges, or linear features, such as canals and rivers, locations are given for the position of the type as it appears on the map.

Index

Novosibirskiye Ostrava (New Siberian Is.), Russia ...75N 141E **141**
Novyy Port, Russia ...67N 72E **140**
Nowy Sǒcz, Pol. ...50N 21E **117**
Ntwetwe Pan, Basin, Bots. ...20S 25E **130**
Nubian Des., Sudan ...21N 33E **129**
Nuevo Laredo, Mex. ...27N 99W **96**
Nuevo San Juan, Pan. ...9N 80W **96**
Nullarbor Plain, Austl. ...32S 128E **156**
Nunavut, Ter., Can. ...70N 95W **73**
Nurata, Uzb. ...41N 65E **140**
Nürnberg, Ger. ...49N 11E **117**
Nushki, Pak. ...29N 66E **143**
Nyala, Sudan ...12N 25E **129**
Nyasa, L., Afr. ...12S 35E **130**
Nyíregyháza, Hung. ...48N 22E **117**

O

Oakland, Ca., U. S. ...38N 122W **84**
Oak Park, Il., U. S. ...42N 88W **90**
Oak Ridge, Tn., U. S. ...36N 84W **92**
Oaxaca, Mex. ...17N 97W **96**
Ob', R., Russia ...63N 67E **140**
Occidental, Cordillera, Ra., Peru ...10S 77W **104**
Odemiş, Tur. ...38N 28E **121**
Odense, Den. ...55N 10E **116**
Odesa (Odessa), Ukr. ...46N 31E **115**
Ogbomosho, Nig. ...8N 4E **128**
Ogden, Ut., U. S. ...41N 112W **83**
Ogilvie Mts., Yk., Can. ...65N 139W **72**
Ohio, State, U. S. ...40N 83W **77**
Ohio, R., U. S. ...37N 88W **90**
Okayama, Japan ...35N 134E **147**
Okha, Russia ...54N 143E **141**
Okhotsk, Sea of, Japan-Russia ...57N 147E **141**
Oklahoma, State, U. S. ...36N 98W **76**
Oklahoma City, Ok., U. S. ...35N 98W **87**
Okovango Swamp, Bots. ...19S 23E **130**
Olavarría, Arg. ...37S 60W **106**
Old Crow, Yk., Can. ...68N 140W **72**
Oldenburg, Ger. ...53N 8E **117**
Olds, Ab., Can. ...52N 114W **72**
Olean, N. Y., U. S. ...42N 78W **91**
Olekminsk, Russia ...61N 121E **141**
Ol'ga, Russia ...44N 136E **141**
Olhão, Port. ...37N 8W **120**
Olinda, Braz. ...8S 35W **105**
Olivos, Arg. ...34S 58W **106**
Olomouc, Czech Rep. ...50N 17E **117**
Olot, Spain ...42N 3E **120**
Olsztyn, Pol. ...54N 20E **116**
Olympia, Wa., U. S. ...47N 123W **82**
Omaha, Ne., U. S. ...41N 96W **87**
Oman, Ctry., Asia ...19N 57E **142**
Oman, G. of, Asia ...25N 57E **142**
Omdurman, Sudan ...16N 32E **129**
Omsk, Russia ...55N 73E **140**
Öndörhaan, Mong. ...47N 111E **147**
Onega, Russia ...64N 38E **115**
Onezhskoye Ozero (L. Onega), Russia ...62N 37E **115**
Onitsha, Nig. ...6N 6E **128**
Ontario, Prov., Can. ...50N 89W **73**
Ontario, L., Can. -U. S. ...44N 78W **91**
Oostende, Bel. ...51N 3E **117**
Opole, Pol. ...51N 18E **117**
Oradea, Rom. ...47N 22E **121**
Oral, Kaz. ...51N 51E **115**
Oran, Alg. ...36N 1W **128**
Orange, R., Afr. ...29S 18E **130**
Oranjemund, Nmb. ...29S 16E **130**
Ordu, Tur. ...41N 38E **121**
Örebro, Swe. ...59N 15E **116**
Oregon, State, U. S. ...44N 120W **76**
Orekhovo-Zuyevo, Russia ...56N 39E **140**
Orël, Russia ...53N 36E **115**

Orenburg, Russia ...52N 55E **115**
Oriental, Cordillera, Ra., S. A. ...14S 68W **104**
Orinoco, R., Col. -Ven. ...8N 65W **104**
Oristano, Italy ...40N 9E **117**
Orizaba, Mex. ...19N 97W **96**
Orkney Is., Scot., U. K. ...59N 2W **116**
Orlando, Fl., U. S. ...29N 81W **93**
Orléans, Fr. ...48N 2E **117**
Orsk, Russia ...51N 59E **115**
Oruro, Bol. ...18S 67W **104**
Ōsaka, Japan ...35N 135E **147**
Osh, Kyrg. ...40N 73E **140**
Oshawa, On., Can. ...44N 79W **73**
Oshkosh, Wi., U. S. ...44N 89W **89**
Oshogbo, Nig. ...8N 4E **128**
Osijek, Cro. ...46N 19E **121**
Oslo, Nor. ...60N 11E **116**
Osorno, Chile ...41S 73W **106**
Ostrava, Czech Rep. ...50N 18E **117**
Ostrowiec Swiętokrzyski, Pol. ...51N 21E **117**
Ostrów Wielkopolski, Pol. ...52N 18E **117**
Otaru, Japan ...43N 141E **147**
Ottawa, On., Can. ...45N 76W **73**
Ottawa, R., Can. ...46N 77W **73**
Ottumwa, Ia., U. S. ...41N 92W **89**
Ouagadougou, Burkina ...12N 2W **128**
Oujda, Mor. ...35N 2W **128**
Oulu, Fin. ...65N 26E **116**
Outardes, R. aux, R., Qc., Can. ...52N 70W **73**
Oviedo, Spain ...43N 6W **120**
Owensboro, Ky., U. S. ...38N 87W **90**
Oxford, Eng., U. K. ...52N 1W **117**
Oxford, Oh., U. S. ...39N 85W **90**
Oyo, Nig. ...8N 4E **128**
Ozieri, Italy ...41N 9E **117**

P

Pachuca, Mex. ...20N 99W **96**
Pacific Ocean ...10S 150W **52**
Padang, Indon. ...1S 100E **148**
Padova, Italy ...45N 12E **117**
Padre I., Tx., U. S. ...27N 97W **95**
Paisley, Scot., U. K. ...56N 4W **116**
Pakistan, Ctry., Asia ...30N 71E **143**
Pakokku, Myan. ...21N 95E **146**
Palana, Russia ...59N 160E **141**
Palau, Ctry., Oc. ...8N 135E **158**
Palembang, Indon. ...3S 105E **148**
Palencia, Spain ...42N 5W **120**
Palermo, Italy ...38N 13E **117**
Palestine, Reg., Asia ...32N 35E **139**
Palma, Spain ...40N 3E **120**
Palmira, Col. ...4N 76W **104**
Palúa, Ven. ...9N 63W **104**
Pamirs, Mts., Asia ...38N 73E **142**
Pampa, Tx., U. S. ...36N 101W **86**
Pampa, Reg., Arg. ...35S 64W **106**
Panaji (Panjim), India ...16N 74E **143**
Panamá, Pan. ...9N 80W **97**
Panama, Ctry., N. A. ...8N 80W **97**
Panama, G. of, Pan. ...8N 80W **97**
Panama City, Fl., U. S. ...30N 86W **92**
Pančevo, Serb. ...45N 21E **121**
Pápa, Hung. ...47N 17E **117**
Papua New Guinea, Ctry., Oc. ...7S 142E **149**
Paraguay, Ctry., S. A. ...24S 57W **106**
Paraguay, R., S. A. ...25S 58W **106**
Paramaribo, Sur. ...5N 55W **105**
Paraná, Arg. ...32S 60W **106**
Paraná, R., S. A. ...25S 54W **106**
Paris, Fr. ...49N 2E **117**
Paris, Tx., U. S. ...34N 96W **87**
Parkersburg, W. V., U. S. ...39N 82W **90**
Parma, Italy ...45N 10E **117**
Parma, Oh., U. S. ...41N 82W **90**

Parnaíba, Braz. ...3S 42W **105**
Pärnu, Est. ...58N 24E **116**
Parsons, Ks., U. S. ...37N 95W **87**
Pasadena, Ca., U. S. ...34N 118W **84**
Passaic, N. J., U. S. ...41N 74W **91**
Pasto, Col. ...1N 77W **104**
Patagonia, Reg., Arg. ...44S 46W **106**
Pathein, Myan. ...17N 95E **148**
Patiāla, India ...30N 76E **143**
Patna, India ...26N 85E **143**
Patos, Lago dos, L., Braz. ...31S 53W **106**
Pátra, Grc. ...38N 22E **121**
Patterson, N. J., U. S. ...41N 74W **91**
Pau, Fr. ...43N 0 **117**
Pavia, Italy ...45N 9E **117**
Pavlodar, Kaz. ...52N 77E **140**
Pavlohrad, Ukr. ...49N 36E **121**
Pawtucket, R. I., U. S. ...42N 71W **91**
Paysandú, Ur. ...32S 58W **106**
Peabody, Ma., U. S. ...43N 71W **91**
Peace, R., Can. ...57N 117W **72**
Pebane, Moz. ...17S 38E **131**
Peş, Serb. ...43N 20E **117**
Pechenga, Russia ...70N 31E **114**
Pecos, R., U. S. ...31N 103W **76**
Peş, Hung. ...46N 18E **121**
Peiraiás, Grc. ...38N 24E **121**
Peleduy, Russia ...60N 113E **141**
Pelly Mts., Yk., Can. ...62N 134W **72**
Pelotas, Braz. ...32S 52W **106**
Pembroke, On., Can. ...46N 77W **73**
Pendleton, Or., U. S. ...46N 119W **82**
Pennsylvania, State, U. S. ...41N 78W **77**
Pensacola, Fl., U. S. ...30N 87W **92**
Penticton, B. C., Can. ...49N 119W **72**
Penza, Russia ...53N 45E **115**
Penzhino, Russia ...64N 168E **141**
Peoria, Il., U. S. ...41N 90W **90**
Pereira, Col. ...5N 76W **104**
Pergamino, Arg. ...34S 61W **106**
Perigueux, Fr. ...45N 1E **117**
Perm', Russia ...58N 56E **115**
Pernik, Bul. ...43N 23E **121**
Perpignan, Fr. ...43N 3E **117**
Persian G., Asia ...28N 50E **142**
Perth, Austl. ...32S 116E **156**
Perth, Scot., U. K. ...56N 3W **116**
Perth Amboy, N. J., U. S. ...41N 74W **91**
Peru, Ctry., S. A. ...10S 75W **104**
Perugia, Italy ...43N 12E **117**
Pervomais'k, Ukr. ...48N 31E **121**
Pesaro, Italy ...44N 13E **117**
Peshāwar, Pak. ...34N 72E **143**
Peterborough, On., Can. ...44N 78W **73**
Petersburg, Va., U. S. ...37N 78W **93**
Petrich, Bul. ...41N 23E **121**
Petropavlovsk, Kaz. ...55N 69E **140**
Petropavlovsk-Kamchatskiy, Russia ...53N 159E **141**
Petrópolis, Braz. ...23S 43W **106**
Petrozavodsk, Russia ...62N 34E **115**
Phenix City, Al., U. S. ...32N 85W **92**
Philadelphia, Pa., U. S. ...40N 75W **91**
Philippines, Ctry., Asia ...14N 125E **149**
Philippine Sea, Asia ...25N 129E **147**
Phitsanulok, Thai. ...17N 100E **148**
Phnom Penh, Camb. ...12N 105E **148**
Phoenix, Az., U. S. ...33N 112W **85**
Phra Nakhon Si Ayutthaya, Thai. ...14N 101E **148**
Piacenza, Italy ...45N 10E **117**
Piatra-Neamt, Rom. ...47N 26E **121**
Piedras Negras, Mex. ...29N 101W **96**
Pierre, S. D., U. S. ...44N 100W **88**
Pietermaritzburg,, S. Afr. ...30S 30E **130**
Pieve, Italy ...46N 12E **120**
Pilcomayo, R., S. A. ...24S 60W **106**
Pinar del Río, Cuba ...22N 84W **97**
Pine Bluff, Ar., U. S. ...34N 92W **87**

Pinega, Russia ...65N 43E **140**
Pinsk, Bela. ...52N 26E **114**
Piombino, Italy ...43N 11E **117**
Piotrkow Trybunalski, Pol. ...51N 20E **117**
Piracicaba, Braz. ...23S 48W **105**
Pirot, Serb. ...43N 23E **121**
Pisa, Italy ...44N 10E **117**
Pistoia, Italy ...44N 12E **117**
Pitesti, Rom. ...45N 25E **121**
Pittsburg, Ks., U. S. ...37N 95W **87**
Pittsburgh, Pa., U. S. ...40N 80W **91**
Pittsfield, Ma., U. S. ...42N 73W **91**
Piura, Peru ...5S 81W **104**
Plainfield, N. J., U. S. ...41N 74W **91**
Plata, R. de la, Arg. -Ur. ...35S 58W **106**
Platte, R., Ne., U. S. ...41N 100W **88**
Plauen, Ger. ...50N 12E **117**
Pleven, Bul. ...43N 24E **121**
Pljevlja, Serb. ...43N 19E **121**
Ploiesti, Rom. ...45N 26E **121**
Plovdiv, Bul. ...42N 25E **121**
Plymouth, Eng., U. K. ...50N 4W **117**
Plzeň, Czech Rep. ...50N 13E **117**
Po, R., Italy ...45N 11E **117**
Pocatello, Id., U. S. ...43N 112W **83**
Podgorica, Serb. ...42N 19E **121**
Pointe-à-Pitre, Guad. ...16N 62W **97**
Pointe Noire, Congo ...5S 12E **130**
Poitiers, Fr. ...47N 0 **117**
Poland, Ctry., Eur. ...52N 18E **117**
Poltava, Ukr. ...50N 35E **115**
Pomona, Ca., U. S. ...34N 118W **84**
Ponce, P. R. ...18N 67W **97**
Pondicherry, India ...12N 80E **143**
Ponta Delgada, Port. ...38N 26W **128**
Ponta Grossa, Braz. ...25S 50W **106**
Ponta Pora, Braz. ...22S 56W **105**
Pontiac, Mi., U. S. ...43N 83W **90**
Pontianak, Indon. ...0 109E **148**
Poopo, Lago de, L., Bol. ...18S 68W **104**
Popayán, Col. ...2N 77W **104**
Porbandar, India ...22N 70E **143**
Pori, Fin. ...62N 22E **116**
Poronaysk, Russia ...49N 143E **141**
Port Alice, B. C., Can. ...50N 127W **72**
Port Angeles, Wa., U. S. ...48N 123W **82**
Port Antonio, Jam. ...18N 76W **97**
Port Arthur, Tx., U. S. ...30N 94W **95**
Port-au-Prince, Haiti ...19N 72W **97**
Port Elizabeth, S. Afr. ...34S 26E **130**
Port Harcourt, Nig. ...5N 7E **128**
Port Huron, Mi., U. S. ...43N 82W **90**
Portland, Me., U. S. ...44N 70W **91**
Portland, Or., U. S. ...46N 123W **82**
Port Moresby, Pap. N. Gui. ...10S 147E **149**
Porto, Port. ...41N 9W **120**
Porto Alegre, Braz. ...30S 51W **106**
Port of Spain, Trin. ...11N 61W **97**
Porto-Novo, Benin ...7N 3E **128**
Porto Velho, Braz. ...9S 64W **104**
Port Said, Egypt ...31N 32E **129**
Portsmouth, Eng., U. K. ...51N 1W **117**
Portsmouth, N. H., U. S. ...43N 71W **91**
Portsmouth, Oh., U. S. ...39N 83W **90**
Portsmouth, Va., U. S. ...37N 76W **91**
Portugal, Ctry., Eur. ...40N 8W **120**
Posadas, Arg. ...28S 56W **106**
Potenza, Italy ...41N 16E **117**
Poti, Geor. ...42N 42E **115**
Potomac, R., U. S. ...38N 77W **91**
Potosí, Bol. ...20S 66W **104**
Potsdam, Ger. ...52N 13E **117**
Pottstown, Pa., U. S. ...40N 76W **91**
Pottsville, Pa., U. S. ...41N 76W **91**
Poughkeepsie, N. Y., U. S. ...42N 74W **91**
Poyang Hu, L., China ...29N 117E **147**
Poznan, Pol. ...52N 17E **117**